Geopolitics

Recent Titles in
Contemporary Military, Strategic, and Security Issues

Military Doctrine: A Reference Handbook
Bert Chapman

Energy Security Challenges for the 21st Century: A Reference Handbook
Gal Luft and Anne Korin, editors

An Introduction to Military Ethics: A Reference Handbook
Bill Rhodes

War and Children: A Reference Handbook
Kendra E. Dupuy and Krijn Peters

Military Justice: A Guide to the Issues
Lawrence J. Morris

Military Space Power: A Guide to the Issues
Wilson W.S. Wong and James Fergusson

American Missile Defense: A Guide to the Issues
Victoria Samson

Private Armed Forces and Global Security: A Guide to the Issues
Carlos Ortiz

Women in the United States Armed Forces: A Guide to the Issues
Darlene M. Iskra

War Crimes, Genocide, and the Law: A Guide to the Issues
Arnold Krammer

NATO: A Guide to the Issues
Brian J. Collins

Strategic Communication: Origins, Concepts, and Current Debates
Christopher Paul

Geopolitics

A Guide to the Issues

Bert Chapman

Contemporary Military, Strategic, and Security Issues

PRAEGER

AN IMPRINT OF ABC-CLIO, LLC
Santa Barbara, California • Denver, Colorado • Oxford, England

Library of Congress Cataloging-in-Publication Data

Chapman, Bert.
Geopolitics : a guide to the issues / Bert Chapman.
p. cm. — (Contemporary military, strategic, and security issues)
Includes bibliographical references and indexes.
ISBN 978-0-313-38579-7 (alk. paper) — ISBN 978-0-313-38580-3 (ebook)
1. Geopolitics. I. Title.
JC319.C514 2011
320.1'2—dc22 2010052066

ISBN: 978-0-313-38579-7
EISBN: 978-0-313-38580-3

15 14 13 12 11 1 2 3 4 5

This book is also available on the World Wide Web as an eBook.
Visit www.abc-clio.com for details.

Praeger
An Imprint of ABC-CLIO, LLC

ABC-CLIO, LLC
130 Cremona Drive, P.O. Box 1911
Santa Barbara, California 93116-1911

This book is printed on acid-free paper ∞

Manufactured in the United States of America

Contents

Acknowledgments

My introduction to geopolitics began during fall 1981, when I took a political geography course at Taylor University under Professor Roger Jenkinson. During this class I learned about the geopolitical theories of individuals such as Halford Mackinder and Friedrich Ratzel along with concepts such as heartland, rimland, Eurasia, and the Great Game. This knowledge base has helped me immensely as I pursued studies and an academic career incorporating history, library science, and political science.

My training in these fields as been very beneficial to me as I prepared this work, which seeks to emphasize how vitally important geography is in personal, national, and international economics; environmental policy; foreign policy; international security; and political developments locally and globally. This project has been assisted by Adrian Johnson of the University of Texas at Austin Benton Latin American Collection Library, my Purdue Libraries colleague Robert Freeman, and by Steve Catalano and others at Praeger Security International. I want to thank my wife, Becky, for helping prepare the maps used in this book, for her loving support, and for her willingness to travel with me to diverse geographic locations to see and experience natural scenery such as Australia's Blue Mountains, the Canadian Rockies, and Yellowstone National Park; historical sites such as Blenheim Palace, Greenwich's National Maritime Museum, and Sydney's ANZAC Memorial; battlefields such as Quebec and Vicksburg; and waterways such as the St. Lawrence and Thames rivers and Sydney Harbor. I also want to thank my teachers from elementary school through higher education who have inspired and exhorted me to achieve educational excellence and promote lifelong learning.

Introduction

Personal and national economic health, prosperity, and physical security are profoundly affected by geography. Whenever energy-producing nations raise natural gas and oil prices, we pay higher prices when we fill up our cars or purchase other goods and services using energy commodities and their by-products. We live in a globalized economy where tremendous amounts of money are electronically transferred from one corner of the world to another by governmental and private-sector sources for legitimate purposes or to facilitate drug trading and terrorism financing. The U.S. subprime mortgage market crash in 2008 had serious domestic and global repercussions on economic performance and personal prosperity. Political unrest and instability in one country or region can have profound effects throughout the world, as crisis regions such as Afghanistan, Egypt, North Korea, and Somalia demonstrate.

Jet air travel makes it possible for us to reach most areas of the world in a few hours, including Australia, as I found out during my 2010 summer vacation. This expedited travel and transportation also makes it possible to transmit human diseases germs globally and invasive species to unfamiliar ecosystems with serious public health and environmental consequences. Events such as the 2010 Icelandic volcanic eruption and maritime piracy near Somalia and elsewhere can cause significant disruption to personal travel and international maritime trade. Instantaneous communications such as the Internet and satellite television make us aware of these events and allow us to form and express personal analysis of their significance, but disruption of these communication channels through technical malfunction or cyber or terrorist attacks can do severe damage to personal and international economic well-being.

However, these technological advances do not alter the climactic, ethnographic, geographical, and sociopolitical realities of conducting naval and military operations in areas as diverse as the South China Sea, the U.S.-Mexican border, and Afghanistan. Instead, they require "boots on the ground" and long-term historical and cultural understanding of the factors shaping conflicts in these regions, along with a sustained commitment to forging cooperative relationships with individuals and groups in these regions if these problems are to have a chance of somewhat successful resolution. In fact, they increase the importance of understanding how geographical factors shape ongoing and emerging historical and cultural conflicts and mandate increasing the importance of geography and its political aspects at all educational levels from primary through postgraduate.[1]

Political aspects of geography such as geopolitics, which in this work emphasizes international economic, environmental, diplomatic, and security relationships between nation-states, international governments, and nongovernmental organizations, involve

- defining the location of national or multinational territory
- describing all aspects of that territory's physical characteristics
- distinguishing a state's national territory from other states territories
- defining a polity's cultural zone or civilization (e.g., British, French, Portuguese, or Spanish colonization in the Americas)
- conditioning, shaping, and influencing a polity's historical development[2]

Geopolitics can also be defined as describing geographical settings and their relationship to political power and setting out spatial frameworks embracing political power units such as hemispheres, oceans, land and maritime boundaries, natural resources, and culture.[3] As an interdisciplinary field encompassing topics as diverse as anthropology, cartography, demography, economics, geography, international security, military policy, natural resources policy, political science, and other subjects, geopolitics has recovered from the disrepute it fell into due to Nazi Germany's ideological abuse of it. Geopolitics is now a multifaceted topic essential for understanding the multifaceted ways geography and human behavior have shaped and continue shaping historical, current, and emerging international political and security matters.[4]

Early-21st-century geopolitics is roughly, if somewhat simplistically, divided into two camps: classical geopolitics and critical geopolitics. Classical geopolitics, which this writer adheres to, incorporates traditional methodological emphases of this subject as embodied by practitioners such as Halford Mackinder (1861–1947) and Alfred Thayer Mahan (1840–1914). It stresses conventional aspects of national economic, political, and military strategy such as economic strength, the importance of freedom of the seas, the criticality of possessing national military strength with effective striking power, cooperating with allied nations to defend national interests and preventing transnational groups or powers from gaining a competitive strategic advantage that could jeopardize national security and prosperity, and the nation-state's preeminence in international affairs. One prominent proponent of classical geopolitics says that

> geopolitics is not geographic determinism, but is based on the assumption that geography defines limits and opportunities in international politics: states can realize their geopolitical opportunities or become the victims of their geopolitical situation. One purpose of grand strategy is to exploit one's own geographical attributes and an adversary's geographical vulnerabilities.

Geopolitics is dynamic, not static. It reflects international realities and the global constellation of power arising from the interaction of geography on one hand and technology and economic development on the other. Technology and the infusion of capital can modify, though not negate, the strategic importance of a particular geographic space.

Finally, geopolitics clarifies the range of strategic choices, providing a guide for achieving strategic efficiency. While it places particular stress on geographic space as a critically important strategic factor and source of power, it recognizes that geography is only a part of the totality of global phenomena.[5]

Articles representing classical geopolitics perspectives are generally found in government and military publications and traditionalist international relations journals such *Foreign Affairs*, *International Security*, *Journal of Strategic Studies*, and *Naval War College Review*.

Critical geopolitics reflects varied interdisciplinary approaches to geopolitics developed during the 1980s and are reflected in the work of scholars such as Simon Dalby and Geróid Ó Tuathail (Gerard Toal). This perspective, which is leftist in ideological orientation, seeks to challenge traditional geopolitical interpretations. It criticizes what it sees as a state-centric approach to international relations; takes a hostile approach to what it claims are ethnocentric, determinist, and exceptionalist attributes to classical geopolitical writings; it dismisses traditional balance of power and influence analyses of international affairs; it is concerned with geographical aspects of U.S. and other Western interventions in the developing world; it emphasizes rhetorical aspects of geopolitical analysis while seeking to "deconstruct" this literature; it challenges the strategic rationalizations used by the United States and other Western countries to portray countries such as the former Soviet Union and China and transnational terrorist groups such as al-Qaeda as geopolitical threats; and it is concerned with political rhetoric, which its proponents contend maintains Western dominance of international affairs.[6]

Critical geopolitics often uses such obtuse rhetoric that it is difficult for it to advance its influence beyond a narrow sector of academic adherents. However, it wields significant influence on many journal editorial boards and in articles published in journals such as *Geopolitics* and *Political Geography* and is also reflected in works published by some scholarly monographic publishers such as the University of Minnesota Press.

While it may be hyperbolic to say geographic knowledge is a critical national security ingredient,[7] we cannot ignore geography's affect on our personal economic well-being and national and international prosperity and poverty, how climatic changes affect our lives, and how access to or the inability to access natural resources such as water and oil can have drastic impacts on our lives. We also must become more aware of the multiple cultural, economic, historical, military, and political developments and grievances in other countries and global regions and how they can affect our security and living standards in an increasingly globalized and interconnected multipolar world.[8]

This increased understanding of how geography affects our nation and world needs to occur at all levels of the educational system by replacing the vague and diffuse phrase "social studies" with systematic long-term study of economics, geography, history, and political science. The 2001 National Assessment of Education Progress found, in a slight improvement over 1994 test results, that only 20 percent of 4th-grade students, 30 percent of 8th-grade students, and 25 percent of 12th-grade students reached proficient levels in geographic scores, with the typical or average student only scoring at the basic level.[9]

Students in a country with the United States' power, responsibility, and interests, which remain so heavily dependent on cultural, economic, political, and strategic developments in other countries, must do much better than this. Enhancements in geographic and geopolitical education must stress the importance of knowing how to correctly read and interpret maps. This includes not just traditional highway maps of cities and states or political maps of countries. It also needs to include topographic maps describing elevation changes in geographic areas; bathymetric maps describing ocean floor contours; historical maps showing changes in population movement and crop production; and maps showing natural resource locations, sizes, and exploitation practices. It should include the ability to interpret geospatial imagery from aerial or satellite photography; an understanding of how nations and organizations can use maps to argue their political positions to support their agendas for gaining proper political or territorial boundaries and denigrate those of opposing opponents or groups; an understanding of the topographic, physical, and political features of critical strategic choke points where energy supplies must pass through and be vulnerable to cutoff or attack such as the Arabian/Persian Gulf; considerations of the multifaceted implications of aging European populations and burgeoning Muslim and other populations; recognition of the dangers caused by failed states such as Haiti and Somalia; and knowledge of the physical locations of natural disasters such as the 2004 Indian Ocean tsunami and ongoing or possible future theaters of combat operation such as Kandahar, Afghanistan, Waziristan, or the Straits of Taiwan.[10]

This enhanced geographic education can be accomplished through ongoing commitment by all U.S. educational sectors and through the use of cutting-edge technologies such as Geographic Information Systems, geospatial data, Google Earth and Google Maps, DVDs, CD-ROMs, GPS, and even traditional paper maps.

Geopolitics: A Guide to the Issues seeks to introduce students, scholars, and curious readers to the burgeoning literature of geopolitics and how this multidisciplinary subject can enhance their understanding of historical, contemporary, and emerging international diplomatic, economic, environmental, and security developments. It begins with a 20th-century historical overview of global geopolitics and describes some of the individuals shaping this discipline and their key works and ideas. Subsequent chapters will examine the recent historical and current geopolitical practices of countries as varied as Australia, China, India, Russia, and the United States and provide overviews of current and emerging geopolitical "hot spots" such as Arctic Ocean resources, China's "String of Pearls Basing Strategy, and Russian Energy Diplomacy; freely accessible U.S., foreign, and international government organization geopolitical information resources; monographic scholarly literature; databases and scholarly journal articles; gray literature, including dissertations, technical reports, conference proceedings, and social networking utilities; profiles of current geopolitical scholars and their works; and a glossary.

A diverse and multifaceted array of materials and perspectives will be presented in this work and will enable students, scholars, and readers interested in geographical aspects of international affairs to conduct substantive research on how geography influences international diplomacy, economics, environmental policy, foreign country domestic politics, and security policy.

Notes

1. See Harm de Blij, *Why Geography Matters: Three Challenges Facing America: Climate Change, the Rise of China, and Global Terrorism* (New York: Oxford University Press, 2005): 3–23; and Robert D. Kaplan, "The Revenge of Geography," *Foreign Policy*, 196 (May/June 2009): 96–105.

2. Colin S. Gray, "A Debate on Geopolitics: The Continued Primacy of Geography," *Orbis*, 40 (2)(Summer 1996): 248.

3. Saul B. Cohen, *Geography and Politics in a World Divided*, 2nd ed. (New York: Oxford University Press, 1973): 29–33.

4. Leslie W. Hepple, "The Revival of Geopolitics," *Political Geography Quarterly*, 5 (4, suppl.)(October 1986): S21–S36.

5. Mackubin Thomas Owens, "In Defense of Classical Geopolitics," *Naval War College Review*, 52 (4)(Autumn 1999): 73.

6. See Simon Dalby, "Critical Geopolitics," in *Dictionary of Geopolitics*, ed. John O'Loughlin (Westport, CT: Greenwood Press, 1994): 56–58; Gerard Toal, *Critical Geopolitics* (Minneapolis: University of Minnesota Press, 1996).

7. De Blij, *Why Geography Matters*, 21.

8. See George A. Van Otten, "Educating Military Intelligence Professionals to Meet the Challenges of Changing Global Political Realities and Modern Asymmetric Warfare," *Military Intelligence Professional Bulletin*, 28 (3)(July–September 2002): 33–36; Milan N. Vego, "Russia and the Return of Geopolitics," *Joint Force Quarterly*, 45 (April 2007): 8–15; Kaplan, "The Revenge of Geography"; and Iveta Solova and William C. Brehm, "Education and Geopolitics in a Changing Europe: Forty Years of Scholarship in *European Education*," *European Education*, 41 (2)(Summer 2009): 7–30.

9. U.S. Department of Education, National Center for Education Statistics, "Fourth-and Eighth-Grader Scores Higher in NAEP 2001 Geography," http://nces.ed.gov/pressrelease/rel2002/6_21_02.asp.

10. See Mary Lynette Larsgaard, *Map Librarianship: An Introduction*, 3rd ed. (Littleton, CO: Libraries Unlimited, 1998); Edoardo Boria, "Geopolitical Maps: A Sketch History of a Neglected Trend in Cartography," *Geopolitics*, 13 (2)(Summer 2008): 278–308; Mark Monmonier, *Spying with Maps: Surveillance Technologies and the Future of Privacy* (Chicago: University of Chicago Press, 2002); and Mark Monmonier, *Rhumb Lines and Map Wars: A Social History of the Mercator Projection* (Chicago: University of Chicago Press, 2004).

CHAPTER 1

History of Geopolitics and Biographies of Key Personalities (20th Century)

The term *geopolitics* is generally regarded as being first used by Swedish political scientist Rudolf Kjellén (1864–1922) in an 1899 article in the Swedish geographical journal *Ymer,* and Kjellén used the German term *Geopolitik* in a 1905 article in the German journal *Geographische Zeitschrift*. Kjellén defined geopolitics as describing the role of geographical factors in determining national behavior and was also a Swedish nationalist sympathetic to German World War I efforts.[1]

Political geography is also used to describe the relationship between physical environment and politics and has both domestic policy and international implications, but *geopolitics*, as used in this work, will refer to the international economic, environmental, diplomatic, and security relationships between nation-states, international government organizations, and nongovernmental organizations. While geopolitics has been practiced by nation-states throughout history, its rise as a scientific discipline and formalized governmental policy-making instrument begins in the early 20th century. Key emphases of geopolitics include the belief that states have boundaries, capitals, communication lines, consciousness, and culture; the belief that a state's size and resources can determine its strength; and the belief that states are in continual competition and that larger states seek to expand to consolidate their power. It is also an interdisciplinary subject encompassing topics such as demographic movement, economic development, land use, and natural resource distribution.[2]

U.S. geopolitical theory and practice during this time were heavily influenced by Alfred Thayer Mahan (1840–1914), who contended that nations with superior sea power consisting of a navy, merchant marine, maritime-oriented populaces, well-distributed bases, and control of narrow waterways could dominate international affairs by using this power to blockade and choke rivals.[3] British geopolitics, most prominently articulated by Halford Mackinder (1861–1947), was concerned about Germany's emerging naval challenge and sought to prevent national decline by uniting with Britain's overseas territories into a league of democracies with common defense and foreign policies as well as giving trade preferences to these countries by imposing higher tariffs on products from other countries.[4]

Geopolitics would achieve its greatest use and controversy in Germany during the 20th century's earliest decades. Numerous individuals were involved in developing German geopolitical thought, including Karl Haushofer (1869–1946) and Friedrich Ratzel (1844–1904). German geopolitical thought was influenced by Germany's central European location; its recurring historical antagonism with France and Russia; an acute emphasis on the unity of the German *Volk* (people or nation); national desires for a "place in the sun," including dominance of Europe; the zeal to rectify World War I defeat and avenge themselves for the reparations imposed by the Treaty of Versailles; the desire to gain additional lebensraum (living space) through a *Drang nach Osten* (drive to the east) by conquering territory in Eastern Europe and Russia to populate a growing German population; and a sense of racial superiority, influenced by the writings of Heinrich von Treitschke (1834–1896) and others who believed that Germany was entitled to European dominance and that the Jews and other foreign and domestic "traitors" were responsible for keeping Germany from reaching what they saw as its Manifest destiny, to be a preeminent global power.[5]

Geopolitics would receive its most prominent and negative association with Nazi Germany. Hitler's regime incorporated traditional aspects of German national and international security policy making with its nauseating ideology of racial superiority toward Jews and Slavic peoples, whom it considered to be genetically inferior. Lebensraum and other aspects of Nazi ideology were incorporated into educational curricula at all levels and into geographical, historical, and political science research, as evidenced by journal publication practices and Haushofer's regular contact with Nazi officials. Although geopolitics was a legitimate scholarly discipline incorporated into the academic research in the United States, France, and other major countries at this time, its strong association with Nazi Germany resulted in it being discredited in World War II's aftermath.[6]

Geopolitics was largely neglected in North America and Europe, though not in South America, in the four decades after World War II because of the Nazi stigma, although there were detailed scholarly analyses of international security and strategy published during this time. The German journal *Zeitschrift für Geopolitik* was published from 1951 to 1968, and the U.S. Air Force produced *Military Aspects of World Political Geography* (1958) as part of its education programs. Key factors prompting renewed interests in geopolitics include bipolar cold war U.S.-Soviet competition encompassing many geographic regions; the Sino-Soviet split; the rise of third world nationalism and Islamic fundamentalism; the inflexibility of nuclear weapons in dealing with regional problems; and economic changes, including the rise of energy prices and the emergence of the Organization of Petroleum Exporting Countries. Nazi Germany's receding into historical memory, Henry Kissinger's extensive use of geopolitics as a scholar and policy maker, and the increasing need to understand geographical factors in international cultural, economic, political, and strategic development all contributed to a reemergence of geopolitics in scholarly analysis by the 1980s.[7]

The next two decades would see the increasing importance of geography in international affairs. The Soviet Union's collapse created an increasingly multipolar world, producing an environment conducive to the recurrence of tribally based conflicts in the Balkans, Caucasus, and Rwanda; the emergence of transnational terrorist groups such as al-Qaeda; natural disasters such as the 2004 Indian Ocean tsunami; concern and controversy over climate change and how to respond to it; rising energy prices due to increased demand from growing economies such as China and India; increasing nuclear proliferation evidenced by the desire of countries such as Iran and North Korea to acquire weapons of mass destruction; and the creation of new nation-states such as East Timor, Kazakhstan, and Macedonia. A world increasingly connected by transportation; instantaneous communication systems such as the Internet; and increasingly interlocked economic, environmental, and military-strategic interactions made it impossible for engaged citizens to ignore geography as an increasingly critical factor in personal, national, and international economics and security.

One prominent writer has described this development as "The Revenge of Geography" and goes on to argue that geography will determine the success of political ideas, that wealth and political and social order will erode, and that natural frontiers and human passions will determine who can coerce whom. He goes on to maintain:

> We all must learn to think like Victorians. . . . Geographical determinists must be seated at the same honored table as liberal humanists, thereby merging the analogies of Vietnam and Munich. Embracing the dictates and limitations of geography will be especially hard for Americans, who like to think that no constraint, natural or otherwise, applies to them. But denying the facts of geography only invites disasters that, in turn, make us victims of geography.[8]

Numerous figures have contributed to geopolitics global development, and this chapter will profile them, their work, and the multiple perspectives they bring to this topic, which still resonate with contemporary geopolitical issues.

Isaiah Bowman (1878–1950)

Bowman became prominent during World War I for his role in U.S. preparation for postwar reconstruction and redrawing European national boundaries. He served as director of the American Geographical Society and was responsible for assembling cartographic and geographical data used by Woodrow Wilson at the Versailles Peace Conference. Additional professional honors Bowman also received included his 1930 election to the National Academy of Sciences and becoming president of the Johns Hopkins University in 1935. Land settlement was one of his areas of scholarly expertise, and his prominent writings on this and other geopolitical subjects include *The New World* (1921), *Geography in Relation to the Social Sciences* (1934), and *The Limits of Land Settlement: A Report on Present-Day Possibilities* (1937), along with articles examining the relationships between geopolitics, political geography, and power.

During World War II, he advised the Roosevelt administration and helped design many aspects of postwar U.S. foreign policy, including development of the United Nations and formulation of postwar European territorial reconstruction. Although critical of Nazi Germany's use of geopolitics, Bowman believed it was important to learn historical lessons and played influential academic and policy-making roles in ensuring that geopolitical questions are inherently political and are recognized as such, instead of being viewed only as scientific questions.[9]

James Burnham (1905–1987)

Burnham began his political career as a radical leftist actively involved in Trotskyite circles, where he regularly contributed to the Marxist journal *New International*, advocated socialist revolution in the United States, and published *Managerial Revolution* (1941), which contended that the world's industrial countries would be ruled by managers, instead of capitalists or communists. During World War II, Burnham served in the Office of Strategic Services (OSS), and his politics began shifting in a more conservative direction; in 1944, he wrote an analysis for the OSS warning of an emerging Soviet geopolitical threat to Western democracies.

This work, *The Struggle for the World* (1947), was published the same week President Truman announced the U.S. assistance program to Greece and Turkey, which would become known as the Truman Doctrine. In this work, Burnham warned that the Soviets sought to achieve control of Eastern Europe,

Eurasia, and Mackinder's World Island, consisting of Eurasia and Africa, and effectively to dominate the world. He criticized early cold war containment policy as being excessively defensive in *The Coming Defeat of Communism* (1949) and *Containment or Liberation?* (1951) and urged U.S. adaptation of policies to undermine Soviet power in Eastern Europe by exploiting inherent Communist structural vulnerabilities.

Burnham consulted for the Central Intelligence Agency and increasingly began writing for conservative publications such as William Buckley's *National Review*, in which he analyzed a variety of geopolitical issues. Burnham's last major work, *Suicide of the West* (1964), warned that Western civilization was killing itself due to religious decline and excessive material luxury and was becoming tired and worn out pursuing material gain. He received the Presidential Medal of Freedom from President Reagan in 1983 and should be remembered as an influential figure in conservative American geopolitical thought and analysis.[10]

Julian Corbett (1854–1922)

Corbett was a prominent naval historian whose work influenced British military history writing and the conduct of British naval geopolitics. He also wrote fiction, and it's possible that his service as a war correspondent for the *Pall Mall Gazette* during the 1896 Dongola expedition to Sudan caused him to think about the conduct of war as a writing topic. His first serious military writing was *Drake and the Tudor Navy* (1898), which, along with other works, got him involved in the naval educational reform movement and made himself known to Admiral John Fisher (1841–1920), who would eventually serve as First Sea Lord, Britain's highest-ranking naval officer.

Corbett became a history lecturer at the Royal Naval College in Greenwich in 1902 and published *England in the Mediterranean, 1603–1714* (1904), which was a comprehensive analysis of naval strategy. Additional Corbett books include *England in the Seven Years War* (1907), *Some Principles of Maritime Strategy* (1911), *Maritime Operations in the Russo-Japanese War* (2 volumes; 1915), and a three-volume analysis of World War I naval battles titled *Naval Operations* (1920–1923), in which he had to mute his criticisms of British strategy and tactics at the 1916 Battle of Jutland due to their political sensitivity.

Corbett was a valuable advisor to Fisher and Lord of the Admiralty Winston Churchill (1874–1965) during World War I, writing persuasive official memoranda providing valuable naval policy-making advice. He favored using British sea power in a limited way, recognizing the limits it placed on its user during wartime. Corbett saw military history as an intrinsic part of national history and international politics dating back to the Elizabethan age and, like Alfred Thayer Mahan, considered sea power synonymous with national power.[11]

Albert Demangeon (1872–1940)

Demangeon was a French geographer with a strong interest in geography's political aspects. During his career, he taught at the University of Lille, the Sorbonne, and École des Hautes Études Commercialles; served as an advisor on frontier problems at the Versailles Peace Conference and as editor of *Géographie Universelle* and *Annales de Géographie*; and was also involved in the Annaliste historical movement.

Following World War I, Demangeon came to believe that Europe's dominant world position was ending due to the rise of the United States; Japan's growing power in the Far East, which would turn the Pacific into a "new Mediterranean" and an East-West meeting place; and the rise of militant Islam, which he viewed as being highly dangerous to Europe's international strategic position. These sentiments were articulated in *The Decline of Europe* (1920) and other works.

He was also concerned that the post–World War I establishment of new European states would have a negative impact on continental security; wanted regional agreements established as a means of enhancing political stability; was skeptical that the League of Nations would be able to achieve lasting peace; was concerned about Germany's growing assertiveness in the 1930s; wanted France to modernize its agriculture, industry, and colonization practices to serve as a counterweight to Germany; and ultimately believed greater continental cooperation, instead of confrontation, was in Europe's long-term interests, even being an early user of the terms *European Community* and *United States of Europe*.[12]

Yann Morvran Goblet (1881–1955)

This French geographer taught at the École Supérieure de Commerce, École des Hautes Études Sociales, and Institut Universitaire des Hautes Études in Geneva. Goblet considered geopolitics to be a subtle and complex subject and that theories must be based on rigorously examined existing conditions. He wanted to keep international relations analysis grounded in concrete reality and proposed developing new and more sophisticated geopolitical analysis techniques to resolve international problems.

His works, including *Twilight of Treaties* (1935), condemned German geopolitics for wrong ideas of geographical determinism that treated nations as metaphysical beings, and he believed that its proponents were modern alchemists who added somber fanaticism to their ideas. Goblet also wrote *Political Geography and the World Map* (1955) and was very interested in Irish geopolitics, on which he wrote extensively. His interests in regionalism and small states rights became increasingly irrelevant in the bipolar post–World War II European security environment.[13]

Golbery do Couto e Silva (1911–1987)

This Brazilian geopolitical writer served in his country's military forces, participated in the Italian campaign during World War II, and was a member of the Brazilian military's Sorbonne Group, who were military officers closely associated with Brazil's Higher War College. This group supported Brazil's military government between 1964 and 1985 and favored an anti-Communist foreign policy but tended to be more moderate, supportive of free enterprise, and desirous of a long-term return to democracy. Golbery also was a key advisor to these military governments between 1964 and 1981 and served as Brazil's equivalent to the White House chief of staff.

His geopolitical thinking, articulated in works such as *Brazilian Geopolitics* (1981), saw Golbery advocate exclusive Brazilian leadership in South America. He favored an anti-Communist partnership with the United States to protect South Atlantic maritime waters from Soviet attack between the Atlantic Narrows and West African Bulge. Golbery distrusted neighboring Spanish-speaking countries, such as Argentina, Colombia, and Peru, which he believed wanted to encircle Brazil. He also advocated expanding internal Brazilian frontiers by developing the Amazon and Brazil's northeastern and southern regions.

Golbery believed Brazil could not escape from the U.S.-Soviet confrontation; that it could not pursue cold war nonalignment, as advocated by some Latin American foreign policy thinkers; that Brazil should collaborate with other Portuguese-speaking nations; and that it should seek to expand its influence beyond South America. He incorporated insights from Mackinder and Mahan into his writings and is an example of how geopolitics played an important role in Brazilian foreign and national security policy making during an era when it was deemphasized in U.S. and European policy making.[14]

Sergei Gorshkov (1910–1988)

Gorshkov was a Soviet admiral and commander-in-chief of the Soviet Navy from 1956 to 1985. He joined the navy in 1927 after graduating from the Frunze Higher Naval School, served in destroyers in the Black Sea and

Pacific fleets during the 1930s, became rear admiral in 1941 after the German invasion, and distinguished himself in several World War II commands. In 1956, Soviet leader Nikita Khrushchev (1893–1971) appointed him to lead the Soviet Navy and to implement nuclear weapons into this force and its doctrine. Gorshkov began this process and is also best known for transforming the Soviet Navy from a coastal force to a blue water maritime striking power with aircraft carriers and nuclear submarines capable of challenging U.S. naval supremacy in many global arenas.

Gorshkov wrote about his geopolitical philosophy in works such as *Red Star Rising at Sea* (1974) and *Seapower of the State* (1983) as well as various articles in the journal *Military Thought*. He wanted to achieve parity with U.S. and NATO navies and sea control in the world ocean and expanded the size of the Soviet shipbuilding industry to build various surface vessels, including aircraft carriers and nuclear submarines. His incentive to build this force was heavily influenced by the 1962 Cuban Missile Crisis demonstrating the Soviets did not have the long-range fleet to thwart the U.S. quarantine of Cuba. Gorshkov was also involved in Soviet efforts to build naval bases in friendly developing countries like Angola, Cuba, and Vietnam; believed in the importance of aircraft carriers and tactical aviation to achieve balanced fleet forces; and sought to strengthen discipline in the Soviet Navy to enable it to achieve its geopolitical aspirations of counterbalancing U.S. maritime power.

High financial costs made it impossible for the Soviet Navy to sustain its large size, and Gorshkov's fleet was losing its strength at the time of his death. The Russian Federation has not been able to rebuild its fleet to its halcyon days under Gorshkov, although it is seeking to increase its assertiveness in the Arctic Ocean and other areas. Gorshkov should be remembered as a significant military leader and strategist who was able to launch the Soviet Navy on a trajectory of at least partial parity with the United States during the cold war.[15]

Enrique Guglialmelli (1922–1983)

This Argentine held several important political and military appointments including the Superior War College and Center for Advanced Military Studies. He also commanded the Fifth Army Corps, served as National Development Council Secretary between 1966 and 1971, directed the Argentinean Institute of Strategic Studies and International Relations, and served as editor of the journal *Estrategia*.

Guglialmelli's writings in this journal and books such as *Argentina, Brazil, and the Atomic Bomb* (1976) and *Geopolitics and the Southern Cone* (1979) focused on national and regional geopolitics with particular emphasis on what he saw as Brazilian expansionism and Argentina's inability to counter it. He was a nationalist policy advocate, and his writings addressed the historical development of Argentine geopolitical writing, the potential impact of nuclear weapons in the Southern Cone, and the armed forces' proper role in national development. He favored protectionist tariffs and governmental industrial subsidies and believed that national resources should be devoted to developing southern frontier regions like Patagonia and northern frontier regions adjacent to Bolivia and Brazil to counter what he saw as Brazilian attempts to control natural resources and gain access to the Pacific.

Guglialmelli also believed Argentina should develop nuclear weapons if Brazil did; that the United States would support Brazil in any dispute with Argentina; and that advocates of free trade and capitalism from Brazilian, British, and U.S. multinational corporations made Argentina economically dependent on them, which he regarded as dangerous to Argentine national economic development, security, and social cohesion.[16]

Karl Haushofer (1869–1946)

Haushofer is one of geopolitics's seminal historical figures. He served as a German military commander during World War I and wrote several books and articles, including *Western Pacific Ocean Geopolitics* (1925), *World Politics Today* (1934), and *Japan Builds Its Empire* (1941). Haushofer also edited the *Zeitschrift für Geopolitik* (1924–1944), served as professor of geography at the University of Munich (1921–1939), and was president of the German Academy (1934–1937), which was Germany's premier scientific research and German culture–promoting institution.

Haushofer had only sporadic contact with Adolf Hitler (1889–1945) but was close friends with Hitler's deputy Rudolf Hess (1894–1987), which allowed his geopolitical theories to gain significant influence in Nazi policy-making circles. Haushofer's geopolitical ideology had clear imperialist proclivities by the 1920s as he sought to increase German territory. He believed there was an Eurasian continental block stretching from Germany through Russia to Japan that Germany could use to conduct a land power–oriented foreign policy against maritime nations such as France and the United Kingdom, and he argued for building such an alliance in 1940. Having spent time in Japan between 1908 and 1910, Haushofer also admired that country and its politicians.

He increasingly began seeing sea power as an important element in his geopolitical *Weltanschauung*, and his thought and writings would divide the earth into three north-south regions with a core and periphery and Arctic, temperate, and tropical environments. These regions, which had the potential for economic self-sufficiency, were

- Pan-America, with the United States as the core
- Eurafrica, with Germany as the core
- East Asia, with Japan as the core and Australia as the periphery

Haushofer never constructed a concrete geopolitical theoretical concept in order to retain intellectual and political flexibility. He and his editorial colleagues at *Zeitschrift für Geopolitik*, along with a Geopolitics Study Group founded in 1932, sought to expand geopolitics's popular appeal, serve as a foreign policy propaganda mechanism, and educate the general public in what they regarded as proper political thought in order to rectify incorrect political views which they believed produced German defeat in World War I. He was involved in preparing the November 1936 Anti-Comintern agreement between Germany and Japan and lost much of his political influence with the Nazis following Hess's 1941 flight to Scotland.

After World War II, Haushofer was interrogated by the U.S. Office of Chief of Counsel concerning his activities and writings but was not accused at the Nuremberg Military Tribunals and released. He and his wife committed suicide on March 10, 1946, and his legacy is being one of the individuals responsible for promoting the intellectual groundwork for Nazi ideology and policies and preparing Germans for World War II's aggressive violence.[17]

Rudolf Kjellén (1864–1922)

As mentioned earlier, Kjellén is credited with coining the term *geopolitics* in an 1899 journal article on Swedish boundaries. During his career, Kjellén served as a political science and geography professor at Gothenburg University and Uppsala University, a Conservative MP in the Swedish parliament, and a foreign affairs columnist for conservative Swedish newspapers.

His geopolitical thought was influenced by German idealist philosophy, social Darwinism, and prevailing imperialist views. Kjellén rejected the prevailing view of the state as a legal object and viewed it as a power in foreign affairs with particular emphasis on using organic analogy, which stressed that nation-states like Sweden were more important than individuals residing within those countries. Key tenets of his thought stressed that a state's attributes include

1. geopolitics as studying a state's territory
2. demographic politics involving studying a state's population
3. the critical importance of a state's economy
4. societal politics, including traditions held for generations
5. governmental-constitutional politics, including relationships between states and their peoples

He defined geopolitics as the study of the state as a geographical organism or spatial phenomenon with particular emphasis on a state's location in relation to other states, its territorial form, and its size. Kjellén envisioned a future of fewer but larger territorial states, believed that territorial size was crucial for states in their relationship with other powers, emphasized the importance of freedom of movement in state policy making such as not being constrained by other states blocking straits of water, and emphasized the importance of a state being in one territorial piece to promote cohesion. He also believed that the nation was a state's soul; that national homogeneity involved common culture, identity, and values instead of race; and that a state's ability to become economically self-sufficient was crucial to its success.

He also believed that, barring incompetent leadership, states possessing the greatest power resources would win wars, saw Germany and Japan as increasingly powerful and England and France and declining before World War I, and saw the United States and Russia as being the only two powers capable of fulfilling his category of becoming world powers. Although a Swedish nationalist, Kjellén supported many of Germany's World War I aims, and Haushofer and other German geopolitical theorists incorporated many of his elements into their thinking, with particular emphasis on Kjellén's organic theory of state power. Besides inventing the term *geopolitics*, his work is significant for emphasizing environmental traditions influencing state-to-state relationships and emphasizing a state's physical character, size, and location as keys to its international political power position.[18]

Halford Mackinder (1861–1947)

Mackinder is arguably the most historically influential geopolitical strategist. During his career he held faculty appointments at Oxford University and the London School of Economics; served as a Conservative MP representing Glasgow's Camlachie constituency from 1910 to 1922; was appointed British high commissioner to south Russia in 1919, where he was charged with finding ways to stop Bolshevik expansion; and chaired the British government's Imperial Shipping Committee between 1920 and 1945.

He was an assiduous promoter of geographic education and favored strengthening the British Empire by granting preferential trading rights to countries and territories within the empire. His geopolitical writings began with *Britain and the British Seas* (1902), which showed the strategic and imperial implications of the British Isles physical location and natural resource endowment. His ascension to geopolitical prominence began with his essay "The Geographical Pivot of History," published by the Royal Geographical Society's *Geographical Journal* in 1904. This seminal work stressed his concern that one power or alliance of powers could gain control of Eurasia and use that region's resources to dominate the world. It stressed factors such as Asiatic influences on Europe dating back to the Mongols; the importance of river water drainage on national economies and international security; how settlement patterns and agronomy influence political and economic development; the importance of climate and railroads in determining human settlement and inhabitation; Russia's geographically advantageous position, which makes it possible to strike out in all directions and be attacked from all directions except the north; and China's and Japan's possible future potential to challenge Russia.[19]

Another significant exposition of Mackinder's geopolitical thinking was reflected in *Democratic Ideals and Reality* (1919). This work was written hastily for the Versailles Conference and expanded his geographical pivot ideas. Analyzing the weakness of the emerging postwar order, he contended that power was becoming centralized in large states and that mass political movements were emerging but that populations would be susceptible to manipulation by organizers controlling state machinery. He favored creating new nation-states from the defeated German and Austro-Hungarian empires but saw that countries such as Czechoslovakia, Hungary, and Poland would be vulnerable to aggression and subversion from Germany and Russia.

It also supported national self-determination and the League of Nations and established the concept of the Heartland, which included all of Eastern Europe, and that Germany and Russia would vie for control of this region, contending that

1. who rules East Europe commands the Heartland
2. who rules the Heartland commands the World Island
3. who rules the World Island commands the world[20]

The World Island included separate regions such as Arabia covering as far north as the Turkish border, European coastland extending from Scandinavia to North Africa, Monsoon coastland extending from India through Southeast Asia and China and northeast Russia, the southern Heartland region consisting of most of Africa, and North and South America as part of an oceanic realm. *Democratic Ideals and Reality* had little immediate impact in the United States and United Kingdom and was not consulted by Isaiah Bowman and the U.S. delegation at Versailles. However, it received more detailed scrutiny in Germany, where Haushofer approved of it and advocated a German-Soviet alliance to defeat maritime powers such as the United Kingdom and the United States. Hitler, though, did not see the Soviet Union as an ally but as a region to be plundered for its resources.[21]

Mackinder has been the source of laudatory and negative assessments in historical and geopolitical literature, depending on the prevailing thinking and geopolitical conditions of subsequent historical periods. He can be praised for being a pioneer in attempting to establish and communicate a reasonably coherent geopolitical theory of international politics and economics. Some critics see him as an apologist for the British Empire and for what they regard as Western imperialism. Mackinder had a major influence on geographic education within the United Kingdom and commonwealth countries. Although he failed to gain lasting support for a unified and modernized empire to offset continental European powers which might threaten Britain, his work remains highly influential and instructive reading as we enter and immerse ourselves in a globalized era where geography is becoming increasingly important in international economic, environmental, natural resources, and security policy making and the impact these activities have on our lives.[22]

Alfred Thayer Mahan (1840–1914)

Mahan is one of the world's premier naval and maritime geopolitical strategists, and his work continues influencing U.S. naval planning. The son of West Point military engineering professor and faculty dean Dennis Hart Mahan (1802–1871), Alfred Thayer Mahan graduated from the U.S. Naval Academy in 1859 and served on blockade and shoreline duty during the Civil War, despite being susceptible to seasickness. He gradually rose through the ranks and was promoted to captain in 1885. While serving at Brooklyn's Navy Yard in 1883, he was asked by Scribner's publishing to produce a book on the navy in the civil war, which was published that year as *The Gulf and Inland Waters*.

This work contained no illuminating strategic insights but demonstrated his writing ability and was noticed in 1884 by Stephen B. Luce (1827–1917), who was the founder and president of the newly opened U.S. Naval War College in Newport, Rhode Island. Luce appointed Mahan to write and teach naval history, and his class lecture notes were published in 1890 as *The Influence of Sea Power upon History, 1660–1783*, which had a stunning impact on global foreign ministries and war departments. A two-volume sequel, *The Influence of Sea Power upon the French Revolution and Empire, 1793–1812*, appeared in 1892.

The first book is a classic of maritime and geopolitical strategy. It asserted that naval and merchant marine assets were the primary reasons England, France, Holland, and Spain won wars, permitting them to seize overseas colonies, eliminate enemy access to these colonies, and exploit their natural resources. The publication timing of these works also proved fortuitous as European powers were dissecting Africa and, along with Japan, had similar objectives for China and East Asia. Expansionist-oriented Americans such as Secretary of State John Hay (1838–1905), Senator Henry Cabot

Lodge (1850–1924), and Theodore Roosevelt (1858–1919) read this work and asserted that the United States would be economically and politically disadvantaged internationally until it abandoned its post–Civil War isolationism. These individuals went on to argue that the United States should increase its agricultural and industrial exports to overseas markets such as the Far East and would gradually come to advocate larger U.S. naval forces.

Mahan would come to advocate a larger navy to patrol and defend the Gulf and Caribbean coasts; believed that a canal would soon penetrate Central America, attract global merchant and naval shipping, and be militarily controlled by the United States; and favored establishing an eastern Pacific naval perimeter to permit Japan or any other country from establishing a naval presence within 3,000 miles of San Francisco.

A prodigious literary output would emanate from Mahan in the late 19th and early 20th centuries, including works such as *Lessons of the War with Spain* (1899). Viewpoints stressed in these writings include the inadvisability of arms limitations, treaties, international arbitration courts, and rules of war because they compromised combat effectiveness and the chance of achieving fast and victorious wars; the imperative of navies using tactical concentration to combine their firepower on enemies weaker firepower assets; and welcoming Hawaii's and Puerto Rico's annexation and reluctantly accepting Philippine annexation as part of expanding the United States' security perimeter while forecasting that the Philippines could not be militarily defended against Japan.

However, he believed the United States' open door policy in China and Monroe Doctrine in the western hemisphere overextended U.S. resources; disagreed with Roosevelt's desire of building HMS *Dreadnought* big-gun battleships between 1906 and 1914, believing that naval ships should have varied sizes and arsenals; and failed to see the emerging tactical and strategic significance of the airplane, submarine, and wireless telegraphy. He also believed that good political and naval leadership counterbalanced geography, favored free trade over autarchy, appreciated contingency's power to affect geopolitical outcomes, and believed that sea transport and trade's fundamental importance needed to be examined within the relationship of continental and land structures and that national policy on these subjects must be set within the parameters of transnational perspectives.[23]

Augusto Pinochet Ugarte (1915–2006)

Pinochet is best known for his controversial tenure as Chile's president between 1973 and 1990. He also was a career army officer who began serving the Chilean armed forces in 1933 and taught at Chile's war college on geopolitics and was credited with writing works such as *Military Geography: Military Interpretations and Geographical Factors* (1980) and *Geopolitics* (1984).

Pinochet argued that Chile had three regions, Andean, Pacific, and Antarctic, and he desired a closer integration of the core central valley with geographically peripheral and less-developed areas and sought to build land and maritime highways to reach remote southern territories without having to cross into Argentina. He established the Chilean Pacific Ocean Institute and a national ocean policy to emphasize the importance of oceans in Chilean national policy. He also sought to promote geographic education in all levels of Chilean society and emphasized Chilean claims in Antarctica.

Additional attributes of Pinochet's geopolitical thinking included bolstering Chile's presence in the Antarctic and Beagle Channel; negotiating with Bolivia to give that country a Pacific access corridor; advocating exchanging maritime land for space and guaranteeing a security zone in cooperation with Peru; and preventing Argentina, Bolivia, and Peru from encircling Chile. Pinochet also wanted to increase Chile's merchant marine and enhance national port facilities, promote increased use of oceanic food and mineral resources, and enhance Chile's interior industrial manufacturing capabilities. He was concerned the United States lacked the will to contain communism in South America; favored national self-reliance and an independent bloc of third world nations to restrain great power actions; and believed Chile was entering a Pacific era that would bring increased wealth from the Antarctica and the Orient.[24]

Friedrich Ratzel (1844–1904)

Ratzel was a major German geographer and is regarded as a founder of modern human and political geography. He began his professional career as a chemist's assistant, did graduate work in the natural sciences, and was also a journalist. Limited professional opportunities in these fields in Germany and 1870s travels in the United States and elsewhere turned his interest to geography, and he became a professor of geography at the University of Munich in 1876, before taking a similar position in 1886 at the University of Leipzig, which he held until his death.

"Laws of the Spatial Growth of States," published in 1896, described the state's expansion through war as a natural and progressive tendency. It went on to assert that a state's territory grows with its culture and that expansionist politics's greatest success depends on its effective use of geography. Ratzel's preeminent work, *Political Geography* (1897), is credited with laying the foundations for geopolitics. This work saw him introduce the concept of lebensraum to German political discourse and present what he considered seven laws on state growth:

1. State space increases with cultural growth.
2. Territorial growth follows other developmental aspects.
3. A state grows by absorbing other, smaller units.
4. Frontiers are peripheral state organs reflecting a state's strength and growth and are not permanent.
5. States seek to absorb politically valuable territory as they grow.
6. A primitive states's incentive to grow comes from a more highly developed state.
7. Tendencies toward territorial growth increase as they pass from state to state.

Haushofer was one of Ratzel's most influential followers and helped spread his beliefs throughout German academic and governmental circles. Ratzel published *The Sea as a Source of the Greatness of a People* (1900) as a written demonstration of Germany's commitment to *Weltpolitik* as a maritime and expansionist foreign policy. Besides space and distance, Ratzel was concerned with the importance of environmental influences, including climate, resources, terrain, and vegetation. He believed that the world is inherently conflict ridden; that competition for living space is part of a nation-state's life cycle; that powerful states must become larger over time; that *Grossraum* (large space states) is the world's future; and that Germany had to compete for lebensraum to become a world power. These beliefs would be reflected in *The Geography of States, Traffic, and War* (1903) and solidify Ratzel's legacy as a proponent of Wilhelmine nationalism, which would eventually be adopted by the Nazis for their own political purposes.[25]

Alexander P. De Seversky (1894–1974)

Seversky was a Russian American naval aviator who played a critical role in publicizing how airpower transformed national security and militarily extended the geographic reach and striking power of national militaries. He initially came to the United States on a military mission in 1918, where he defected and became an advisor to military aviation pioneer Billy Mitchell (1879–1936). Seversky founded what eventually became Republic Aircraft, which built the P45 fighter. In the early 1940s, he began publicizing the potential for American military victory through air power and long-range aircraft, which he articulated in *Victory through Air Power* (1942).

His argument stressed using polar projection to enhance global U.S. air control extending over an offensive radius of 6,000 miles and a defensive radius of 3,000 miles controlled from what he regarded as an impregnable superfortress. In later works, such as *Air Power: Key to Survival* (1950) and *America: Too Young to Die* (1961), he argued that whoever gained control of airspace overlapping Europe, the Middle East, North Africa, and North America could achieve global dominance and that the United States needed to make its heartland an invincible base so it could project offensive power to all corners of the world.

Seversky criticized the importance of armies and navies and was a tireless advocate of air power, although he exaggerated the extent of its effectiveness. Nevertheless, he helped expand geopolitics to a subject that must include the application and projection of aerospace power along with land and maritime power.[26]

Nicholas J. Spykman (1893–1943)

Spykman was a Dutch-born American scholar and geopolitical writer who was a professor of international relations at Yale University's Institute of International Relations. His two principal works, *America's Strategy in World Politics: The United States and the Balance of Power* (1942) and *The Geography of Peace* (1944), are updated versions of Mahan's quest for a realistic sea power–based foreign policy.

Spykman believed that geography was the preeminent factor in international relations because it was this subject's most enduring characteristic. His key philosophical tenet was that U.S. foreign policy objectives would be best served by dropping its traditionally idealistic and isolationist view of world affairs and adopting European balance of power principles. He believed the United States should protect its security by pursing an active foreign policy so it could influence events, prevent threats to its interests, and be prepared for dangerous confrontations.

He believed that the Old World and New World were the two principal geographical entities in international politics. Spykman asserted that the Old World included the Eurasian continent, Africa, Australia, and smaller offshore islands adjacent to these areas and that the New World included the Americas in the western hemisphere. He believed both of these worlds interacted with each other across the Atlantic and Pacific and that this interaction could determine if one of these worlds could "strangle" the other.

Spykman contended that the New World was not a cohesive alliance but that it was dominated by the United States, and if one state achieved dominance in the Old World and acquired and mobilized eastern hemisphere human power and resources, it could threaten the United States and western hemisphere. Consequently, he believed U.S. foreign policy should focus on dividing the Old World by striving for alliances with weaker states against potentially hegemonic states.

His description of the Old World went on to divide it into four geographical features. The Heartland was Eurasia's core and patterned after Mackinder's heartland. The Rimland was generally similar to Mackinder's inner crescent, covering European coastland, Arab–Middle Eastern deserts, and Asiatic monsoon territory. Spykman believed a third Old World feature was a "great circumferential maritime highway" covering the Baltic, North Sea, and Mediterranean to the Sea of Okhotsk and that a fourth feature was offshore islands, including England, Africa, Australia, and Japan. His Rimland was the most strategically critical because it had been involved in all large-scale historical military conflicts and because it served as an intermediate zone between the Heartland, circumferential maritime highway, and offshore islands. Consequently, he believed the United States should project its power in the Rimland to prevent the expansion of a states or alliance of states such as the Soviet Union and believed that Germany, Japan, and the United Kingdom would be critical U.S. allies even during the early days of World War II.[27]

Robert Strausz-Hupé (1903–2002)

Strausz-Hupé was born and grew up in Austria before immigrating to the United States following World War I. Parleying a Wall Street career as a political risk analyst for Americans holding European bonds, Strausz-Hupé became increasingly concerned about Hitler and Nazi Germany and that their policies would replace the traditional European balance of power. His professional contacts brought him in contact with Isaiah Bowman, and he eventually became an international relations professor at the University of Pennsylvania and a research chief for a Roosevelt administration project on refugee affairs and natural resources. These contacts gave him the opportunity to work closely with eventual secretary of state Dean Acheson (1893–1971) and with Secretary of the Navy James Forrestal (1892–1949).

Strausz-Hupé detested communism as being a crude scientific fraud for maintaining and holding political power and suggested to Forrestal that George Kennan be used to write the "MR. X" 1947 containment article in *Foreign Affairs*, outlining U.S. cold war containment strategy toward the Soviet Union. Strausz-Hupé would produce a significant corpus of works on geopolitical strategy over the next few decades. Examples of these works included *The Zone of Indifference* (1952), which depicted Europe as weak and vulnerable to the products of technological prowess such as mass organization and atomized societies but capable of being rescued by the United States and NATO, and *The Protracted Conflict* (1963), which argued that the West needed to fight a long-term conflict with the Soviet Union and that it needed to regain its lead in advanced military weaponry.

He was also involved in establishing the Foreign Policy Research Institute (FPRI) in 1955 at the University of Pennsylvania to conduct scholarship to advance U.S. interests. FPRI is now independent of this university, but one of its enduring publications is the scholarly journal *Orbis*, established in 1957.

Strauz-Hupé criticized the belief that foreign assistance and state building could benefit developing countries, warned that the guilt complex developed in these countries by Western benefactors created a large psychological gulf enabling them to attack the free-market West even as they desired its material benefits, and asserted that there would always be a gap between these countries rising expectations and the amount of assistance the West could provide them. He remained influential in Republican administrations, serving as U.S. ambassador to countries such as Belgium, Sri Lanka, Sweden, and Turkey through the 1980s. He also served as U.S. ambassador to the NATO Council and gained U.S. military access to the United Kingdom Indian Ocean military base Diego Garcia, which has been used in numerous military operations in that part of the world and advocated deploying Pershing II ballistic missiles in Western Europe to counter Soviet SS-20 missiles in Eastern Europe.

He concluded his career at FPRI and began writing on geopolitical issues such as urging improved relations with Russia to curtail China; advocating enhanced U.S. relations with India; favoring Turkish membership in the European Union; and urging the Arabs, Israelis, and Turks to work together to enhance Middle East water supplies.[28]

Paul Vidal De La Bache (1845–1918)

This French geographer was educated and taught at the École Normale Supéruere and also lectured and taught at the University of Nancy and the Sorbonne. He founded and edited the journal *Annales de Géographie* and edited *Géographie Universelle*. His background was in history and classics, and he saw geography as being a synthesis and a unifying discipline whose objective should be studying the creative relationship between humans and their environment.

Vidal de la Bache was particularly interested in regional synthesis and the geographic roles played by *pays*, or country. He believed that the interaction of civilization and milieu produced ways of live which he believed were the foundations of human geography. In works such as *France and the East* (1917) and *Principles of Human Geography* (1922), he recognized the importance of political factors in shaping human landscapes and argued that political geography or geopolitics was best understood within a wider human geographic context. He disagreed with Ratzel's attempts to formulate geopolitical behavioral laws and emphasized the roles played by frontiers such as Alsace-Lorraine in national spatial development. He went on to view provinces in a wider European context, was concerned about the potential for German continental hegemony, and ultimately believed transnational groups should substitute for sovereign states in conducting international affairs.[29]

Notes

1. See Sven Holdar, "The Ideal State and the Power of Geography: The Life-Work of Rudolf Kjellén," *Political Geography*, 11 (3)(May 1992): 307–9, 319–20; and Greg Russell, "Theodore Roosevelt, Geopolitics, and Cosmopolitan Ideals," *Review of International Studies*, 32 (3)(July 2006): 543–44.

2. See Klaus Dodds and David Atkinson, eds., *Geopolitical Traditions: A Century of Geopolitical Thought* (London: Routledge, 2000); Harm De Blij, *Why Geography Matters: Three Challenges Facing America: Climate Change, the Rise of China, and Global Terrorism* (New York: Oxford University Press, 2005): 9; and Russell, "Theodore Roosevelt," 542–44.

3. Alfred Thayer Mahan, *The Influence of Sea Power upon History, 1660–1783* (New York: Dover, 1987).

4. Brian W. Blouet, "The Political Career of Sir Halford Mackinder," *Political Geography Quarterly*, 6 (4)(October 1987): 355–67.

5. See Norman Levine, "Gerhard Ritter's Weltanschauung," *The Review of Politics*, 30 (2)(April 1968): 209–27; David Thomas Murphy, *The Heroic Earth: Geopolitical Thought in Weimar Germany, 1918–1933* (Kent, OH: Kent State University Press, 1997); and Marcel Stoeltzer, *The State, the Nation, and the Jews: Liberalism and the Antisemitism Dispute in Bismarck's Germany* (Lincoln: University of Nebraska Press, 2008).

6. See Henning Heske, "German Geographical Research in the Nazi Period: A Content Analysis of the Major Geography Journals," *Political Geography Quarterly*, 5 (3)(July 1986): 267–81; Leslie W. Hepple, "The Revival of Geopolitics," *Political Geography Quarterly*, 5 (4 Suppl.)(October 1986): S21–36; Hepple, "Karl Haushofer: His Role in German Geopolitics and in Nazi Politics," *Political Geography Quarterly*, 6 (2)(April 1987): 135–44; and Geoffrey Parker, "French Geopolitical Thought in the Interwar Years and the Emergence of the European Idea," *Political Geography Quarterly*, 6 (2)(April 1987): 145–50.

7. Hepple, "The Revival of Geopolitics."

8. Robert D. Kaplan, "The Revenge of Geography," *Foreign Policy*, 196 (May–June 2009): 96–105.

9. See Geoffrey J. Martin, *The Life and Thought of Isaiah Bowman* (Hamden, CT: Archon Books, 1980); and Neil Smith, "Isaiah Bowman: Political Geography and Geopolitics," *Political Geography Quarterly*, 3 (1)(January 1984): 69–76.

10. See Francis P. Sempa, "Geopolitics and American Strategy: A Reassessment," *Strategic Review*, 15 (2)(1987): 26–38; Daniel Kelly, *James Burnham and the Struggle for the World: A Life* (Wilmington, DE: ISI Books, 2002); Philip Abott, "'Big' Theories and Policy Counsel, James Burnham, Francis Fukuyama and the Cold War," *Journal of Policy History*, 14 (4)(October 2002): 417–30; Francis Sempa, *America's Global Role: Essays and Review on National Security, Geopolitics, and War* (Lanham, MD: University Press of America, 2009): 59–62.

11. See Donald M. Schurman, *Julian S. Corbett, 1854–1922: Historian of British Maritime Policy from Drake to Jellicoe* (London: Royal Historical Society, 1981); James Goldrick and John B. Hattendorf, eds., *Mahan Is Not Enough: The Proceedings of a Conference on the Works of Sir Julian Corbett and Admiral Sir Herbert Richmond* (Newport, RI: Naval War College Press, 1993); and G.A.R. Callender and James Goldrick, "Corbett, Sir Julian Stafford," in *Oxford Dictionary of National Biography*, ed. H.C.G. Matthew and Brian Harrison (Oxford: Oxford University Press, 2004): 400–401.

12. See Geoffrey Parker, "French Geopolitical Thought in the Interwar Years and the Emergence of the European Idea," *Political Geography Quarterly*, 6 (2)(April 1987): 145–50; and Parker, "Demangeon, Albert," in *Dictionary of Geopolitics*, ed. John O'Loughlin (Westport, CT: Greenwood Press, 1994): 61–62.

13. Geoffrey Parker, "Goblet, Y.-M.," in O'Loughlin, *Dictionary of Geopolitics*, 99–100.

14. See David M. Schwam-Baird, *Ideas and Armaments: Military Ideologies in the Making of Brazil's Arms Industries* (Lanham, MD: University Press of America, 1983): 30–33; Thomas E. Skidmore, *The Politics of Military Rule in Brazil, 1964–85* (New York: Oxford University Press, 1988): 21; and Philip Kelly, *Checkerboards and Shatterbelts: The Geopolitics of South America* (Austin: University of Texas Press, 1997): 88–92.

15. See Robert Warring Herrick, *Soviet Naval Theory and Policy: Gorshkov's Inheritance* (Newport, RI: Naval War College Press, 1988); U.S. Navy, Chief of Naval Operations, *Understanding Soviet Naval Developments*, 6th ed. (Washington, DC: U.S. Navy, 1991): 11–22; Ronald J. Kurth, "Gorshkov's Gambit," *Journal of Strategic Studies*, 28 (2)(April 2005): 261–280; and Sergei Chernyavskii, "The Era of Gorshkov: Triumph and Contradictions," *Journal of Strategic Studies*, 28 (2)(April 2005): 281–308.

16. Kelly, *Checkerboards and Shatterbelts*, 96–100.

17. See Donald H. Norton, "Karl Haushofer and the German Academy," *Central European History*, 1 (1)(March 1968): 80–99; Henning Heske, "Karl Haushofer: His Role in German Geopolitics and Nazi Politics," *Political Geography Quarterly*, 6 (2) (April 1987): 135–44; David Thomas Murphy, *The Heroic Earth: Geopolitical Thought in Weimar Germany, 1918–1933* (Kent, OH: Kent State University Press, 1997); and Holger Herwig, "*Geopolitik*: Haushofer, Hitler, and Lebensraum," *Journal of Strategic Studies*, 22 (2–3)(June 1999): 218–41.

18. See Sven Holdar, "The Ideal State and the Power of Geography: The Life-Work of Rudolf Kjellén," *Political Geography*, 11 (3)(May 1992): 307–23; Ola Tunander, "Geopolitics of the North: *Geopolitik* of the Weak: A Post–Cold War Return to Rudolf Kjellén," *Cooperation and Conflict*, 43 (2)(June 2008): 164–84.

19. See Brian W. Blouet, "Mackinder, Sir Halford John," in *Oxford Dictionary of National Biography*, ed. H.C.G. Matthew and Brian Harrison (Oxford: Oxford University Press, 2004), 35: 648–51.

20. See Halford John Mackinder, *Democratic Ideals and Reality*, ed. Anthony J. Pierce (New York: Norton, 1919/1962): 74–77; and Brian W. Blouet, *Halford Mackinder: A Biography* (College Station: Texas A&M University Press, 1987): 165–72.

21. See Blouet, "Mackinder," 35: 650–51; and Blouet, *Halford Mackinder*, 177–80.

22. Literature on Mackinder and his significance, besides that already cited, includes Arthur Butler Dugan, "Mackinder and His Critics Reconsidered," *Journal of Politics*, 24 (2)(May 1962): 241–57; Brian W. Blouet, "The Political Career of Sir Halford Mackinder," *Political Geography Quarterly*, 6 (4)(October 1987): 355–67; Gearóid Ó Tuathail, "Putting Mackinder in His Place: Material Transformations and Myth," *Political Geography*, 11 (1)(January 1992): 100–18; Mackubin Thomas Owens, "In Defense of Classical Geopolitics," *Naval War College Review*, 52 (4)(Autumn 1999): 60–77; and Gerry Kearns, *Geopolitics and Empire: The Legacy of Halford Mackinder* (Oxford: Oxford University Press, 2009).

23. See Richard W. Turk, *The Ambiguous Relationship: Theodore Roosevelt and Alfred Thayer Mahan* (Westport, CT: Greenwood Press, 1987); Robert Seager II, "Mahan, Alfred Thayer," in *American National Biography*, ed. John A. Garraty and Mark C. Carnes (New York: Oxford University Press, 1999): 14: 336–38; and Jon Sumida, "Alfred Thayer Mahan, Geopolitician," *Journal of Strategic Studies*, 22 (2–3) (1999): 39–61.

24. See Stephen M. Gorman, "The High Stakes of Geopolitics in Tierra Del Fuego," *Parameters*, 7 (2)(June 1978): 45–56; Kelly, *Checkerboards and Shatterbelts*, 114–16; and Mary Helen Spooner, *Soldiers in a Narrow Land: The Pinochet Regime in Chile*, updated ed. (Berkeley: University of California Press, 1999): 22.

25. See Woodruff D. Smith, "Friedrich Ratzel and the Origins of Lebensraum," *German Studies Review*, 3 (1)(February 1980): 51–68; J.M. Hunter, *Perspectives on Ratzel's "Political Geography,"* (Lanham, MD: University Press of America, 1983); Stephen Kern, *The Culture of Time and Space 1880–1918* (Cambridge, MA: Harvard University Press, 1983): 224–26; Klaus Kost, "The Conception of Politics in Political Geography and Geopolitics in Germany until 1945," *Political Geography Quarterly*, 8 (4)(October 1989); Henning Heske, "Ratzel, Friedrich," in O'Loughlin, *Dictionary of Geopolitics*, 205; Geoffrey Parker, "Ratzel, the French School and the Birth of Alternative Geopolitics," *Political Geography*, 19 (8)(November 2000): 957–69; and Sebastian Conrad, "Globalization Effects: Mobility and Nation in Imperial Germany, 1880–1914," *Journal of Global History*, 3 (1)(March 2008): 43–66, for assessments of Ratzel and the rise of German nationalism.

26. See Neil Smith, "De Seversky, Major Alexander P," in O'Loughlin, *Dictionary of Geopolitics*, 62–63; Philip S. Meilinger, "Proselytiser and Prophet: Alexander P. de Seversky and American Airpower," *Journal of Strategic Studies*, 18 (1)(March 1995): 7–35; and David L. Butler, "Technogeopolitics and the Struggle for Control of World Air Routes, 1910–1928," *Political Geography*, 20 (5)(June 2001): 635–58.

27. See Geoffrey R. Sloan, *Geopolitics in United States Strategic Policy 1890–1987* (New York: St. Martin's Press, 1988): 16–19; and Jan Nijman, "Spykman Nicholas," in O'Loughlin, *Dictionary of Geopolitics*, 222–23.

28. See Walter McDougall, "The Wisdom of Robert Strausz-Hupé," *FPRI Wire*, 7 (4)(1999); and Harvey Sicherman, "Robert Strausz-Hupé: His Life and Times," *Orbis*, 49 (2)(Spring 2003): 195–216.

29. See Geoffrey Parker, "Vidal de la Bache, Paul," in O'Loughlin, *Dictionary of Geopolitics*, 232–33; and Parker, "Ratzel, the French School, and the Birth of Alternative Geopolitics," *Political Geography*, 19 (8)(November 2000): 959.

CHAPTER 2

Selected Countries and Their Recent Historical and Current National Government Geopolitical Practices

This chapter examines the diverse factors prompting individual national governments to pursue current geopolitical policies. These policies are influenced by various historical factors, including economics, foreign policy, intelligence and military assessments of national security interests, national culture, and individual leaders' personalities. It will emphasize recent history along with current and emerging geopolitical practices and trends. At the same time, it recognizes that centuries-long national historical traditions and political convictions also influence national geopolitical strategies and how such strategies and beliefs have been reflected in cartography, atlases, and other publications promoting national geopolitical interests.[1] Where possible, this chapter will stress how current and emerging national geopolitical strategies are articulated in government and military publications.

Australia

This continental country in the southern hemisphere plays a significant role in regional Asia-Pacific and even global geopolitics, despite having a population of less than 23 million.[2] As an island country, Australia is surrounded by the Pacific Ocean, Indian Ocean, and Timor and Arafura seas and is located near many strategically important maritime areas such as the South China Sea and Straits of Malacca. Although its initial primary non-indigenous settlers were British convicts, Australia has become a multicultural Anglocentric parliamentary democracy with historical legacy ties to the United Kingdom, critically important economic and security ties to the United States, and growing trade ties and security interests with countries as diverse as China, Indonesia, and other Oceanic island states. All these combine to make maritime security particularly important in determining Australian economic and strategic interests.[3]

The distinguished Australian historian Geoffrey Blainey describes the critical importance of geographic distance in analyzing Australian geopolitical development and evolution. He notes that Australia's northwestern coast is closer to the Philippines than the national capitol Canberra; that Darwin is as close to Singapore as to Melbourne; that Australia's "boomerang coast," where 80 percent of Australians live, is far away from this northern coastal strip adjacent to Southeast Asia; that Asian trading partners must cross oceanic and land barriers to reach the bulk of the Australian market; and that most Australian trade is with more distant northeast Asia instead of Southeast Asia.[4]

Australia has sought to perform a complex balancing act in its international geopolitical relationships. It remains a close security partner with the United States, having participated in military operations in Afghanistan and Iraq, hosts U.S. intelligence gathering sites, is concerned with Persian Gulf security developments, and is desirous of having unfettered access to Antarctica and its resources. Australia has also become a major regional power in the southern Pacific, having recently committed forces to combat operations or directly intervened to influence domestic political developments in East Timor, Papua New Guinea, and the Solomon Islands. It has a growing but challenging security partnership with Indonesia based on concerns over Islamist terrorism and is heavily dependent on natural resources trade with China. There is considerable and evolving debate within the Australian governmental and strategic communities as to whether it should be an Asian-oriented nation or continue orienting its security ties primarily toward the United States. Recent Australian governments of varied political shades, such as Paul Keating (1991–1996), John Howard (1996–2007), Kevin Rudd (2007–2010), and Julia Gillard (2010–), have all sought to articulate how they will promote and defend Australia's complex and multifaceted geopolitical interests in a variety of publications and proclamations.[5]

Brazil

Brazil has emerged as South America's premier geopolitical power, with a population of 193 million,[6] and in 2009 was ranked as the world's 10th leading economic power, with an estimated gross domestic product (GDP) exceeding $2 trillion.[7] Within its borders, Brazilian geopolitics have historically focused on territorial expansion, including international controversy over its development of the mineral-rich Amazonian north; attempts to develop the agricultural but drought-prone northeast extending into the Atlantic Ocean; and developing additional agricultural, high-tech, mineral, and industrial resources in the southeast, south, and central west.[8]

Internationally, Brazilian geopolitics have stressed its fear of being surrounded by potentially hostile Spanish-speaking countries such as Argentina; its desire to control the Southern Atlantic, have access to Antarctica, and promote South American economic development and cooperation through the Southern Common Market Customs Union (MERCOSUR); be seen as a great power internationally; and to have a collaborative but independent security relationship with the United States. Additional Brazilian geopolitical objectives include keeping the southern hemisphere free of weapons of mass destruction and combating terrorism and drug trafficking and overcoming historical problems caused by periodic military rule.[9]

Key geopolitical emphases of Brazil's 2008 defense white paper include maintaining a desire for peaceful relations with its neighbors, peaceful conflict resolution and nonintervention in external affairs, and a national desire to become a world power without promoting hegemony or domination.[10] It goes on to mention that its armed forces will be built on protecting Brazilian airspace, territory, and jurisdictional waters; reorganizing the defense industry to ensure that military technological needs are met and mastered; and strengthening national cyberinfrastructure, nuclear, and space sectors for national security exigencies; on recognizing that Brazil's most critical national defense concerns are in the country's north (particularly the Amazon), west, and the South Atlantic, with appropriate armed services deployment to these areas to respond to crisis situations; promoting regional security cooperation with other South American countries; naval development of multipurpose vehicles that can be used as aircraft carriers; and producing satellite-launching vehicles along with developing low- and high-orbit multiple-use geostationary satellites.[11]

Canada

Canadian geopolitical interests have been motivated by the desire to serve in United Nations peacekeeping operations as a way of bolstering a positive international image; longtime participation with the United States in the North American Aerospace Defense Command (NORAD) to detect and prevent ballistic missile attacks against North America; increased North American economic and defense cooperation with the United States and Mexico as part of the Security Partnership of the Americas; the desire to preserve Canadian sovereignty in the Arctic region, although this has seldom been backed up financially or with sufficient military resources and has complicated the U.S.-Canadian security relationship; concern over how climate change in the Arctic Ocean may affect its northern populations; and concern over the possibility of increased international trade traffic in the Arctic and competition for natural resources with other Arctic nations, which could produce confrontations.[12]

The most recent and current official explication of Canadian geopolitical strategy was the *Canada First Defence Strategy* issued in April 2008 by Prime Minister Stephen Harper's Conservative government. It is an ambitious 20-year plan to enhance the Canadian military's size, defense spending, and operational capabilities, including asserting enhanced sovereignty in the Arctic. The document reviews how international security developments such as terrorism, regional tensions in the Middle East, and the buildup of conventional forces in northeast Asia may affect Canadian security interests. Where the Arctic is concerned, *Canada First* declares,

> In Canada's Arctic, changing weather patterns are altering the environment making it more accessible to sea traffic and economic activity. Retreating ice cover has opened the way for increased shipping, tourism, and resource exploitation, and new transportation routes are being considered, including through the Northwest Passage. While this promises substantial economic benefits for Canada, it has also brought new challenges from other shores. These changes in the Arctic could also spark an increase in illegal activity, with important implications for Canadian sovereignty and security and a potential requirement for additional military support.[13]

Canadian forces will respond to these demands by increasing Arctic patrols; cooperating with the U.S. military's Northern Command; continuing ongoing Afghanistan operations and developing the ability to respond to a major domestic terrorist event; doubling defense spending over the next 20 years; increasing troop strength and combat aircraft and ship numbers; and equipping the Canadian defense industry to meet current and emerging national security technological challenges.[14]

China

One century ago, China was a weak and divided country highly vulnerable to foreign exploitation. Its international power strengthened after the 1949 Communist revolution and after developing nuclear weapons in the 1960s. A critically important indicator of China's growing importance and economic prosperity was its 1978 decision to begin moving from an exclusively governmentally directed to a more market-oriented economy. This resulted in a quadrupling of China's GDP over the next two decades and an increase in its international trade from 10 percent of GDP in 1978 to 36 percent of GDP two decades later.[15]

China's economic growth has accelerated over the past decade. Its estimated 2009 GDP is $8.789 trillion, ranking it third internationally; its 2009 annual GDP growth rate is estimated at 8.7 percent, ranking it fourth internationally; and its 2009 per capita personal income is estimated to be $6,600.[16] China has used its increasing wealth to acquire growing amounts of U.S. debt, increase its energy imports to fuel its economic growth from the Middle East, Africa, and Latin America; enhance its global foreign investment acquisitions globally; increase its political influence globally through less restrictive foreign economic assistance; and increase its military spending by 2009 to almost 10 times its 1989 level at higher rates than its annual GDP growth to enhance its power projection and war-fighting capabilities with state-of-the-art equipment.[17]

China has historically been interested in expanding northwest in order to contain threats from Russia and central Asia.[18] Its interest in securing its northwestern territories and access to central Asian energy and mineral resources continues today as it battles Islamic Uighur separatists in Xinjiang Province.[19] China is steadily seeking to expand its strategic influence beyond East Asian waters by building a "string of pearls" of bases in countries adjacent to waterways as diverse as the Indian Ocean, South China Sea, Straits of Malacca, and areas adjacent to the Persian Gulf.[20]

China is acutely concerned with maintaining the security of its energy supply lines, enhancing national prosperity, and maintaining domestic political instability and the governmental status quo against what it sees as the subversive influences of Western democracy. China's 2008 defense white paper maintains that its national defense policy is purely defensive in nature and seeks to protect national security sovereignty and territorial integrity, and its defenders also cite its membership in the World Trade Organization as indication of its desire to promote international stability.[21]

However, its military continues building up military forces across Taiwan and periodically threatens military action against this "renegade province"; Chinese forces continue enhancing their space and cyberwarfare assets, including making information attacks against U.S. and Indian computers; a Chinese submarine stalked the USS *Kitty Hawk* aircraft carrier battle group in October 2006 and surfaced within five miles of this force near Okinawa and within firing range of its torpedoes before being detected; and in March 2009, Chinese navy ships harassed the USS *Impeccable* while it was openly conducting surveillance operations outside China's 12-mile territorial limit in the South China Sea. China has geopolitical interests in the Korean Peninsula; periodically has diplomatic disputes with Japan over ownership of the Senkaku/Diaoyutai Islands in the South China Sea; is interested in Spratly Islands oil resources; is concerned with developments in Southeast Asian countries such as Indonesia and Thailand; has close ties with Pakistan; and may eventually compete with India for maritime supremacy in the Indian Ocean. Some foreign policy observers also believe the Chinese-dominated Shanghai Cooperation Organization seeks to create a security architecture antithetical to U.S. interests in central Asia. China also seeks to challenge U.S. naval preeminence in the western Pacific and believes that possessing Taiwan will give it control of the western Pacific's "first island chain" and give Beijing the chance to challenge U.S. control of waters next to the "second island chain" consisting of U.S. territories of Guam and the Northern Mariana Islands.[22]

Whether China's rise in international economic, military, and political influence signifies its emergence as a traditional great power desirous of enhancing international economic growth and stability, or whether it desires to become a hegemonic power threatening the security of its neighbors and even U.S. national security and its multifaceted global geopolitical interests, is this century's most important geopolitical problem.

France

Although France concentrates most of its defense policies through the European Union (EU), it still possesses significant geopolitical interests for various reasons, including a desire to remain independent of American and NATO military structures and retain historical aspects of its *mission civilatrice*. It retains a consultative relationship with NATO, which has increased slightly during President Nicholas Sarkozy's administration; continues maintaining a nuclear weapons deterrent consisting of air and submarine launched ballistic missiles; has historical and ongoing security ties with former colonies in Africa, the Caribbean, and South Pacific; possesses a significant foreign arms export market; and often decides to intervene directly when security situations in these countries deteriorate. France participates in the NATO-led forces in Afghanistan; faces challenges dealing with North African immigrants within its borders, which has produced riots and controversial legislation to prevent Muslim women from publicly wearing burkas; and believes that threats to vital national interests stem more from instability on the European periphery, such as Iran's nuclear program, than from other European countries.[23]

The 2008 *French White Paper on Defence and National Security* mentions that France can be threatened by environmental damage, pandemics, terrorists, ballistic missile proliferation around Europe, and attacks on information and communication systems. It goes on to say that France desires to be in a position where it does not have to submit to uncertainty but has the ability to anticipate, influence, and respond to international developments. It notes the decline in European armed conflicts and the EU's enhancement while also noting that globalization and communication advances increase the possible spread of diseases and economic, financial, and political crises and the growing role of nonstate actors such as computer networks, media, and international criminal organizations and private military organizations.[24]

France's responses to these geopolitical developments include global assessment of French national interests; the need for flexibility in anticipating, deterring, and responding to these threats; changing air, land, sea, and space surveillance methods to enhance national abilities to respond to these threats; enhancing conflict prevention and intervention capabilities on a geographical axis encompassing the Atlantic, Mediterranean, Persian Gulf, and Indian Ocean; recognizing Asia's increasing national security importance; preserving its freedom of action in Africa including the Sahel; retaining nuclear deterrence as foundational to national security; taking complementary approaches to EU and NATO security objectives; and increasing defense spending 1 percent annually above inflation between 2012 and 2020.[25]

Germany

Germany has a complicated historical relationship with the word geopolitics because of 20th-century Germany's historical military aggression, rhetorically symbolized by the term *lebensraum* (living space), and geopolitics abuse by Nazi theoreticians and policy makers. Reunited Germany still faces difficulty in developing a coherent and effective national geopolitical strategy that can command the support of domestic public opinion. However, as the EU's largest economy with global economic interests, early-21st-century Germany is gradually developing an appreciation of the critical role geography plays in fulfilling national economic, political, and security objectives and cannot escape the reality that geopolitics will continue influencing its national development.[26]

Since its 1990 reunification as a democracy, Germany has sought to increase its integration into EU and NATO security architectures while also tentatively beginning to formulate a renewed national geopolitical identity. An early example of Germany demonstrating a unique national geopolitical identity was its December 23, 1991, decision to unilaterally recognize Croatia's and Slovenia's independence before most of the international community thought those countries were ready for independence.[27] Early characteristics of reunified German geopolitical thinking include rhetorical attempts to transcend Germany's middle position in Europe, whether Germany will attempt to reposition itself within a globalized international system instead of by spatial boundaries, Germany's relationships with Eastern Europe and the EU, and how Germany's military will adapt to these changing roles.[28]

Emerging issues in German geopolitics, some of which are addressed in the 2006 German Defense White Paper, include playing a leadership role in handling European economic crises, as demonstrated by Chancellor Angela Merkel during the spring 2010 Greek financial crisis; maintaining good bilateral relations with Russia while looking for alternative energy supply sources to lessen Berlin's dependence on Russian natural gas and oil; restraining Russian assertiveness against former Soviet republics in the "near abroad"; maintaining an active role in international pressure on Iran to prevent it from acquiring nuclear weapons; striking a balance between EU and NATO defense policies; and developing the willingness to use its military forces outside of Europe with less restrictive rules of engagement than it has applied to its forces operating in Afghanistan, which now restrict them to conducting defense-oriented operations in relatively safer northern Afghanistan.[29]

India

In its more than six decades of independence, India has gone from an impoverished country that barely survived its separation from Pakistan to an increasingly important player in the global economy and is developing an increased military capability to expand its influence beyond the South Asian subcontinent. India's estimated July 2010 population is 1.173 billion, making it the world's second most populous country; its population is growing at a faster rate than China and is projected to surpass China's population in 2025 to become the world's highest.[30]

Its increasingly liberalized economy has experienced 7 percent average annual growth rates since 1997; its annual per capita GDP was $3,900 in 2009, ranking it 164th globally; it possesses the world's second largest labor force, and its military expenditures were 2.5 percent of GDP in 2006, ranking it 62nd in the world, just ahead of the United Kingdom.[31] India is a nuclear weapons power and has a nuclear agreement with the United States giving it access to nuclear fuel and technology, including reprocessing U.S. nuclear material under International Atomic Energy Safeguards. It also possesses a wide variety of geopolitical challenges, including its relationships with Pakistan and their bilateral dispute over Kashmir; relationships with China, Afghanistan, Tibet, Bangladesh, and the South Asian Association for Regional Cooperation (SAARC); and hydropolitics concerns with neighboring countries over rivers such as the Ganges and Indus.[32]

India's increasing willingness to assert its maritime presence in the Indian Ocean will become an increasingly important geopolitical issue and could lead to enhanced rivalry with China as that country increases its oil and natural gas imports from the Middle East and Africa. It is likely that security cooperation between India and United States will increase to hedge against possible Chinese efforts to acquire military supremacy in the Indian Ocean and to maintain the security of sea lanes against maritime piracy emanating from sources as far-flung as the Horn of Africa and Straits of Malacca. India has increased its security cooperation with Singapore. The Indian Navy has made port visits to countries such as Japan, the Philippines, South Korea, and Vietnam; conducted a 2007 Malabar training exercise with Australia, Japan, Singapore, and the United States; and may adopt its own version of the Monroe Doctrine to ensure that no hostile power or combination of powers restricts its access to the Indian Ocean. Consequently, India may seek to enhance its naval forces and presence in this body of water thousands of miles beyond the subcontinent in subsequent decades.[33]

The most recent edition of the Indian Ministry of Defence's *Annual Report* notes that India is a maritime and continental entity with mountainous and oceanic frontiers; that the Andoman and Nicobar islands are 1,300 kilometers from its east coast and the eastern parts of the Persian Gulf and Red Sea are 450 kilometers from its west coast; that India represents a bulwark of economic dynamism, functional stability, and plural democracy in an unstable region; that its "Look East" policy toward Southeast Asia seeks to enhance economic prosperity and security ties with these countries; and that it seeks to expand ties and confidence-building measures with China's military.[34]

This document goes on to add that regional maritime security concerns have been enhanced by the November 2008 Mumbai terror attacks and that nearly $260 billion in oil passes annually through the Straits of Hormuz and Malacca. India's 2007 *National Maritime Strategy* stresses that the Indian Navy's major 21st-century task will be using warships to support national foreign policy and that aerial and space-based assets will be integrated into national maritime strategy; stresses the presence of numerous potential maritime traffic choke points; acknowledges the Chinese Navy's desire to become a blue water force and India's need to have secure access to its energy resources given the Indian Ocean's increasing importance as a energy supply corridor; acknowledges the need to promote naval interoperability with friendly forces and conduct rescue operations such as its evacuation of Indian nationals from Lebanon in 2006; and its desire to enhance naval force capabilities in maritime domain awareness, including uninhabited aerial vehicles, enhanced expeditionary operations capabilities, and other scientific and technological developments.[35]

Indonesia

Indonesia is a vast national island archipelago serving as a buffer between China and Indonesia, located near countries such as Brunei, East Timor, Singapore, and Thailand, and is also located near strategically important waterways such as the South China Sea and Straits of Malacca. It also is the world's largest Islamic country, with a July 2010 population of nearly 243 million, ranking it the world's fourth most populous country. Its economy grew 6 percent in 2007–2008 and an estimated 4 percent in 2009, joining China and India as the only G20 nations posting economic growth during the international economic crisis, and its estimated 2009 GDP purchasing power parity is $969.2 billion, ranking it 16th in the world.[36]

Indonesian geopolitical concerns include unresolved maritime and boundary problems with East Timor after that country separated from Indonesia in 2002; some maritime disputes with Malaysia; immigration problems with Papua New Guinea; addressing how China will use hard and soft power in bilateral and Southeast Asian regional relations; periodic bouts with Islamist terrorism such as the October 12, 2002, bombings in Bali, killing over 200, including many Australians; Malacca Strait piracy; the Islamist separatist rebellion in Aceh province; the rise of the Jemaah Islamiya terrorist group responsible for the Bali bombings and subsequent bombings of Jakarta's Marriott Hotel and Australian Embassy; efforts to achieve mutually satisfactory security relationships with Australia over security cooperation and illegal aliens attempting to reach Australia by boat; and developing and sustaining democratic governance after the Suharto government's 1998 collapse.[37]

How Indonesia addresses and resolves these matters, particularly Islamist terrorism, will have an important impact on Southeast Asian regional and maritime economic and geopolitical stability and U.S. relations with the Islamic world. The United States began a comprehensive partnership with Indonesia in 2009, and Defense Secretary Robert Gates met his Indonesian counterpart in Singapore on June 4, 2010, to discuss ways of enhancing this relationship. Indonesia's most recent defense white paper mentions the importance of enhancing professionalism among its military forces; how piracy, human smuggling, drug trafficking, and transnational criminal networks have become national security threats; that Indonesia's strategic location will cause it to face traditional and nontraditional security threats; and that terrorism and communal conflict are also national security threats that must be addressed by national power and international cooperation.[38]

Israel

Since its modern 1948 establishment, Israel has faced numerous geopolitical challenges despite being one of the Middle East's most prosperous and democratic countries. It has had to fight major wars for survival with its major Arab neighbors in 1948, 1956, 1967, and 1973, along with conventional combat and antiterrorist operations at various times in locales as diverse as Lebanon, Iraq, Tunisia, and Uganda, which have produced mixed results. It conducts intelligence operations against a wide variety of enemies and in 2010 received international opprobrium for its secret service Mossad falsifying the passports of civilians from countries as diverse as Australia, France, and the United Kingdom in order to kill a Hamas terrorist leader in Dubai.[39]

Israel continues facing a variety of geopolitical problems entering the 21st century's second decade. One of these includes maintaining good relations with the United States, its principal supporter, at a time when there are differences between the Obama administration and Prime Minister Benjamin Netanyahu's government over the Middle East peace process. Israel faces continual challenges maintaining its national security from Palestinian terrorist attacks originating in Gaza, the West Bank, and Lebanon. Such attacks have compelled Israel to build an internationally controversial wall to prevent unauthorized individuals from entering Israel. It also has had to impose an economic blockade on Gaza to prevent arms shipments from being smuggled into that community by Iran and terrorist organizations such as Hamas to be used in attacks against Israel. It has also conducted military operations in Lebanon against Iranian-supported groups such as Hezbollah.

Additional geopolitical problems facing Israel include a once cooperative but steadily deteriorating relationship with Turkey, which was exacerbated by the May 31, 2010, Israeli storming of a boat with Turkish nationals purportedly carrying humanitarian aid to Gaza; concern over Iran's nuclear program and the growing belief that it represents an existential threat to Israel and may require risky unilateral or multilateral military action to disable or destroy; its four-decade-long dispute with Syria over the Golan Heights; and increasing concerns over water scarcity in this region covering areas such as the Dead Sea and Jordan River and whether Israel and its neighbors can manage this problem without resorting to conflict. Israel has also faces problems in its relationships with European countries that have attempted to criminally prosecute Israeli officials or prevent them from entering their countries for dubious international law reasons because of Israeli policies toward Palestinians.[40]

Japan

As an island nation, Japan faces many geopolitical issues, with particular emphasis on maintaining maritime security due to its heavy dependence on importing natural resources to sustain its economy, which includes its being the world's second largest oil importer and largest importer of liquefied natural gas. At the same time, Japan has been reluctant to use its general economic prosperity to promote expanded military power as a result of its defeat in World War II and its postwar constitution prohibiting Japanese defense forces from engaging in operations other than self-defense. Consequently, it has depended on the United States for most of its national security requirements.[41]

This Japanese reticence to build and project military power has slowly begun to change in the 21st century. After the 9/11 terrorist attacks, Japan deployed its Maritime Self Defense Force to the Indian Ocean to support U.S. and coalition operations in Afghanistan; dispatched 600 troops to Iraq in 2004 to participate in humanitarian reconstruction operations; changed its International Peace Cooperation Law in 2001 limiting its Self Defense Force

Participation to core peace-keeping force operations; and joined the U.S.-led Proliferation Security Initiative as part of its concern with weapons of mass destruction and ballistic missile proliferation.[42]

Japan has also sought to enhance its sea power by posturing its new destroyer units for more effective response to security contingencies; forming submarine units to emphasize responding to new threats and emerging contingencies; and improving the efficiency of combat aircraft units. The September 26, 2006, election of Prime Minister Abe Shinzo (the first Japanese prime minister born after World War II) also signified that Japan would become more outspoken on regional security issues with countries such as China and North Korea and that it will seek to compete with China on regional security matters.[43]

Subsequent years will see Japan confront a number of geopolitical security matters despite the August 2009 election of a more pacific Democratic Party of Japan government. These include Japan's long-standing territorial dispute with Russia over the Kurile and Sakhalin islands; its concern with China's growing military power and dispute with China over ownership of the Senkaku/Diaoyuti Islands; concerns over North Korea's ballistic missile program, which have made Japan interested in acquiring ballistic missile defense systems, and North Korean abduction of Japanese citizens; concern over the consequences of a Chinese attack on Taiwan and the security implications for Japan; disputes with the United States over stationing U.S. troops on Okinawa; the security of energy supply lines, including beginning participation in antipiracy efforts in the Horn of Africa; and how assertive a foreign policy to pursue considering its post–World War II pacifist tradition balanced with emerging geopolitical security concerns and the diplomatic sensitivity such assertiveness will have on countries victimized by Japan's World War II–era aggression.[44]

Japan's most recent defense white paper says it will promote regional security cooperation through regional Asia-Pacific nations, the United Nations, and its security alliance with the United States. This document goes on to stress that Japan is not interested in becoming a nuclear military power; that it will retain civilian control of the military; that it will commit to peaceful uses of space while also increasing its C4ISR capabilities; that it will strengthen its maritime security and antipiracy capabilities; and that it will continue the long-standing practice of keeping its defense expenditures at less than 1 percent GDP.[45]

Russia

The Russian Federation remains an important player in international and Eurasian geopolitical matters due to its military strength and significant oil and natural gas resources. Although it experienced a downturn in its geopolitical power following the Soviet Union's 1991 collapse, it has begun reasserting its power in various years, as demonstrated by its increasing delivery of natural resources to European countries to influence their foreign economic policies; its planting of the Russian flag on the ocean seafloor below the North Pole in August 2007 to assert its sovereignty over the Arctic seabed; its 2008 war with Georgia to seize that country's separatist regions of Abkhazia and South Ossetia; its efforts to keep Ukraine from joining NATO and expanding this alliance's eastern reach; its expanding access to Caspian Sea natural gas and oil resources; its influencing of former Soviet central Asian republics to distance themselves from U.S. antiterrorism initiatives; its cooperating with China through the Shanghai Cooperation Organization; its selectively cooperating with the United States in the G20 but seeking to maintain freedom of action even if that is contrary to U.S. interests; and its taking a reluctant approach to sanctioning Iran for its nuclear weapons program.[46]

There is extensive debate within Russia's government, military, and geopolitical strategic community over what future directions Russian foreign and national security policies should follow. Some favor closer cooperation with the European Union, NATO, and the United States and even seek to counterbalance China; some favor strengthening Russian influence in the "near abroad," which includes former Soviet bloc countries; others favor enhancing Russian ties with Turkey, the Middle East, and other central Asian countries; while others believe it is in Russia's national interest to strengthen its ties with China due to its growing economic and military power and its increasing demographic and economic presence in the Russian Far East, which may threaten Russian control of that area and access to the Pacific Ocean. Russian geopolitics, whether it is under Vladimir Putin, Dmitri Medvedev, or some other leader, will be torn between factions advocating these perspectives and various intermediate viewpoints. Russia will likely seek to prevent the deployment of an expanded U.S.-led ballistic missile defense system and may continue resisting Western efforts to impose tough economic or military sanctions against Iran's nuclear program. It is also likely to keep increasing its own military assertiveness as financial resources permit and to use such forces when it believes it will encounter relatively cost-free international disapproval or retaliation.[47]

United Kingdom

Geopolitics has played a critical role in the United Kingdom's rise from an isolated northwestern European island state to the world's greatest empire, spanning 25 percent of the globe and the world's population, where it extended the English language and parliamentary democracy to global areas as diverse as Africa, Hong Kong, India, Oceania, and the United States. Britain lost its empire in the wake of the costs of two world wars and granting independence to most of its former colonies. However, it remains a nuclear weapons power with significant conventional military assets and a military presence in Afghanistan.[48]

British geopolitical interests have been bisected by two competing intellectual strands. An idealistic strand seeks to promote democratization and human rights and cooperate with international government organizations, while a more realistic strand emphasizing assertive and even unilateral diplomatic, economic, and military assertion of national power was best personified on March 1, 1848, by Prime Minister Viscount Palmerston (1784–1865), who declared, "We have no allies, and we have no perpetual enemies. Our interests are eternal and perpetual, and those interests it is our duty to follow."[49]

Regardless of existing geopolitical global situations, the domestic economic British economic situation, or the real or perceived value of its military power and its allies, the British have sought to follow a number of consistent principles in their application and use of national power, which has been demonstrated in all global areas. These include maintaining unrestricted access to the seas and the freedom of international maritime traffic due to the superior power of the Royal Navy or this force being allied with the U.S. Navy and ensuring that no power or combination of powers could dominate Europe or other critical global regions such as India and the Middle East to endanger British national interests. Britain has used these principles to promote its highest national ideals, commercial interests, and national survival at considerable cost in blood and treasure throughout the centuries with differing degrees of emphasis, regardless of the political preferences of its governments.[50]

The past three decades have seen Britain fight a 1982 war to reclaim the Falkland Islands from Argentina; fight counterinsurgency campaigns in Northern Ireland; participate in peace-keeping operations in the Balkans and Sierra Leone; actively participate in U.S.-led antiterrorism wars in Afghanistan and Iraq. Conservative and Labour governments have had to face criticism that they are to subservient to U.S. geopolitical interests; decide on how closely Britain should ally itself with the EU; attempt to balance its special relationship with the United States and relationships with NATO and the EU; determine how much resources it can allocate to national security and armed forces (including maintaining and enhancing its nuclear missile submarines as recommended by a 2006 Defense White Paper) at a time of acute financial constraints; and have periodic diplomatic disputes with Argentina and Spain over the Falkland Islands and Gibraltar. These issues will also continue and impact emerging concerns, including determining how to integrate its growing Muslim population, which has shown radical tendencies, as demonstrated by the July 7, 2005, London mass transit bombings, and advocacy by some radical British Muslims of turning Britain into an Islamic state. Concerns over Britain's ability to financially sustain future national security obligations were expressed on July 22, 2010, by Defense Secretary Liam Fox, who said Prime Minister David Cameron's government may have to reduce force size by 30,000; remove 25,000 troops from Germany; reduce the arsenal of warships, fighter jets, and armored vehicles and cut the defense budget by 20 percent; structure the military for "realistic potential future threats"; and get funding for the Trident submarines from outside of the Ministry of Defence's core budget.[51]

United States

In its rise from a small western Atlantic seaboard revolutionary upstart to the world's preeminent military power, the United States has experienced tremendous and ongoing evolution in its geopolitical aspirations and practices. This has occurred from the George Washington to Barack Obama presidential administrations and reflects continually evolving national economic, foreign policy, and national security beliefs and realities.[52]

The United States gradually gained control of the North American continent; became a global presence with its 1898 Spanish-American War victory; and became the world's preeminent global power after its victorious leadership in two world wars. Following 1945, the subsequent four and half decades of the cold war saw it involved in a nuclear stalemate with the former Soviet Union, in which it used various strategies, including containment, détente, the maintenance of a strong nuclear weapons deterrent, and the Reagan Doctrine supporting anti-Communist liberation movements, to weaken and ultimately defeat the Soviet Union.[53]

Victory over the Soviet bloc briefly produced the illusory view that this triumph of liberal democratic capitalism represented the "end of history."[54] Despite the United States' military preeminence, the cold war's end would cause long-suppressed conflicts to reappear in the Balkans and the Middle East, which would require the attention of U.S. geopolitical strategists and policy makers during the 1990s. These strategists and policy makers would also debate when and if U.S. military forces should be deployed to defend national interests.[55]

The September 11, 2001, terrorist attacks shattered U.S. beliefs in immunity from international troubles and prompted a series of foreign military interventions in Afghanistan and Iraq that are ongoing and controversial and that have achieved mixed success. In 2002, the George W. Bush administration released its controversial national security strategy that advocated taking preemptive action against potential military threats; working collaboratively with nations and international law as needed but being willing to take unilateral action if necessary; stressing the dangers of weapons of mass destruction terrorism; emphasizing that key international cultural and normative differences remain between countries despite globalization; and advocating the expansion of democracy as the best means of enhancing U.S. national security.[56]

This document reflects a continuation of the long-standing American geopolitical strategy of seeking to expand its security perimeters, which now encompass the entire world. It has its supporters, who praise its recognition of what they see as an astute understanding of emerging geopolitical realities, and critics, who contend it has bogged down the United States in costly Middle Eastern wars that have weakened our economy, cost innocent lives, damaged U.S. international standing, and endangered domestic constitutional freedoms and international law. Debate over appropriate global U.S. foreign and military policy continues in the Obama administration, which has criticized Bush administration policies but retained many of them in its 2010 *National Security Strategy* report, including advocacy of the potential need for preemptive military force.[57]

A particularly vivid illustration of geography's role in American strategic planning is the U.S. military's unified combatant command structure dividing military forces and theaters into regional and functional commands. These include Central Command (CENTCOM), covering Middle Eastern and central Asian countries such as Afghanistan and Iraq; Pacific Command (PACOM), covering most of the Pacific and Indian Oceans and including countries such as India and China; and commands for North America, South America, Africa, and Europe, including the Russian Federation. This command structure, which includes many bureaucratic components, also includes functional entities such as Strategic Command (STRATCOM), which seeks to deter and defeat global threats to U.S. security such as ballistic missile strikes and cyberwarfare.[58]

U.S. geopolitical activities will overlap and/or conflict with many of the other national government geopolitical situations described in this chapter. However, since the United States is the only global superpower, despite its current military challenges in the CENTCOM region and domestic financial problems, it will remain geopolitically preeminent throughout the world for the foreseeable future, though China may become a dangerous competitor. It will continue having military forces in Afghanistan past July 2011, despite the Obama administration's objective of beginning to withdraw U.S. forces then. It will continue fighting against al-Qaeda and its affiliated forces throughout the world; seek to prevent the development and use of Iranian nuclear weapons; attempt to deter North Korean conventional and nuclear aggressiveness, as evidenced by its late July 2010 participation in joint naval exercises with South Korea featuring the aircraft carrier USS *George Washington*; and combat maritime piracy and seek to maintain freedom of the seas and the security of strategic choke points against terrorist attacks that could disrupt energy supplies and international trade.

It will also seek to develop more environmentally and energy-effective technologies to lessen dependence on unreliable and hostile foreign energy sources; improve international environmental cooperation in addressing climate change; seek to prevent Venezuela's Chavez regime from destabilizing Latin America and the Southern Caribbean; seek to constructively engage China, where possible, but also hedging against a rise of Chinese hostility by strengthening security cooperation with Australia, India, Indonesia, Japan, and South Korea; attempt to engage constructively with Russia while strengthening security with European and other nations if Russian foreign policy turns hostile; support Israel's security while trying to advance the Middle East process; and seek to promote international recovery and economic growth while wrestling with its own fiscal profligacy, which has created a public debt of nearly $13.25 trillion as of July 22, 2010, and an anticipated 2010 federal budget deficit of $1.3 trillion, representing 9.2 percent of GDP. These domestic economic problems are increasing and will also affect the United States' ability to meet its international geopolitical interests and obligations and may require it to surrender some of these interests or delegate them to other countries or groups of countries.[59]

Notes

1. See Jeremy Black, *Maps and History: Constructing Images of the Past* (New Haven, CT: Yale University Press, 1997); and Walter Goffart, *Historical Atlases: The First Three Hundred Years, 1570–1870* (Chicago: University of Chicago Press, 2003).

2. Australian Bureau of Statistics, "Population Clock," http://www.abs.gov.au/.

3. See Frank Broeze, *Island Nation: A History of Australians and the Sea* (St. Leonards, NSW: Allen and Unwin, 1998); Dennis Rumley, *The Geopolitics of Australia's Regional Relations* (Dordrecht, Netherlands: Kluwer, 1999); Sean McDonald and Bruce Baughn, "Australia's Strategic Posture: A Spatial Orientation under the Howard Government," *Geographical Bulletin*, 43 (1)(May 2001): 16–27; Bilveer Singh, *Defense Relations between Australia and Indonesia in the Post–Cold War Era* (Westport, CT: Greenwood Press, 2002); and Clive Schofield, "Australian Interventionism Grows in the South Pacific," *Jane's Intelligence Review*, 17 (5)(May 2005): 40–43.

4. Geoffrey Blainey, *The Tyranny of Distance: How Distance Shaped Australia's History* (Sydney: Pan Macmillan, 2001): 369.

5. See Simon Dalby, *Continent Adrift: The Changing Strategic Parameters of Australian Discourse* (Canberra: Australian Defence Studies Centre, 1995); Klaus Dodds, *Geopolitics in Antarctica: Views from the Southern Oceanic Rim* (New York: John Wiley, 1997): 77–106; Nicholas Thomas, ed., *Re-orienting Australia-China Relations: 1972 to the Present* (Burlington, VT: Ashgate, 2004); Australia, Department of Defence,

Defence 2000: Our Future Defence Force (Canberra: Department of Defence, 2000); Australia, Department of Defence, *Australia's National Security: A Defence Update 2007* (Canberra: Department of Defence, 2007); Australia, Department of Defence, *Defending Australia in the Asia-Pacific Century: Force 2030* (Canberra: Department of Defence, 2009); John Mortimer and David Stevens, *Presence, Power Projection and Sea Control: The RAN in the Gulf 1990–2009* (Canberra: Department of Defence Sea Power Centre, 2009); Sam Bateman and Anthony Bergman, *Our Western Front: Australia and the Indian Ocean* (Barton, ACT: Australian Strategic Policy Institute, 2010); and Richard Leaver and Karl Ungerer, *A Natural Power: Challenges for Australia's Resources Diplomacy in Asia* (Barton, ACT: Australian Strategic Policy Institute, 2010).

6. Brazil, Institute of Geography and Statistics, homepage, http://www.ibge.gov.br/english/.

7. Central Intelligence Agency (CIA), "World Factbook 2009," https://www.cia.gov/library/publications/the-world-factbook/geos/br.html.

8. Philip Kelly, *Checkerboards and Shatterbelts: The Geopolitics of South America* (Austin: University of Texas Press, 1997): 48–51.

9. See Klaus-John Dodds, "Geopolitics, Cartography, and the State in South America," *Political Geography*, 12 (4)(July 1993): 374–77; Kelly, *Checkerboards and Shatterbelts*, 1997, 51–54; Arie M. Kacowicz, "Geopolitics and Territorial Issues: Relevance for South America," *Geopolitics*, 5 (1)(Summer 2000): 81–100; Luis Bitencourt, "Security Issues and Challenges to Regional Security Cooperation: A Brazilian Perspective," in *Perspectives from Argentina, Brazil, and Colombia* (Carlisle, PA: U.S. Army War College, Strategic Studies Institute, 2003): 13–34; and Leslie W. Hepple, "South American Heartland: The Charcas, Latin American Geopolitics and Global Strategies," *Geographical Journal*, 170 (4)(December 2004): 359–67.

10. Brazil, Ministry of Defense, *National Strategy for Defense: Peace and Security for Brazil* (Brasilia: Ministry of Defense, 2008): 8, http://merln.ndu.edu/whitepapers/Brazil_English2008.pdf.

11. Ibid., 10, 12–13, 17, 21, 25.

12. See J. L. Granatstein, *A Friendly Agreement in Advance: Canada-U.S. Defense Relations Past, Present, and Future* (Toronto, ON: C. D. Howe Institute, 2002); Brian S. MacDonald and David S. McDonough, eds., *The New World of Robust International Peacekeeping Operation: What Roles for NATO and Canada?* (Toronto, ON: Royal Canadian Military Institute, 2005); Donald McRae, *Arctic Sovereignty? What Is at Stake?* (Toronto, ON: Canadian Institute of International Affairs, 2007); Security and Prosperity Partnership of North America, homepage, http://www.spp.gov/; Gerry Madigan, "Canada First-Defence Strategy: A Retrospective Look. Too Much? To Little? Or Just Right?" *Canadian Military Journal*, 10 (3)(Summer 2010): 27–36; and Charles Emmerson, *The Future History of the Arctic* (New York: Public Affairs, 2010).

13. Canada, Department of National Defence, *Canada First Defence Strategy* (Ottawa, ON: Department of National Defence, 2008): 4, 6.

14. Ibid., 8, 11–12, 21–22.

15. Mark A. Groombridge, *China's Long March to a Market Economy: The Case for Permanent Normal Trade Relations with the People's Republic of China* (Washington, DC: CATO Institute, 2000): 3.

16. See CIA, "World Factbook 2009," https://www.cia.gov/library/publications/the-world-factbook/geos/ch.html.

17. See Bernard D. Cole, *"Oil for the Lamps of China": Beijing's 21st Century Search for Energy* (Washington, DC: National Defense University, Institute for National Strategic Studies, 2003); Wayne M. Morrison and Marc Labonte, *China's Holdings of U.S. Securities: Implications for the U.S. Economy* (Washington, DC: Library of Congress, Congressional Research Service, 2008); U.S. Congress, Senate Committee for Foreign Relations, Subcommittee on African Affairs, *China in Africa: Implications for U.S. Policy* (Washington, DC: Government Printing Office, 2008); Miria Pigato, *Strengthening China's and India's Trade and Investment Ties to India and North Africa* (Washington, DC: World Bank, 2009); U.S. Department of Defense, *Annual Report to Congress: Military Power of the People's Republic of China* (Washington, DC: U.S. Department of Defense, 2009): 31; and U.S.-China Economic and Security Review Commission, "U.S. Debt to China: Implications and Repercussions," http://www.uscc.gov/hearings/2010hearings/hr10_02_25.php.

18. Peter C. Perdue, *China Marches West: The Qing Conquest of Central Asia* (Cambridge, MA: Belknap Press of Harvard University Press, 2005).

19. See Haava Kok, "China and the Geopolitics of Oil in East Turkestan," *Turkish Review of Eurasian Studies*, 4 (2004): 255–72; U.S. Department of Energy, *Energy Policy Act 2005, Section 1837: National Security Review of International Energy Requirements* (Washington, DC: U.S. Department of Energy, 2006); and U.S. Congress, House Committee on Foreign Affairs, Subcommittee on International Organization, Human Rights, and Oversight, *Exploring the Nature of Uighur Nationalism: Freedom Fighters or Terrorists?* (Washington, DC: Government Printing Office, 2009).

20. Christopher J. Pehrson, *String of Pearls: Meeting the Challenge of China's Rising Power across the Asian Littoral* (Carlisle, PA: U.S. Army War College, Strategic Studies Institute, 2006).

21. See Kam C. Chan, Hung-gay Fung, and Qingfeng 'Wilson' Liu, eds., *China's Capital Markets: Challenges from WTO Membership* (Northampton, MA: Edward Elgar, 2007); and China State Information Council, "China National Defense in 2008," http://www.china.org.cn/government/whitepaper/2009-01/21/content_17162883.htm.

22. See Toshi Yoshihara and James R. Holmes, "Command of the Seas with Chinese Characteristics," *Orbis*, 49 (4)(Fall 2005): 677–94; "China Sub Stalked U.S. Fleet," *Washington Times*, November 13, 2006; James R. Holmes and Toshi Yoshihara, "China's Naval Ambitions in the Indian Ocean," *Journal of Strategic Studies*, 31 (3) (June 2008): 367–94; U.S. Congress, Commission on Security and Cooperation in Europe, *The Shanghai Cooperation Organization: Is It Undermining U.S. Interests in Central Asia* (Washington, DC: Government Printing Office, 2008); U.S. Department of Defense, *Annual Report to Congress*, 51–53; Tuomo Kuosa, *Future of U.S. Power: Is China Going to Eclipse the United States? Two Possible Scenarios to 2040* (Singapore: S. Rajaratnam School of International Studies, 2010); and Robert D. Kaplan, "The Geography of Chinese Power," *Foreign Affairs*, 89 (3)(May/June 2010): 22–41.

23. See Anton Andereggen, *France's Relationship with Subsaharan Africa* (Westport, CT: Praeger, 1994); Stephen A. Kocs, *Autonomy or Power? The Franco-German Relationship and Europe's Strategic Choices, 1955–1995* (Westport, CT: Praeger, 1995);

Avery Goldstein, *Deterrence and Security in the 21st Century: China, Britain, France, and the Enduring Legacy of the Nuclear Revolution* (Stanford, CA: Stanford University Press, 2000); Joseph Philippe Gregoire, *The Bases of French Peace Operations Doctrine: Problematical Scope of France's Military Engagements within the U.N. or NATO Framework* (Carlisle, PA: U.S. Army War College, Strategic Studies Institute, 2002); Sten Rynning, "Potent or Paralyzing? Nuclear Weapons in Contemporary French Military Strategy," *Defense and Security Analysis*, 19 (1)(March 2003): 55–68; Daniel Keohane, "Defensive Realignment," *ISS Opinion* (September–October 2008): 38–40; and Tom Sauer, "A Second Nuclear Revolution: From Nuclear Primacy to Post-existential Deterrence," *Journal of Strategic Studies*, 32 (5)(October 2009): 745–67.

24. France President, *The French White Paper on Defense and National Security* (Paris: President of the Republic, 2008): 22–24.

25. Ibid., 301–6.

26. See David Murphy, *The Heroic Earth: Geopolitical Thought in Weimar Germany, 1918–1933* (Kent, OH: Kent State University Press, 1997); and Guntram H. Herb, "Double Vision: Territorial Strategies in the Construction of National Identities in Germany, 1949–1979," *Annals of the Association of American Geographers*, 94 (1) (March 2004): 140–64.

27. Alan Hanson, "Croatian Independence from Yugoslavia, 1991–1992," in *Words over War: Mediation and Arbitration to Prevent Deadly Conflict*, ed. Melanie C. Greenburg, John H. Barton, and Margaret E. McGuinness (New York: Carnegie Commission on Preventing Deadly Conflict, 2000): 78.

28. See Jonathan Bach and Susanne Peters, "The New Spirit of German Politics," *Geopolitics*, 7 (3)(Winter 2002): 1–18; Vassilis K. Fouskass, "Germany and the Passage from War to Peace in Eurasia," *Debatte: Review of Contemporary German Affairs*, 15 (2)(August 2007): 195–210; and Louis Simon and James Rodgers, "The Return of European Geopolitics," *RUSI Journal*, 155 (3)(June/July 2010): 58–64.

29. See Francis T. Miko, *Germany's Role in Fighting Terrorism: Implications for U.S. Policy* (Washington, DC: Library of Congress, Congressional Research Service, 2005); Hanns W. Maull, ed., *Germany's Uncertain Power: Foreign Policy of the Berlin Republic* (New York: Palgrave Macmillan, 2006); Germany, Federal Ministry of Defense, *White Paper 2006 on German Security Policy and the Future of the Bundeswehr* (Berlin: Federal Ministry of Defense, 2006); Paul Belkin, *German Foreign and Security Policy: Trends and Transatlantic Implications* (Washington, DC: Library of Congress, Congressional Research Service, 2009); Nik Hynek, Vit Stricky, Vladimir Handl, and Michael Koran, "The US-Russian Security 'Reset': Implications for Central-Eastern Europe and Germany," *European Security*, 18 (3)(September 2009): 263–85; and Gerrit Wiesman, "Voters Accept Bitter Medicine," *Financial Times*, May 25, 2010: 10.

30. See CIA, "World Factbook 2009," http://www.cia.gov/library/publications/the-world-factbook/geos/in.html; and U.S. Census Bureau, "International Data Base: Country Rankings," http://sasweb.ssb.census.gov/idb/ranks.html.

31. CIA, "World Factbook 2009," http://www.cia.gov/library/publications/the-world-factbook/geos/in.html.

32. See Graham P. Chapman, *The Geopolitics of South Asia: From Early Empires to the Nuclear Age*, 2nd ed. (Burlington, VT: Ashgate, 2002): 241–80; David van Praagh, *The Greater Game: India's Race with Destiny and China* (Montreal, QC:

McGill-Queen's University Press, 2003); Jayshree Bajoria, *The U.S.-India Nuclear Deal* (New York: Council on Foreign Relations, 2009): 1–6.

33. See Zhang Guihong, "U.S.-India Strategic Partnership: Implications for China," *International Studies*, 42 (3–4)(July–December 2005): 277–93; James R. Holmes and Toshi Yoshihara, "Strongman, Constable, or Free-Rider? India's 'Monroe Doctrine' and Indian Naval Strategy," *Comparative Strategy*, 28 (4)(2009): 332–48; and David Brewster, "India's Security Partnership with Singapore," *Pacific Review*, 22 (5)(December 2009): 597–618.

34. India, Ministry of Defence, *Annual Report 2009–2010* (New Delhi: MOD, 2010): 2–4, 7.

35. Ibid., 8; India, Navy, *Freedom to Use the Seas: India's Maritime Military Strategy* (New Delhi: Indian Navy, 2007): 11–12, 27–28, 41, 46, 81, 117, 119; and Ashok W. Sawney, *Indian Naval Effectiveness for National Growth* (Singapore: R. Rajaratnam School of International Studies, 2010).

36. See CIA, "World Factbook 2009," http://www.cia.gov/library/publications/the-world-factbook/geos/id.html.

37. See Ibid.; P. Flynn, "Indonesian Islamic Fundamentalism and Acch in the Twentieth Century," *Australian Defence Force Journal*, 141 (March/April 2000): 29–35; M.C. Ricklefs, *A History of Modern Indonesia since c. 1200*, 4th ed. (Stanford, CA: Stanford University Press, 2000); Angel Rabasa and Peter Chalk, *Indonesia's Transformation and the Stability of Southeast Asia* (Santa Monica, CA: RAND, 2001); Greg Fealy and Aldo Borgu, *Local Jihad: Radical Terrorism and Islam in Indonesia* (Barton, ACT: Australian Strategic Policy Institute, 2005); Peter Chalk and Carl Ungerer, *Neighbourhood Watch: The Evolving Terrorist Threat in Southeast Asia* (Barton, ACT: Australian Strategic Policy Institute, 2008); and Parama Sinha Palit, *China's Soft Power in Asia* (Singapore: R. Rajaratnam School of International Studies, 2010).

38. See Indonesia, Minister of Defense, *Defending the Country Entering the 21st Century* (Jakarta: Minister of Defense, 2003), 4, 6: 26–29; John B. Haseman and Eduardo Lachia, "Getting Indonesia Right: Managing a Security Partnership with a Nonallied Country," *Joint Force Quarterly*, 54 (July 2009): 87–91; and White House, Office of the Press Secretary, "The U.S.-Indonesia Comprehensive Partnership," http://www.whitehouse.gov/the-press-office/us-indonesia-comprehensive-partnership/.

39. See Michael B. Oren, *Six Days of War: June 1967 and the Making of the Modern Middle East* (New York: Oxford University Press, 2002); Benny Morris, *1948: A History of the First Arab-Israeli War* (New Haven, CT: Yale University Press, 2009); Sheera Frenkel, "Two More British Passport-Holders among New Hamas Killer Suspects," *Times of London*, May 8, 2010.

40. See Stephen D. Kiser, *Water: The Hydraulic of Conflict in the Middle East and North Africa* (Colorado Springs, CO: U.S. Air Force Academy, Institute for National Security Studies, 2000); Robert G. Rabil, *Embattled Neighbors: Syria, Israel, and Lebanon* (Boulder, CO: Lynne Rienner, 2003); Sheria Zuhur, *Hamas and Israel: Conflicting Strategies of Group-Based Politics* (Carlisle, PA: U.S. Army War College, Strategic Studies Institute, 2008); *Contemporary Israel: Domestic Politics, Foreign Policy, and Security Challenges*, ed. Robert O. Freedman (Boulder, CO: Westview Press, 2009); Scott C. Farquahar, ed., *Back to Basics: A Study of the Second Lebanon War*

and Operation CAST LEAD (Fort Leavenworth, KS: Combat Studies Institute Press, U.S. Army Combined Arms Center, 2009); Clive Lipchen, Deborah Sandler, and Emily Cushman, eds., *The Jordan River and Dead Sea Basin: Cooperation Amid Conflict* (Dordrecht, Netherlands: Springer, 2009); Gian P. Gentile, "Learning, Adapting, and the Perils of the New Counter-Insurgency," *Survival*, 51 (6)(December 2008–January 2009): 189–202; United Nations, Human Rights Council, *Human Rights in Palestine and Other Occupied Arab Territories: Report of a United Nations Fact Finding Commission on the Gaza Conflict* (New York: United Nations, 2009); U.S. Congress, House Committee on Foreign Affairs, Subcommittee on the Middle East and South Asia, *Update on Lebanon* (Washington, DC: Government Printing Office, 2009); Alexander Murinson, *Turkey's Entente with Israel and Azerbaijan: State Identity and Security in the Middle East and Caucasus* (New York: Routledge, 2010); Damien McElroy and Tom Whitehead, "Britain to Prevent Abuse of War Crime Warrants," *London Daily Telegraph*, March 4, 2010: 19; and F. Stephen Larrabee, "Turkey's New Geopolitics," *Survival*, 52 (2)(April–May 2010): 157–80.

41. See Yoriko Fukushima, "Japanese Geopolitics and Its Background: What Is the Real Legacy of the Past?" *Political Geography*, 16 (5)(1997): 407–21; *Toward a True Alliance: Restructuring U.S.-Japan Security Relations*, ed. Mike M. Mozizuki (Washington, DC: Brookings Institution Press, 1997); and U.S. Energy Information Administration, *Country Analysis Brief Japan* (Washington, DC: EIA, 2008).

42. Naoko Sajima and Kyochi Tachikawa, *Japanese Sea Power: A Maritime Nation's Struggle for Identity* (Canberra: Department of Defence Sea Power Centre, 2009): 83.

43. See ibid., 85; and Kenneth B. Pyle, *Abe Shinzo and Japan's Change of Course* (Seattle, WA: National Bureau of Asian Research, 2006): 3, 6.

44. See William E. Rapp, *Paths Diverging? The Next Decade in the U.S.-Japan Security Alliance* (Carlisle, PA: U.S. Army War College, Strategic Studies Institute, 2003); Peter J. Wooley, *Geography and Japan's Strategic Choices: From Seclusion to Internationalization* (Washington, DC: Potomac Books, 2005); Peter J. Katzenstein, *Rethinking Japanese Security: Internal and External Dimensions* (New York: Routledge, 2008); and U.S. Department of State, "Background Note: Japan," http://www.state.gov/r/pa/ei/bgn/4142.htm.

45. Japan, Ministry of Defence, *Defense of Japan 2009: Annual White Paper* (Tokyo: Ministry of Defense, 2009): 118, 121, 123, 126, 164.

46. See Ertan Efegil, "Struggle for Power in Central Asia after the September 11 Attacks," *Turkish Review of Eurasian Studies*, 5 (2005): 5–25; Younkyoo Kim and Gu-Ho Eom, "The Geopolitics of Caspian Oil: Rivalries of the US, Russia, and Turkey in the South Caucasus," *Global Economic Review*, 37 (1)(March 2008): 85–106; Pavel K. Baev, "Troublemaking and Risk-Taking: The North in Russian Military Activities," in *Russia and the North*, ed. Elana Wilson Rowe (Ottawa, ON: University of Ottawa Press, 2009): 17–34; and George Joffé, "The EU and Natural Gas: The New Security Agenda," *Issues*, 31 (March 2010): 5.

47. The vast literature on potential trends in Russian geopolitics includes William C. Green, "The Historic Russian Drive for a Warm Water Port: Anatomy of a Geopolitical Myth," *Naval War College Review*, 46 (2)(Spring 1993): 80–102; Dmitri Trenin, *The End of Eurasia: Russia on the Border between Geopolitics and Globaliza-*

tion (Washington, DC: Carnegie Endowment for International Peace, 2002); Andrej Kreutz, "The Geopolitics of Post-Soviet Russia and the Middle East," *Arab Studies Quarterly*, 24 (1)(Winter 2002): 49–61; Mark Brassin, "Classical Eurasianism and the Geopolitics of Russian Identity," *Ab Imperio*, 2 (2003): 257–66; Richard Weitz, "Why Russia and China Have Not Formed an Anti-American Alliance," *Naval War College Review*, 54 (4)(Autumn 2003): 39–61; A. P. Tsygankov, "Mastering Space in Eurasia: Russia's Geopolitical Thinking after the Soviet Break-Up," *Communism and Post-Communist Studies*, 36 (1)(March 2003): 101–27; Fatih Oabay and Bulent Aras, "Polish-Russian Relations: History, Geography, and Geopolitics," *East European Quarterly*, 42 (1)(March 2008): 27–42; Andrei Kazantsev, "Russian Policy in Central Asia and the Caspian Sea Region," *Europe-Asia Studies*, 60 (6)(August 2008): 1072–88; "Arming the Arctic," *Jane's Defence Weekly*, 47 (12)(March 24, 2010): 24–25; and Stephen Blank and Richard Weitz, eds., *The Russian Military Today and Tomorrow: Essays in Memory of Mary Fitzgerald* (Carlisle, PA: U.S. Army War College, Strategic Studies Institute, 2010).

48. See Trevor Owen Lloyd, *The British Empire, 1558–1983* (New York: Oxford University Press, 1983); Lawrence Friedman, Martin S. Navias, and Nicholas J. Wheeler, *Independence in Concert: The British Rationale for Possessing Strategic Nuclear Weapons* (College Park, MD: Center for International Security Studies, School of Public Affairs, 1989); Goldstein, *Deterrence and Security*, 2000; Niall Ferguson, *Empire: The Rise and Demise of the British World Order and the Lessons for Global Power* (New York: Basic Books, 2003); Des Browne and Stephen Carter, "Afghanistan: The Change We Need," *RUSI Journal*, 154 (3)(June 2009): 30–34.

49. See Edward Heath, "Realism in British Foreign Policy," *Foreign Affairs*, 48 (1) (October 1969: 39–50); and *Hansard's Parliamentary Debates*, 3rd ser., 97 (March 1, 1848): Column 122.

50. See Ferguson, *Empire*, 221–90; Eric Grove, *The Royal Navy Since 1815: A New Short History* (New York: Palgrave Macmillan, 2005); Nicholas Saratakes, "One Last Crusade: The British Fleet and Its Impact on the Anglo-American Alliance," *English Historical Review*, 121 (491)(April 2006): 429–66; and James Kraska, "Grasping 'the Influence of Law on Sea Power,'" *Naval War College Review*, 62 (3)(Summer 2009): 113–35.

51. See Max Hastings and Simon Jenkins, *The Battle for the Falklands* (New York: W. W. Norton, 1983); David Dimbleby and David Reynolds, *An Ocean Apart: The Relationship between Britain and America in the Twentieth Century* (New York: Random House, 1988); Jeremy Stocker, *Britain's Role in U.S. Missile Defense* (Carlisle, PA: United States Army War College, Strategic Studies Institute, 2004); United Kingdom, Ministry of Defense and Foreign and Commonwealth Office, *The Future of the United Kingdom's Nuclear Deterrent*, Command Paper 6994 (London: MOD, 2006); Melanie Phillips, *Londonistan: How Britain Is Creating a Terror State Within* (London: Gibson Square, 2008); Alex Carlile, *Report on the Operation in 2008 of the Terrorism Act 2000 and Part I of the Terrorism Act 2006* (London: TSO, 2009); United Kingdom, Parliament, House of Commons, Defence Select Committee, *The Strategic Defence and Security Review: Uncorrected Evidence* (London: House of Commons Defence Select Committee, July 21, 2010); and Thomas Hardings, "Britain No Longer Has the Cash

to Defend Itself from Every Threat, says Liam Fox," *London Daily Telegraph*, July 22, 2010.

52. See Ira Katznelson and Martin Shefter, eds., *Shaped by War and Trade: International Influences on American Political Development* (Princeton, NJ: Princeton University Press, 2002); John Lewis Gaddis, *Strategies of Containment: A Critical Appraisal of American National Security Policy during the Cold War* (New York: Oxford University Press, 2005); Peter W. Rodman, *The Emerging Pattern of Geopolitics* (Carlisle, PA: United States Army War College, Strategic Studies Institute, 2007); Simon Bromley, *American Power and the Prospects for International Order* (Cambridge: Polity, 2008); and Francis B. Sempa, *America's Global Role: Essays and Reviews on National Security, Geopolitics, and War* (Lanham, MD: University Press of America, 2009).

53. See Joseph S. Roucek, "The Development of Political Geography in Geopolitics in the United States," *Australian Journal of Politics and History*, 3 (2)(1958): 204–17; Jay Winik, *On the Brink: The Dramatic, Behind-the-Scenes Saga of the Reagan Era and the Men and Women Who Won the Cold War* (New York: Simon and Schuster, 1996); Katzelson and Shefter, *Shaped by War and Trade: International Influences on American Political Development* (2002); D. W. Meining, *The Shaping of America: A Geographical Perspective on 500 Years of History*, vol. 4, *Global America, 1915–2000* (New Haven, CT: Yale University Press, 2004); Gaddis, *Strategies of Containment*, 2005; and Alfred McCoy and Francisco Scarano, eds., *Colonial Crucible: Empire in the Making of the Modern American State* (Madison: University of Wisconsin Press, 2009).

54. Francis Fukuyama, *The End of History and the Last Man* (New York: Free Press, 1992).

55. See Samuel P. Huntington, *The Clash of Civilizations and the Remaking of World Order* (New York: Simon and Schuster, 1996); President of the United States, *A National Security Strategy for a Global Age* (Washington, DC: White House, 2000); Stephen J. Flanagan, Ellen L. Frost, and Richard L. Kugler, *Challenges of the Global Century: Report of the Project on Globalization and National Security* (Washington, DC: National Defense University Institute for National Strategic Studies, 2001); and Frederick H. Fleitz, *Peacekeeping Fiascoes of the 1990s: Causes, Solutions, and U.S. Interests* (Westport, CT: Praeger, 2002).

56. Ibid.; President of the United States, *The National Security Strategy of the United States* (Washington, DC: White House, 2002).

57. See John Lewis Gaddis, *Surprise, Security, and the American Experience* (Cambridge, MA: Harvard University Press, 2004); Chalmers Johnson, *The Sorrows of Empire: Militarism, Secrecy, and the End of the Republic* (New York: Metropolitan Books, 2004); Robert G. Kaufman, *In Defense of the Bush Doctrine* (Lexington: University Press of Kentucky, 2007); Patrick M. Cronon, ed., *Global Strategic Assessment 2009: America's Security Role in a Changing World* (Washington, DC: National Defense University, 2009); and President of the United States, *National Security Strategy* (Washington, DC: White House, 2010).

58. See *United States Government Manual, 2009–2010* (Washington, DC: National Archives and Records Administration, 2009): 151; U.S. Department of Defense, "The World with Commanders Areas of Responsibilities," http://www.defense.gov/home/features/0109_unifiedcommand/images/unified-command_world-map.jpg; and U.S. Strategic Command, http://www.stratcom.mil/.

59. See Mackubin Thomas Owens, "In Defense of Classical Geopolitics," *Naval War College Review*, 52 (4)(Autumn 1999): 59–76; Svante E. Cornell, "The United States and Central Asia: In the Steppes to Stay?" *Cambridge Review of International Affairs*, 17 (2)(July 2004): 239–54; Eric Talmadge, "U.S. Shows Its Power to N. Korea with Carrier Drills," *Washington Times*, July 26, 2010; Antulio J. Echevarria II, ed., *2010 Key Strategic Issues List* (Carlisle, PA: U.S. Army War College, Strategic Studies Institute, 2010); see U.S. Bureau of the Public Debt, *Treasury Direct: The Debt to the Penny and Who Holds It*, http://www.treasurydirect.gov/NP/BPDLogin?application=NP; and U.S. Congressional Budget Office, *The Budget and Economic Outlook: Fiscal Years 2010 to 2020* (Washington, DC: Congressional Budget Office, 2010).

CHAPTER 3

Current and Emerging Geopolitical "Hot Spots"

Geography has gained renewed importance in international affairs, international economic policy, and international security in the post–cold war era and the aftermath of 9/11 and ongoing domestic and global financial crises. One international affairs analyst has described geography's increased renaissance in international affairs as "the revenge of geography." This prescient analysis maintains that geography determines domestic and international events more than people and ideas; that we must recognize that there are forces such as culture, tradition, history, and dark human passions that are beyond human control and constrain human actions; that permanent environmental forces such as poor soil and drought-afflicted climates can produce conflict; that control of global maritime areas heavily influences international trade, national power, access to natural resources, and international security; that migration of peoples and contests between divergent religions may also drive conflict; that countries ranging in a geographic arc from Israel to North Korea are developing ballistic missiles; that Chinese and Indian naval forces are now able to project power beyond their immediate geographic regions; and that failed states such as Somalia and "shatter zones" such as the Arabian Peninsula and the Indian subcontinent can be sources of regional and global strategic conflict.[1]

This analyst concludes by asserting that humans will initiate but nature will control, that geography will determine the success of individualism and liberal universalism, and that global wealth and political and social order will erode in many areas and leave natural frontiers as the arbiters of "who can coerce whom?" He goes on to add:

> We thought globalization had gotten rid of this antiquarian world of musty map, but it is now returning with a vengeance. We must learn

> to think like Victorians. This is what must be our guide and inform our newly rediscovered realism. Geographical determinists must be seated at the same honored table as liberal humanists, thereby merging the analogies of Vietnam and Munich. Embracing the dictates and limitations of geography will be especially hard for Americans, who like to think that no constraint, natural or otherwise, applies to them. But denying the facts of geography only invites disasters that, in turn, make us victims of geography.[2]

Keeping this insight in mind, this chapter will provide succinct overviews of current and emerging geopolitical "hot spots" that may produce U.S. or other national and international military or financial intervention. It makes no attempt to propose solutions to these problems and is not necessarily comprehensive. However, it seeks to introduce readers to the issues involved and direct them to other resources in this book and on the Internet that provide more detailed analysis and statistics on these areas.

Afghanistan/Pakistan

As of this writing in summer 2010, no geopolitical issue has more attention in the United States and many other countries than the challenging security situation in Afghanistan/Pakistan. Under the leadership of the United States and NATO's International Security Assistance Force (NATO/ISAF), nearly 120,000 troops from 46 nations are in all regions of Afghanistan fighting tenacious Taliban and al-Qaeda forces seeking to return to power after they were ousted by U.S.-led forces in 2001 and trying to build a governmental and economic infrastructure that is economically and politically sustainable and less corrupt.[3]

A number of factors complicate this situation and enhance its geopolitical importance. Afghanistan is located next to geopolitically contentious areas such as Iran, Pakistan, and central Asian republics such as Uzbekistan and Tajikistan. While some progress has been made fighting the Taliban and al-Qaeda due to recent and ongoing increases in U.S. force levels, there is acute concern in Washington and other ISAF capitals about the corruption of Afghan president Hamid Karzai's government; restrictive rules of engagement many ISAF countries have placed on their military forces, and the operational quality of Afghan military and police forces; lingering questions about the extent of support and sanctuary provided to Taliban and al-Qaeda by renegade elements of Pakistan's government in that country's tribal regions such as Waziristan, particularly the Interservices Intelligence Agency; and how serious Pakistan is about fighting its own home-grown Taliban insurgency. Additional concerns cover the flourishing opium trade that helps finance Taliban operations; the security of Pakistan's nuclear weapons arsenal against terrorist infiltration and targeting; civilian casualties in Afghanistan as a result of inaccurate intelligence and U.S. predator drone missile strikes; political turmoil and personality conflicts between the Obama administration and the U.S. military, as demonstrated by the June 2010 forced resignation of commanding U.S. general Stanley McChrystal and his replacement by General David Petraeus; and among Afghans as to the willingness of ISAF forces to stay in Afghanistan for the long haul, as demonstrated by U.S. and Canadian announcements that they hope to begin withdrawing their forces sometime in 2011.[4]

Besides these historical and contemporary cultural, military, and strategic factors, Afghanistan's economic and geopolitical importance could be heightened further by recent U.S. discoveries of potentially $1 trillion worth of previously unknown mineral resources in this country. These resources include large amounts of copper, iron, gold, and lithium, which are concentrated in areas such as Ghazni Province near Pakistan, and have been the scene of intense combat between ISAF forces and the Taliban. General Petraeus has described these resources as possessing "stunning potential," and an internal Pentagon document says Afghanistan could become the "Saudi Arabia of lithium," which is a key battery component of laptops and Blackberrys. These resources will increase the interest, not only of existing participants in Afghanistan's internecine conflict, but of neighboring countries such as China and India, which are seeking mineral resources to augment their economic and political growth and further increase Afghanistan's geopolitical importance.[5]

Arctic Natural Resources

The Arctic Ocean has become a source of international competition in recent years due to its rich natural resources and to warmer temperatures, allowing for increased shipping traffic to occur in its waters such as the Northwest Passage. Several nations, including Canada, Denmark, Norway, the Russian Federation, and the United States, are particularly interested in having access to Arctic Ocean resources, including oil and natural gas, and clearly determining where the boundaries of these countries need to be demarcated on the Arctic Ocean floor is of particular international legal importance.[6]

A late 2009 U.S. Energy Information Administration (EIA) assessment presented a mixed evaluation of this Arctic Ocean's energy resources:

> The Arctic presents a "good news, bad news" situation for oil and natural gas development. The good news is that the Arctic holds about 22 percent of the world's undiscovered conventional oil and natural gas resources, based on the USGS [U.S. Geological Survey] mean estimate. The bad

> news is that: (1) the Arctic resource base is largely composed of natural gas and natural gas liquids, which are significantly more expensive to transport over long distances than oil; (2) the Arctic oil and natural gas resources will be considerably more expensive, risky, and take longer to develop than comparable deposits found elsewhere in the world; (3) unresolved Arctic sovereignty claims could preclude or substantially delay development of these oil and natural gas resources where economic sovereignty claims overlap; and (4) protecting the Arctic environment will be costly. The high costs and long lead-times of Arctic oil and natural gas development undercut the immediate importance of these sovereignty claims, while at the same time diminishing the economic incentive to develop these resources.[7]

The potential of these Arctic natural resources has caused the aforementioned countries to take increase interest in asserting national sovereignty in this region. The most recent Canadian defense policy document maintains that its forces will be resourced and equipped to have the ability conduct daily domestic and continental operations in the Arctic to monitor air and maritime threats to national security and demonstrate a visible presence in this resource-rich region.[8] Russia and its military have become particularly interested in staking national claims in this region. Increasing oil prices have heightened this already oil-rich country's interest in Arctic Ocean reserves, which helped influence a Russian mission to plant its national flag on the ocean floor seabed below the North Pole in August 2007 and to increase Russian aerial and naval activity to buttress national territorial and natural resources claims.[9]

The Obama administration, in its May 2010 *National Security Strategy* document, declares that the United States is an Arctic nation with "broad and fundamental interests" in this region, where it will seek to meet its national security needs, protect the environment, manage resources, and strengthen international cooperation.[10] This followed up a comparable policy document issued a year earlier by the outgoing George W. Bush administration stressing the Arctic's increasing importance to U.S. national security policy making and stressing that the United States would seek to preserve the global mobility of its civilian and military vessels in this area; project a sovereign national maritime presence to support vital national interests; increase U.S. ability to protect its Arctic air, land, and sea borders; and work to peacefully resolve international disputes.[11]

Ownership of the Northwest Passage has been an area of particular dispute. Canada contends it is in Canadian territorial waters. However, the United States and European Union (EU) contend the passage should be considered part of international waters. In 2009, Russia announced that it was going to spend $578 million on a nuclear powered icebreaker by 2015, and Russia, the

United States, Canada, Norway, Sweden, and Denmark plan to increase the their military presence and exercises in the Arctic Ocean.[12]

Caspian Sea

The Caspian Sea is an area of geopolitical interest because it possesses oil reserves estimated as being between 17 and 44 billion barrels and natural gas reserves of 232 trillion cubic feet. Countries surrounding the Caspian Sea include Azerbaijan, Iran, Kazakhstan, Russia, and Turkmenistan, and additional countries seeking access to its mineral resources and control of the infrastructure transporting these resources include Afghanistan, Armenia, China, EU countries, Georgia, India, Pakistan, Turkey, the United States, and Uzbekistan. Uncertainty over the territorial and seabed demarcations of the Caspian seabed and control of infrastructure such as oil and natural gas pipelines have resulted in disputes between these littoral powers and could produce additional conflicts if not resolved.[13]

Central Asian Instability

Central Asian countries, many of them part of the former Soviet Union, and located adjacent to or between major countries such as China, India, and Russia, along with Pakistan and Afghanistan, are also subjects of interest and desired influence among these powers and the United States due to their mineral resources, economic problems, and periodic political instability.[14]

Examples of regional volatility occurred in Kyrgyzstan during the first half of 2010 when antigovernment anger, economic distress, and ethnic rioting resulted in the government being toppled, which is important to the United States due to the presence of Manas Air Base, which has supplied U.S. troops in Afghanistan. This country also has an unresolved 2001 boundary delimitation with Kazakhstan, an Isfara Valley boundary dispute with Tajikistan, a similar dispute with Uzbekistan and serves as a partial cultivation and supply source for cannabis and opium for neighboring countries and as a transit point for southwest Asian narcotics bound for Russia and Europe.[15]

The United States, Russia, and China also compete for political influence and seek to gain diplomatic, economic, and strategic advantages in other regional countries, such as Kazakhstan, Tajikistan, and Uzbekistan, whose intensity is likely to accelerate in the future, depending on developments in Afghanistan and the energy supply needs of these countries and adding additional complexities to the geopolitical "great game" in which major world powers have demonstrated acute interest in this region's developments.[16]

China in Africa

In its quest for energy sources to meet increasing demand for natural resources to fuel its growing economy, which can no longer domestically supply its natural resource requirements, China is also expanding its political and economic influence in African countries. It is doing this without imposing political democratization, economic development, and human rights conditions often imposed by Western countries. Chinese interest in Africa dates from the 1960s and 1970s, when it began supporting national liberation forces such as UNITA in Angola and ZANU in Zimbabwe, which were seen as anti-Soviet. These relationships continued to develop after movements like ZANU came to power. China has also sought to develop energy, transportation, and military ties with countries as diverse as Algeria, Angola, Ethiopia, Nigeria, South Africa, Sudan, and Zimbabwe. Along with increased U.S. interest in cultivating military ties and access to African natural resources, this could produce potential tension, if not conflict, with China and these African countries during the 21st century, although general cooperation has been the norm so far.[17]

China in Latin America

China has also sought to expand its political, economic, and security influence in Latin America. Beijing has sought to use economic aid to convince some Latin American countries to end diplomatic relations with Taiwan and begin relations with Beijing. It is also interested in the oil resources possessed by Ecuador and Venezuela, expanding its trade relationships with regional countries, with particular emphasis on enhancing ties with Cuba and acquiring properties in the Panama Canal region. Between 1999 and 2007 Chinese-Latin trade rose from $8.2 billion to $102 billion. During 2002, a small Chinese naval flotilla sailed around the world, visiting Latin American countries such as Brazil, Ecuador, and Peru; in 2004 China became one of Brazil's top three export origins, with Brazilian steel being a particularly important export; the China National Petroleum Corporation has acquired holdings in Peru and Venezuela; and China invested more than $19 billion over 10 years on closer trade ties with Argentina, with $5 billion of this allocated to oil exploration. There are also Chinese nationals living in the border region of Argentina, Brazil, and Paraguay, with some of these potentially being involved in import-export fraud and human smuggling. How these Chinese activities in Latin America play out, particularly if there are security crises affecting U.S. interests in this region, is a matter of debate that represents another area of potential global geopolitical contention.[18]

China's "String of Pearls" Basing Strategy and Future Military Objectives

China's increasing need to import natural resources such as oil and natural gas from the Middle East, Africa, and Latin America have made it acutely vulnerable to supply disruptions. These disruptions may be due to political instability in supplier countries but are especially due to long sea lines of communication. The need for their tanker fleet to pass through strategic choke points such as the Persian Gulf, Straits of Malacca, and the South China sea, where they could be vulnerable to terrorist or hostile nation blockade or attack, has led Beijing to develop its "string of pearls" basing strategy to ensure the stability of these resources and develop alternative mechanisms for delivering these resources.[19] A more detailed description of this strategy follows:

> Each "pearl" in the "String of Pearls" is a nexus of Chinese geopolitical influence or military presence. Hainan Island, with recently upgraded military facilities, is a "pearl." An upgraded airstrip on Woody Island, located in the Paracel archipelago, 300 nautical miles east of Vietnam, is a "pearl." A container shipping facility in Chittagong, Bangladesh is a "pearl." Construction of a deep water port in Sittwe, Myanmar, is a "pearl," as is the construction of a naval base in Gwadar, Pakistan. Port and airfield construction projects, diplomatic ties, and force modernization form the essence of China's "String of Pearls." The "pearls" extend from the coast of mainland China through the littorals of the South China Sea, the Strait of Malacca, across the Indian Ocean and onto the littorals of the Arabian Sea and Persian Gulf. China is building strategic relationships and developing a capability to establish a forward presence along the sea lines of communications (SLOCs) that connect China to the Middle East.[20]

There is considerable debate and controversy over whether China's "string of pearls" strategy is only designed to protect Chinese maritime access to natural resources from the Middle East and Africa by building a large tanker fleet, or whether it heralds Chinese desires to become a global maritime naval power capable of threatening U.S. maritime interests in the western Pacific and Indian maritime interests in the Indian Ocean, or whether this strategy will balance Chinese attempts to acquire these natural resources through pipelines running through central and Southeast Asian countries to avoid strategic choke points such as the Straits of Malacca.[21]

Considerable debate and controversy also exist over the future nature and intentions of Chinese military power. The Defense Department's annual report on Chinese military power says the China's People's Liberation Army is transitioning from a mass army fighting domestic wars of attrition to a high-tech force capable of winning short-duration and high-intensity conflicts along its periphery against high-tech adversaries. This document goes on to note that Chinese nuclear force modernization is enhancing its strategic strike capabilities including its nuclear, space, and cyberwarfare potential and its acquisition of significant foreign weapons; that high investment in domestic science and technology industries has implications beyond the Asia-Pacific region; and that the lack of transparency about Chinese defense spending and inconsistencies between peaceful policy declarations and operational deployments make it difficult to assess accurately Chinese military intentions.[22]

Literature on the geopolitical and strategic aspects of Chinese military powers ranges from assessments contending that China is a rising power that does not seek military confrontation with the United States or to impede U.S. interests to those maintaining that China seeks to challenge and even remove U.S. military influence from waters next to China and take global military supremacy from the United States. This corpus of literature is continually growing and represents the intense debate and analysis over what may be the 21st century's most important geopolitical issue.[23]

China/Taiwan

Another unique East Asian geopolitical challenge is the relationship between China and Taiwan and how the United States and other Asia/Pacific powers would respond if China were to attempt to forcibly incorporate Taiwan, which it considers a "renegade province." Taiwan has been a sovereign country since the defeated remnants of China's anti-Communist nationalist regime fled the mainland following the victorious 1949 Communist revolution. In the ensuing six decades, there have been near military confrontations between these two countries that were deterred by the threat of U.S. military power. The most recent of these was in 1996, when U.S. aircraft carriers were deployed to prevent Chinese missile tests in the Strait of Taiwan from serving as a prelude to a direct Chinese assault on this country.

Most of the world's countries have official diplomatic relations with China and unofficial diplomatic relations with Taiwan out of a desire to accept China's "one China" policy between these countries and out of recognition of China's growing international diplomatic, political, and military power. The United States is pledged to defend Taiwan under the 1979 Taiwan Relations Act if it is militarily attacked by China, and U.S. administrations have to walk a diplomatic tightrope in their desire to maintain good bilateral relations with China while also maintaining good economic relations with Taiwan and selling arms to this country when the United States believes such sales are necessary to maintain the cross-straits military balance.

Despite its relative international diplomatic isolation, Taiwan has become an economically affluent and politically democratic country that remains a thorn in Beijing's side and a geographical barrier to China extending its naval power into the western Pacific. Some cross-straits trade and cultural exchanges occur between these two countries, and Taiwanese domestic politics involves a balancing act between those who favor maintaining the status quo and those who think Taiwan should declare independence from China even if that risks possible Chinese military invasion. The proximity of these countries to neighboring countries such as Japan and to U.S. military assets in the western Pacific makes this a continual source of potential geopolitical conflict.[24]

Climate Change

Climate change, whether from natural or human-caused forces, is being factored into national and international security policy making and its literature, foreign policy, economic development, and natural resources policy making in countries around the world. Regardless of one's position on whether climate change is exclusively caused by carbon dioxide emissions, other forms of human activity, or natural climatological activity, and regardless of individuals positions on potential governmental climate change policy responses such as developing clean energy technologies, carbon trading policies, reducing dependence on fossil fuels, or enhancing national energy independence, climate change is affecting and may continue affecting international economic development, international relations, and international security in a variety of ways.

Examples of these affects could include the emergence of year-round ice-free waters in the Northwest Passage, which could create a new international trade route and affect ecosystems in countries such as Canada, Russia, and the United States; water shortages which may affect public access to this vital liquid and agricultural production in areas such as Australia's Murray-Darling Basin, the American West, and the Middle East; increased natural disasters such as hurricanes and tsunamis in the Gulf of Mexico, Pacific Ocean, and Indian Ocean; volcanic eruptions such as the spring 2010 plumes over Iceland disrupting European and transatlantic air traffic for several days; rising ocean waters in certain areas of the world such as the South Pacific; and human-caused disasters such as the summer 2010 British Petroleum oil spill in the Gulf of Mexico, which was an undesired side effect of global efforts to find fossil fuel resources such as petroleum and natural gas to promote economic growth. All these factors also have the potential to produce regional and widespread international conflict between nation-states trying to acquire dependable access to these resources.[25]

Cyberwarfare

The information revolution and the Internet's ongoing growth and evolution have made it a critical part of the global economy and international security system. This criticality has also made individual Internet nodes, particularly those built and maintained by government agencies, vulnerable to hostile attacks from disgruntled individuals, criminal and other terrorist groups, and hostile military and intelligence agencies. Such attacks can disable or knock out military command and control systems, critical civilian and military infrastructures such as power grids, telecommunications assets including satellites, electronic financial transactions, utilities such as water supply plants, and transportation assets such as traffic lights. The U.S. military established U.S. Cyber Command (CYBERCOM) within its Strategic Command (STRATCOM) on June 23, 2009, to direct the full spectrum of U.S. military defensive and offensive cyberspace operations.[26]

Private-sector agencies, worldwide militaries, and government agencies at all levels must invest significant personnel hours and financial resources to maintain the security and integrity of their computer systems against hostile attack. Countries like China and North Korea are particularly interested in using asymmetric means of warfare such as cyberwarfare to exploit the vulnerabilities of countries such as the United States as a means of achieving economic, political, and security objectives they would be unable to achieve with conventional military assets.[27]

Energy Policy and Competition

Global competition for energy resources, particularly oil and natural gas, along with water and other mineral resources also has the potential to produce international diplomatic, economic, military, and political conflict. Countries experiencing rapid economic growth such as China and India are looking overseas to access resources they need to maintain and expand their economic opportunities. Highly economically developed countries such as the United States and other Organization for Economic Cooperation and Development (OECD) countries seek to maintain their economic growth and access to resources at a time of global economic downturn in order to avoid reducing their economic growth, national living standards, and creating political dissension or unrest within their countries. Areas of potential conflict over energy resources include European dependence on Russia for oil and natural gas, U.S. dependence on Middle Eastern oil, water shortages in Africa and other global regions, and Chinese and East Asian dependence on oil and natural gas from Africa, central Asia, Latin America, and the Middle East. Seeking to prevent this growing demand for existing fossil fuel natural resources and emerging natural resources such as solar and wind power from producing conflict will be a major challenge for national governments and international government organizations during the 21st century.[28]

Failed States

The term *failed state* can be defined in many ways. It generally refers to sovereign governments that are seen as failing to meet basic conditions and responsibilities such as defending national territorial integrity, providing some level of political stability and governmental functionality, and meeting some of their population's basic socioeconomic needs. This can cause internecine strife within these countries that is often ethnically based and make them vulnerable to foreign intervention and exploitation such as supporting rebel groups or pirates in the case of Somalia, becoming support bases for terrorist groups such as al-Qaeda in Afghanistan and Pakistan, and increasing their susceptibility to natural and human-caused disasters that may require neighboring states or the international community to intervene.[29]

Somalia is probably the most blatant example of a failed state, being without a functional government for nearly two decades. Other examples of failed states may include Afghanistan, Bolivia, Democratic Republic of the Congo, East Timor, North Korea, Yemen, and Zimbabwe, depending on the methodologies used to classify failed states.[30] A vast corpus of literature on this concept exists in political science and government literature.[31]

Global Immigration/Migration

Global immigration and migration are contentious geopolitical issues in the United States and many other countries. Arizona's May 2010 passage of legislation to more assertively enforce federal laws against illegal immigration was harshly criticized by Mexico and has resulted in the U.S. Justice Department filing a lawsuit against Arizona's law.[32]

Unstable domestic political and economic conditions in their home countries, poverty, war, and political and religious persecution often force individuals and their families to leave these countries and seek sanctuary in other countries. This often creates great controversy and expense for these sanctuary countries. Besides the United States, countries that have recently or currently are subject to refugee influxes include Australia, France, Germany, Jordan, Pakistan, South Africa, and the United Kingdom. These countries have different laws and customs for dealing with illegal immigrants and their smugglers and have interest groups supporting and opposing the admission of illegal immigrants. There is also shifting political opinion in countries as to whether immigrant refugees will be able to adapt to the cultural norms of host countries, the ability of these countries to financially support immigrants in times of economic and fiscal strain, and whether such immigrants will become threats to national security and societal cohesion. A key issue in Australia's 2001 federal election was the government's decision to deny admission to refugees from the Norwegian-flagged ship MV *Tampa,* which facilitated the reelection of John Howard's government.[33]

Consequently, immigration and migration is a subject with bilateral national security and international security implications that extends beyond the humanitarian and domestic policy concerns of the countries involved. An extensive array of literature on immigration's geopolitical and security aspects exists covering the United States and many other countries.[34]

Globalization

Globalization can be described as the process of increasing the interconnectivity of world markets and businesses. This has been accelerated by technological advances, making it easier for people to travel and conduct business internationally, and by telecommunication advances such as the Internet. Globalization proponents contend that increased opportunities, competition, and service availability enhance product efficiency and consumer choice. Globalization opponents maintain that there are individuals, groups, and countries that cannot function successfully in an increasingly competitive global economic environment, which can include some labor and business organizations and farm groups. Antiglobalization protests, which can become violent, are regular occurrences at most international political and economic gatherings such as the G20 summits. The increasing globalization of the world economy makes it easier for geographically far-flung countries to be affected by economic turmoil in remote countries, as demonstrated by the financial downturn of 2008 to present times.[35]

Global Pandemics

A globalized world also makes it easier to carry bacteria, germs, and viruses, which do not respect national borders, to all corners of the world, where they can affect animals and humans. This can occur through civilian jet airplane travel, international trade cargos, and the deployment of military forces into areas where these forces are not immunized against local diseases. AIDS has had a significant impact on the economy, public health, and national security of many African countries, and diseases such as SARS, dengue, mad cow disease, various forms of influenza, malaria, and other conditions can also reach pandemic proportions in individual countries and internationally if the causes and carriers are not quarantined or regulated effectively. Consequently, world governments and military forces must develop and implement effective epidemiological practices into their policies and operational planning as they interact with other countries and military forces.[36]

India/China

As the world's most populous nations, India and China have a periodically contentious relationship. The countries fought a 1962 war in the Himalayan Mountains that resulted in India losing some territory. India's nuclear weapons arsenal is used to deter China and Pakistan; the two countries disagree over the status of Tibet; India is concerned about developments in neighboring countries such as Nepal, Bangladesh, and Myanmar that might adversely threaten its interests; and India is also increasing the size of its navy and its cooperation with the United States, which could be used counteract China's "string of pearls" strategy and restrict or eliminate Chinese access to Middle Eastern and African oil and natural gas resources in the event of maritime or other security crises in the Indian Ocean region.[37]

India/Pakistan

India and Pakistan are both nuclear weapons states and have had a complicated and sometimes contentious bilateral relationship that has produced wars and near military confrontations between these two countries during their six decades of independence. Both countries have border disputes over the Kashmir region. Although the countries cooperate in many areas, their relationship was exacerbated by the November 26–29, 2008, Pakistani Muslim terrorist attacks in India's Mumbai, which resulted in at least 173 deaths. Pakistan has traditionally had closer diplomatic and security ties with China, while India, after initially having close ties with the former Soviet Union, has increased its ties with the United States, including increasing its economic and security collaboration with the United States through a bilateral nuclear agreement giving India access to nuclear fuel and technology, including reprocessing U.S. nuclear material under International Atomic Energy Agency safeguards. Balancing its relationships with India and Pakistan and helping these countries build secure nuclear deterrence and command and control structures are ongoing mission critical objectives of U.S. foreign policy in this geopolitically sensitive region.[38]

Iran

Since the 1979 Islamic Revolution overthrowing the pro-American Shah and its replacement by an aggressively anti-American and dictatorial Islamist regime, Iran has become a subject of geopolitical and strategic concern to the United States and the broader Persian Gulf and Indian Ocean regions. Its aspirations to achieve nuclear weapons have produced acute concern within the broader international community but have only produced modest rhetorical condemnation and sanctions of questionable economic effect.

Iran has actively supported terrorist groups such as Hamas against Israel and anti-American forces attempting to destabilize Iraq's U.S.-installed and nascent democratic government. It has also sought to build ties with opponents of U.S. policies such as Venezuelan president Hugo Chavez, it has made some attempts to gain political influence in South American countries such as Argentina and Bolivia, and the political influence of its military over national policy making appears to be increasing. Iranian president Mahmoud Ahmadinejad has incurred international fury for his desire to "wipe Israel off the map," denying the Holocaust, and crushing antigovernment demonstrations after his 2009 reelection.

Its failure to genuinely cooperate with international efforts to monitor and determine the exact status of its nuclear programs may eventually result in military attacks against this arsenal by the United States or Israel, which would cause tremendous regional instability and threaten oil supplies from this critical strategic region.[39]

Iraq

Despite the overthrow of Saddam Hussein's regime and its replacement by a nominally democratic government, Iraq remains a country struggling to stabilize its economy, government, and society. It continues confronting sectarian Islamic conflict between its majority Shia and minority Sunni populations, which is aggravated by the presence of al-Qaeda terrorists; U.S. and other international military forces are being withdrawn from Iraq but will still play a critical support role in enhancing and supporting Iraq's domestic security for years to come, Iran will continue trying to gain influence within Iraq and destabilize the government, ethnic conflict between Iraqis and Kurds will continue, political corruption will keep Iraq's government from achieving optimal public support and economic efficiency, and the country's oil reserves and strategic location will make it an area of interest and concern for global energy supplies.[40]

Islamic Integration in Europe

Western Europe's Muslim population has increased in recent decades to an estimated 15–18 million and is expected to grow to at least 10 percent of the continent's population by 2020. While many Muslims have peacefully integrated into the European cultural, economic, and political mainstream, others have chosen to advocate the imposition of Sharia law within these countries and have participated in violent terrorist plots or actions, including the March 11, 2004, bombing of the Madrid train system, the November 2, 2004, murder of anti-Islamist filmmaker Theo van Gogh in Amsterdam, the July 7, 2005, bombing of London's public transport system, and violent protests by Muslims in Europe and internationally following the September 30, 2005, publishing of cartoons offensive to Islam's founder Mohammed in the Danish newspaper *Jyllands-Posten*.

Such growing Islamist activism has generated countervailing responses from many European countries. A Swiss national referendum on November 29, 2009, voted to ban the construction of new mosque minarets; the French legislature is debating and expected to pass a ban on Islamic women wearing burkas in summer 2010; and the June 9, 2010, Dutch elections saw the victory of strongly conservative parties, with particular success being received by Geert Wilder's People's Party for Freedom and Democracy, which favors restricting immigration and establishing new Islamic mosques and schools in order to preserve the Netherlands' Judeo-Christian heritage. Many other commentators have warned of increasingly forceful Islamist sentiment and actions in Europe and have criticized governments they feel are insufficiently concerned about preserving European cultural and religious pluralism. This issue will affect European domestic politics and foreign relations with Islamic countries for the foreseeable future.[41]

Israel/Palestine

Confrontation between Israel and Palestinians aspiring for some level of autonomy or national independence has been a critical feature of Middle East geopolitics for over six decades. Palestinians contend Israel took land from them during its 1948 war of independence and the Six Days' War of 1967. Israel believes it is entitled to its existence under international law and as part of its religious beliefs. Various diplomatic negotiations involving the United States, EU, United Nations, and some regional Arab countries have achieved mixed results. Israel has remained the target of missile attacks from Iranian-supported groups such as Hamas in the Palestinian-held city of Gaza, and Israel has build a fence separating its territory from Palestinian territory on the West Bank of the Jordan River to prevent terrorist attacks inside Israel. The May–June 2010 controversy involving an Israeli raid on a Turkish boat carrying what it said was humanitarian assistance to Gaza has exacerbated an already strained relationship and created domestic contentiousness in Israel and an international uproar, despite there being a history of arms smuggling to Gaza-based Palestinian terrorist groups. The Israeli-controlled Golan

Heights region has been disputed with Syria since 1967. This will remain a front-burner issue in Middle Eastern geopolitics for the foreseeable future.[42]

Latin American Geopolitics

Spanish-, Portuguese-, and French-speaking areas from Mexico on south face a number of geopolitical and security issues. These include violent drug wars in Mexico and Colombia; border disputes in many regions of South America such as the Chaco Triangle in Bolivia; controversy over the Plata River Basin involving Argentina, Bolivia, Brazil, Paraguay, and Uruguay; environmental policies in the Amazonian region; the aggressiveness of Venezuelan's "Bolivarian Revolution," personified by its dictator President Hugo Chavez; uncertainty over the domestic and foreign policies of Cuba after the Castro regime concluded and that regime's ties with Iran; increasing Chinese influence in Latin American countries near the Panama Canal; Iran's desire to use the terrorist group Hezbollah to expand its influence in Latin America; the United States' desire to retain promote democratization and prevent hostile powers from gaining a foothold in this region; and the desire of some Argentines to regain control of the Falkland Islands, despite losing a 1982 war to the United Kingdom.[43]

Maritime Piracy

Maritime piracy or terrorism is no longer a historical relic and has resurfaced as a major contemporary international security problem. The International Maritime Bureau Piracy Reporting Centre announced in July 2009 that the number of worldwide piracy attacks increased from 114 in the first half of 2008 to 240 during the first half of 2009 and that the attacking pirates in the large majority of these incidents were heavily armed and committed violence against crewmembers, including hostage taking, kidnapping, and murder. This problem became particularly visible to Americans when the U.S.-flagged container ship MV *Maersk Alabama* was attacked 250 nautical miles southeast of Somalia and seized by Somali pirates on April 8, 2009, while carrying U.S. government food aid to Mombasa, Kenya. The captain was taken hostage before U.S. military sharpshooters on the USS *Bainbridge* killed his captors and secured his release. On April 14, 2009, the U.S.-flagged MV *Liberty Sun*, with 20 crew members on a similar mission, was attacked 285 nautical miles southeast of Mogadishu, Somalia, but the crew thwarted the attack.[44]

While currently most prevalent in the Gulf of Aden, Red Sea, and Horn of Africa, maritime piracy is a global problem occurring in waters adjacent to Bangladesh, Indonesia, India, Malaysia, South America, and the Strait of

Malacca, where it can affect transportation of essential commerce, including energy supplies.[45] These pirates may be affiliated with terrorist groups, parts of transnational criminal rings, or individual freelance operatives with assorted political or economic grievances. This maritime piracy resurgence has resulted in increased international intelligence sharing and cooperation in conducting antipiracy measures. Concern over attacks on its shipping prompted China to send a naval mission to the Gulf of Aden in late 2008 to participate in international antipiracy interdiction activities, which continue to the present. The United States has stepped up its efforts in this area as well as working to develop measures to protect domestic ports and maritime assets from terrorist attack, and governments worldwide have sought to obtain United Nations legal authorization to step up their antipiracy efforts, including determining appropriate rules of engagement.[46]

Mexico Drug Wars and Central American Gangs

Regular news reports describe the violence produced by Mexican drug wars, which are occurring between various drug gangs for market control, and the Mexican government has increased its efforts against these gangs. This phenomenon has also occurred in other Latin American countries such as El Salvador and Brazil as well as in Caribbean countries such as Jamaica. A 2007 U.S. Army report described the objectives of these gangs as follows:

> Rather than trying to depose a government with a major stroke (*golpe* or coup) or in a prolonged revolutionary war, as some insurgents have done, gangs and their allies (the gang phenomenon) more subtly take control of territory and people one street or neighborhood at a time (*coup d'street*) or one individual, business, or government office at a time. Thus, whether a gang is specifically a criminal or insurgent type organization is irrelevant. Its putative objective is to neutralize, control, or depose governments to ensure self-determined (nondemocratic) ends. This objective defines insurgency, a serious political agenda, and a clash regarding the authoritative allocation of values in a society.[47]

This gang-related violence has had serious economic and security repercussions in these Caribbean and Latin American countries, including many civilian casualties. It has also spread to the United States as many of these gangs have become involved in the U.S. drug trade in numerous cities, causing significant casualties and problems for local, state, and federal law enforcement. This subject also influences public debate over illegal immigration as the ongoing controversy over Arizona's immigration law and charges of lax federal border security indicate. Some of these gangs are also involved in human smuggling across the U.S. border, and it has become necessary to deploy U.S. National Guard units in the Mexican border region. It may also become necessary for U.S. law enforcement or military units to conduct "hot pursuit" missions into Mexico or other countries to apprehend or kill the perpetrators of this violence, which would pose acute diplomatic problems. However, the failure to effectively defeat this violence will have also have serious domestic U.S. political repercussions.[48]

Nigeria's Delta Region

Nigeria is one of Africa's biggest oil and natural gas producers and depends on its oil sector for over 95 percent of its export earnings and approximately 65 percent of government revenue. These reserves are primarily located in the Niger River Delta in this country's southeast. Local antagonism toward the Nigerian government and multinational petroleum companies has resulted in attacks on the production infrastructure and employees of these organizations requiring armed security and escort of these commodities. Oil theft by government and petroleum company opponents produces pipeline damage that severely reduces or stops production and increases pollution. The oil industry has been blamed for this increased pollution, which has damaged air, land, and water, resulting in arable land and fish stock losses, while local critics complain they do not receive sufficient economic benefit from oil and natural gas revenues. Approximately 40 percent of Nigerian crude oil is exported to the United States and 24 percent to Europe, and Nigeria was also the United States' fifth largest foreign oil supplier in 2009. Consequently, any disruptions in the Nigerian production process will have international impact.[49]

North Korea/South Korea

The 38th parallel (demilitarized zone, or DMZ) marking the border between North and South Korea is the world's most dangerous, fortified, and militarized frontier. More than 1.6 million active duty troops from these two countries and 37,000 U.S. troops are stationed on the Korean Peninsula, and any confrontation between these forces would be extremely bloody, even if nuclear weapons are not used. Nearly ⅔ of North Korea's troops are positioned near South Korea's capital city Seoul, with a metropolitan area of nearly 10 million people that is as close as 25 miles to the DMZ and has a major traffic artery to the DMZ.[50]

The United States is legally obligated to come to South Korea's defense as part of a 1953 Mutual Defense Treaty. South Korea is a highly developed economy with a strong military and has provided some economic assistance to North Korea. However, there was never a peace treaty ending the 1950–1953 Korean War, and a sometimes tenuous armistice and the presence of U.S. forces are the only things keeping the peace. North Korea has periodically sought to infiltrate troops into South Korea, and bilateral tensions increased considerably when a North Korean submarine sank a South Korean warship on March 26, 2010, killing 46 sailors.[51]

Geopolitical stakes have been heightened by North Korean efforts to build a nuclear weapons arsenal that regional and international diplomatic negotiations have failed to stop; the highly secretive and dictatorial nature of North Korea's government, led by Kim Jong Il, which has produced a powerful military along with periodic famines; and sometimes naive South Korean efforts to negotiate with and even economically bribe North Korea to preserve peninsula stability. Any war between these two countries would also involve the United States and affect regional countries such as China, Japan, and Russia in multiple ways, such as the security of their energy supplies, and leave enduring physical and psychic damage on the peninsula and within the region. Varying analyses provide divergent viewpoints on how to deal with this geopolitical hot spot.[52]

Persian Gulf

This region is home to major oil-producing countries such as Saudi Arabia, Iraq, Iran, and other Persian Gulf countries. These countries supply oil to the U.S. and Western European countries and to growing energy-consuming powers like China and Japan. In 2006, an estimated 16.5–17 million barrels of oil per day were transported through the Persian Gulf, which is only 21 miles wide at its narrowest point. Within this 21-mile-wide parameter, shipping lanes consist of 2-mile-wide channels for inbound and outbound tanker traffic along with a 2-mile-wide buffer zone. Sea mines were installed in this body of water during the 1980s Iran-Iraq War, and it has been the target of terrorist threats since 9/11.

If the Persian Gulf is closed off, alternative oil and natural gas delivery would have to occur through pipelines crossing Saudi Arabia to the Red Sea or to Turkey through Iraq. Delivery of oil would also be threatened if there were a military confrontation with Iran over that country's nuclear weapons program or if any of this region's countries experienced catastrophic financial downturns. Consequently, this region has been a major focus of U.S. geopolitical strategic concern for several decades, and it is becoming increasingly important to China and other countries as well as ensuring its critical nature in international economic, energy, and strategic policy making.[53]

Russian Energy Diplomacy

Possessing major energy reserves such as natural gas and oil, the Russian Federation has become a major supplier of these resources to countries that were formerly part of the former Soviet Union in central Asia and Eastern Europe and to Western European countries. This has enhanced Russia's economic wealth and given it a certain amount of geopolitical leverage over these countries. During 2007, EU member countries received 34 percent of their oil imports from Russia and 18.3 percent of these imports from the former Soviet republic of Kazakhstan, and during this same year, EU countries received 41 percent of their natural gas imports and 25 percent of their hard coal imports from Russia.[54]

Russian curtailing or eliminating these supplies would force EU countries to turn to the Caspian Sea, Norway, or other resources to fulfill their energy supply needs. Russia has used its energy clout to increase its exports to emerging energy consumers like China and India; may have contributed to restricting NATO expansion to Ukraine; has also used its coercive power to temporarily cut off natural gas supplies to Ukraine in 2009, when that country's former pro-Western government refused to pay considerably higher prices; has coerced other countries, including the former Baltic Republics, Belarus, Georgia, and Poland; has increased military spending; and is heavily involved in international competition with the United States, EU, and central Asian countries for access to Caspian Sea natural resources.[55]

Russian Foreign Policy toward "Near Abroad" Countries

Russia has also sought to use its energy power and increasing economic wealth to consolidate national power and begin to regain influence, if not outright control, over countries that were formerly part of the Soviet Union. During the post-Soviet era from 1991, the Russian government has used the phrase *near abroad* to describe its relations with newly independent countries formerly part of the Soviet Union, who may have significant Russian-speaking populations within their borders, and Moscow's desire to protect the "rights" of these individuals. Moscow is particularly interested in getting the domestic economic, foreign policies, and national security policies of these countries and regions to harmonize with Russian Federation policy and to not be seen as collaborating with hostile Western or American economic, foreign, and national security policies toward Russia.[56]

Examples of Russian efforts to reassert its influence, if not outright control, over the "near abroad" include its wars with Chechen separatists; its close collaboration with Belarus; its 2008 war with Georgia, in which it was able to seize that country's separatist regions of Abkhazia and South Ossetia; its efforts to keep Ukraine from joining NATO; and its influencing of central Asian countries such as Kazakhstan and Uzbekistan to distance themselves from the United States in antiterrorism campaigns in Afghanistan. These examples of increased Russian assertiveness will test the viability of Western security architecture, including the NATO alliance.[57]

South China Sea/Strait of Malacca

Two other potential maritime geopolitical hot spots are the South China Sea and the Strait of Malacca. The South China Sea encompasses a region between southern China, Vietnam, Thailand, West Malaysia's east coast, Singapore, East Malaysia, Brunei, and the Philippines' western archipelago. Since World War II, the area has been dominated by the U.S. Navy, and during the 1990s, this sea's Spratly Islands, consisting of approximately 100 small islands and reefs, were subject to competing claims from these countries and Taiwan and Vietnam due to disputes over national fishing areas and potentially large oil reserves. Some area countries have stationed troops on these islands, and their strategic location on a critical trade route in an economically prosperous and militarily significant region could make them a potential fulcrum of future military conflict.[58]

The Strait of Malacca is located between Indonesia, Malaysia, and Singapore, where it links the Indian Ocean to the South China Sea and Pacific Ocean. This strait provides the shortest sea route between Persian Gulf and West African suppliers and Asian markets, including China, Japan, South Korea, and other Pacific Rim countries such as Indonesia. More than 15 million barrels of oil go through this strait per day, over 50,000 vessels each year, and its narrowest point is 1.7 miles. Pirate attacks are an ongoing threat here, which, if successful in blocking the strait, could require nearly 50 percent of global fleets using alternative routes, and additional problems include collisions, oil spills, and poor visibility from smoke and haze. Possible alternative routes include going through Indonesia's Lombok or Sunda Straits or building pipelines between Malaysia and Thailand, which China is particularly interested in doing in Thailand's Kra Isthmus. Although regional countries, the International Maritime Organization, and the United States regularly share intelligence on potential threats to this body of water, it could become a key source of conflict due the role it plays in transporting energy supplies and the desire of countries as powerful as the China, the United States, and India for these supplies.[59]

Sovereign Debt

Sovereign debt refers to the debt owed by governments, which is a phenomenon that has occurred throughout history. National governments have chosen to place themselves in positions where they have had to borrow money from commercial banks, other national governments, or international government organizations to finance wars, economic development projects, public works, social assistance programs, or other real or perceived national needs. The doctrine of sovereign immunity states that repayment of sovereign debt cannot be compelled by creditors and must be subject to compulsory rescheduling, interest rate reduction, or even forgiveness. Protection available to creditors includes the borrowing nation losing its international economic credibility, the lowering of its global credit rating, and its increased difficulty in borrowing money from creditors in the future.[60]

Although developing countries in Africa, Asia, and Latin America have struggled with repaying debts they have owed to commercial financial institutions and international governmental organizations such as the International Monetary Fund and World Bank for many years, as demonstrated in the 1998 Asian financial crisis, *sovereign debt* has become a more widely used economic and geopolitical term since the onset of the 2008 global financial crisis. Populations and governments, to some degree, in developed countries such as the United States and Great Britain have become concerned over their high levels of national debt and the percentage of this debt as part of their country's overall wealth or gross domestic product.[61]

Severe sovereign debt problems in Greece during spring 2010 forced that country to turn to the EU for financial assistance. That assistance was granted, but with stringent conditions that caused considerable domestic unrest in Greece. During this time, concern also existed over whether Ireland, Portugal, and Spain would also need to seek EU or international economic assistance, the euro's sustainability as an international currency was questioned, and there is also doubt over whether the EU or other international financial lenders possess the capitalization necessary to issue such loans without incurring unsustainable financial risk or domestic political hostility to aiding profligate foreign countries. Concern also exists in the United States as to whether it could experience the same problems and unrest as Greece and whether China or other international creditors would provide the U.S. financial relief with conditions that would be economically and politically sustainable within the United States.[62] The globalized nature of domestic and international economics and the potential for domestic and international violence as a result of financial disruptions caused by sovereign debt will be a critical subject facing international economic, foreign policy, and national security policy makers in the years to come.

Terrorism

Perhaps no issue has broader geopolitical resonance with average citizens and policy makers than terrorism. News reports regularly inform us of violent attacks against civilians, law enforcement personnel, government officials, and military personnel in reprisal for real or imagined injustices and to gain publicity for a cause and its adherents. Targets of terrorist attacks may also include critical infrastructures such as bridges, electrical power stations, water supplies, refineries, and computer networks.

These attacks can occur anywhere in the world and often without warning. Examples of attacks in recent months include the attempted Christmas 2009 bombing of a Northwest Airlines flight approaching Detroit; a January 2, 2010, attack in Aarhus, Denmark, that attempted to kill Danish cartoonist Kurt Westergaard, who drew the controversial Mohammed cartoons; the May 1, 2010, attempted bombing in New York City's Times Square; and the July 11, 2010, attacks in Kampala, Uganda, against fans watching the World Cup championship by the al-Qaeda-allied terrorist group al-Shabab.[63]

Terrorism's impact has been felt in domestic and international economics and with some restrictions on civil liberties in democratic countries. Much more extensive and intrusive security is required to travel by airplane or mass transit. We may have to submit to biometric photo identification, fingerprints or DNA tests, polygraphs, and retinal eye scans to gain access to restricted areas like government office buildings or military facilities or to receive certain kinds of information and services. Government expenditures on security have increased and may contribute to the financial problems many government agencies are currently experiencing. The Internet and social networking sites are targets of terrorist recruitment and activities such as cyberwarfare against nations, military forces, and hated individuals and organizations, including multinational corporations. Terrorist groups representing various political, economic, secularist, and religious beliefs continually seek to conduct sabotage and bloody conventional terrorist attacks and also aspire to acquire weapons of mass destruction such as biological, chemical, and nuclear weapons to achieve their goals. Law enforcement, intelligence agencies, and militaries must continually adopt tactics to deter and defeat terrorist objectives. Public health providers such as hospitals must be prepared to treat mass casualties from terrorist attacks and have limited resources and personnel to do so.[64]

Turkey

Being at the intersection of Europe and Asia, Turkey has historically been an important geopolitical arena. It is a member of NATO, aspires to become an EU member, and, until recently, had close ties with Israel. It also controls the strategic choke point of the Turkish Straits (consisting of the Bosporus and Dardanelles straits), providing access between the Aegean and Mediterranean seas and the Black Sea. In 2006, 2.4 million barrels of oil flowed through this 17-mile-long strait per day, which is 0.5 miles wide at its narrowest point, from the Caspian Sea destined for western and southern Europe. Turkey has the right to close the straits for environmental and safety concerns, and there is no viable maritime alternative for this shipping route, although various pipeline projects are being considered involving countries such as Albania, Bulgaria, Greece, Macedonia, and Russia.[65]

For many decades, Turkey had a secularist government that was generally allied with the United States, with its military playing a particularly strong role in retaining this ideological and policy orientation. This has begun to change in recent years as a more Islamist government led by Prime Minister Recep Tayyap Erdoğan and his Justice and Development Party were elected and consolidated their power and sought to reduce the military's power. Traditionally good U.S.-Turkish relations were strained in 2003 when Turkey refused to allow U.S. forces to use it as a base to launch military operations into Iraq.[66]

Turkish-U.S. relationships have become even more strained in recent years. Turkey believes the U.S. overthrow of Iraq's Saddam Hussein's created instability on its southern border and emboldened the separatist Kurdish Workers Party to increase its operations against the Turkish government. Erdoğan's government has sought to improve Turkey's relationships with Syria and Iran, which is contrary to U.S. desires. Persian Gulf countries see Turkey as an attractive investment alternative and a regional power that can balance Iran. Turkey has become increasingly involved in the Israeli-Palestinian dispute and has vocally supported Hamas to Israel's extreme displeasure, with its outrage over Israel's May 2010 assault on a Turkish ship bringing "humanitarian" aid to Gaza representing the most vivid demonstration of this changing Turkish policy. Turkey has become an increasingly important player in the Caspian and Black Sea energy markets and has sought to improve its ties with countries in this region, including Armenia, Azerbaijian, Georgia, and Russia.[67]

One recent analysis of Turkish geopolitics sees four possible scenarios Turkey could follow. These include a pro-Western Turkey integrating into the EU, which would also anchor Turkey to a broad Euro-Atlantic framework desired by the United States; a more Islamicized Turkey, weakening its ties to the West, strengthening its Muslim identity and ties to Muslim countries, and weakening its commitments to secularism and Western values; a nationalist Turkey that, abandoning its efforts to obtain EU membership while still maintaining strong economic and trade ties with the EU, maintains defense ties with the United States but pursues more independent policies toward the Middle East and central Asia and expands economic and security cooperation with Russia; and a Turkey with escalating domestic political and social tension, leading the Turkish military to intervene and seize power.[68]

Yemen and Bab el Mandeb Strait

The southwestern Arabian Peninsula country of Yemen is another geopolitical flash point. The Bab el Mandeb Strait is a choke point between the Horn of Africa and Middle East as well as serving as a strategic transit point between the Indian Ocean and Mediterranean Sea. Adjacent countries include Djibouti, Eritrea, and Yemen, and this strait connects the Red Sea with the Gulf of Aden. Persian Gulf exports must pass through this strait before entering the Suez Canal. In 2006, an estimated 3.3 million barrels of oil per day went through this waterway toward Asia, Europe, and the United States, with nearly ⅔ flowing toward north toward the Suez Canal.

Bab el Mandeb is 18 miles wide at its narrowest point and is limited to two 2-mile-wide channels for inbound and outbound traffic. An east-west oil pipeline across Saudi Arabia could relieve some of this traffic if the strait were blocked. This area was the scene of the 2000 al-Qaeda terrorist attack on the USS *Cole* and an October 2002 attack on the French tanker *Limburg*.[69]

This area's geopolitical contentiousness and fragility is further highlighted by turmoil in Yemen and its proximity to Somali-based maritime piracy attacks near the Horn of Africa. Yemen remains a poor, sparsely settled, and poorly governed country. Although its government cooperates with the United States on antiterrorism efforts, which have included attacks against terrorist targets in that country, Yemeni demographics include the al-Houthi insurgency, and an al-Qaeda insurgency movement that attacked the U.S. embassy in Sana'a on September 17, 2008, killing several Yemeni security personnel, and claimed responsibility for the attempted December 25, 2009, attack on Northwest Flight 253 over Detroit, which resulted in the U.S. embassy's closure on January 3–4, 2010. This al-Qaeda insurgency has sought to recruit Westerners into its ranks and exploits existing tribal and religious factional disputes and concerns over Yemen's dwindling oil and water resources and resulted in Saudi Arabian military intervention during November 2009.[70]

Notes

1. Robert D. Kaplan, "The Revenge of Geography," *Foreign Policy*, 196 (May/June 2009): 96–105.

2. Ibid., 105.

3. International Security Assistance Force, "Key Facts and Figures," http://www.isaf.nato.int/troops-numbers-and-contributions/index.php.

4. A veritable and continuing flood of literature exists on these topics, including David Hume, *Integration of Weaponized Unmanned Aircraft into the Air-to-Ground System* (Maxwell Air Force Base, AL: Air University Press, 2007); U.S. Government Accountability Office, *Securing, Stabilizing, and Reconstructing Afghanistan: Key Issues*

for Congressional Oversight (Washington, DC: Government Accountability Office, 2007), http://purl.access.gpo.gov/GPO/LPS82737; Abdulkhader H. Sinno, *Organizations at War in Afghanistan and Beyond* (Ithaca, NY: Cornell University Press, 2008); Hans-Georg Erhart and Charles C. Pentland, eds., *The Afghanistan Challenge: Hard Realities and Strategic Choices* (Montreal, QC: McGill-Queens University Press, 2009); U.S. Congress, Senate Committee on Armed Services, *Strategic Options for the Way Ahead in Afghanistan and Pakistan* (Washington, DC: Government Printing Office, 2009); U.S. Congress, House Committee on Armed Services, *Security and Stability in Afghanistan and Iraq: Developments in U.S. Strategy and Operations and the Way Ahead* (Washington, DC: Government Printing Office, 2009); C. Christine Fair and Seth G. Jones, *Securing Afghanistan: Getting on Track* (Washington, DC: U.S. Institute of Peace, 2009), http://purl.access.gpo.gov/GPO/LPS11943; U.S. Congress, Senate Committee on Foreign Relations, *Afghanistan's Narco War: Breaking the Link between Drug Traffickers and Insurgents* (Washington, DC: Government Printing Office, 2009); Hassan Abbas, ed., *Pakistan's Troubled Frontier* (Washington, DC: Jamestown Foundation, 2009); and "The Aftermath of General McChrystal's Ouster," *Washington Post*, June 26, 2010: A14.

5. See James Risen, "U.S. Identifies Vast Mineral Riches in Afghanistan," *New York Times*, June 14, 2010: 1; Steve Ludington, Greta J. Orris, Karen S. Bolm, Stephen G. Peters, and the U.S. Geological Survey-Afghanistan Ministry of Mines and Industry Joint Mineral Resource Assessment Team, *Preliminary Resource Assessment of Selected Mineral Deposit Types in Afghanistan* (Reston, VA: U.S. Geological Survey (USGS), 2007); and USGS, "USGS Projects on Afghanistan," http://afghanistan.cr.usgs.gov/.

6. See Bjørn Brunstad, Givind Magnus, Philip Swanson, Geir Honneland, and Indra Overland, *Big Oil Playground, Russian Bear Preserve, or European Periphery: The Russian Barents Sea Region toward 2015* (Delft, Netherlands: Eburon, 2004); Jessica Robertson, Debbie Hutchinson, and Jonathan Childs, *Scientists Map Unexplored Arctic Sea Floor* (Reston, VA: USGS, 2008): 1, http://soundwaves.usgs.gov/2008/09/fieldwork2.html; U.S. Department of State, Bureau of Oceans and International Environmental and Scientific Affairs, "Defining the Limits of the U.S. Continental Shelf," http://www.state.gov/g/oes/continentalshelf/; U.S. Energy Information Administration, "Arctic Oil and Natural Gas Potential," http://www.eia.doe.gov/oiaf/analysispaper/arctic/; and Elana Wilson Rowe, ed., *Russia and the North* (Ottawa, QC: University of Ottawa Press, 2009).

7. U.S. Energy Information Administration, "Arctic Oil and Natural Gas Potential," 9.

8. Canada, Department of National Defence, *Canada First Defence Strategy* (2008?): 3, 7–8, http://www.forces.gc.ca/site/pri/first-premier/June18_0910_CFDS_english_low-res.pdf.

9. See British Broadcasting Corporation, "Russia Plants Flag under N Pole," http://news.bbc.co.uk/2/hi/europe/6927395.stm; and Pavel K. Baev, "Troublemaking and Risk-Taking: The North in Russian Military Activities," in Rowe, *Russia and the North*, 17–34.

10. President of the United States, "National Security Strategy," http://www.whitehouse.gov/sites/default/files/rss_viewer/national_security_strategy.pdf.

11. President of the United States, "National Security Presidential Directive 66," http://georgewbush-whitehouse.archives.gov/news/releases/2009/01/20090112-3.html.

12. See Elizabeth B. Elliot-Meisel, *Arctic Diplomacy: Canada and the United States in the Northwest Passage* (New York: P. Lang, 1998); "Arming the Arctic," *Jane's Defence Weekly*, 47 (12)(March 24, 2010): 24–25; Rob Huebert, "Polar Frontiers," *Armed Forces Journal*, 147 (7)(March 2010): 20–21, 36; and Gerard Cowen, "Canada Proceeds with Construction of Naval Facility in Disputed NWP," *Jane's Defence Weekly*, 47 (19)(May 12, 2010): 12.

13. See U.S. Energy Information Administration, "Caspian Sea Region: Survey of Key Oil and Gas Statistics and Forecasts," http://www.eia.doe.gov/emeu/cabs/caspian_balances.htm; U.S. Energy Information Administration, "Caspian Sea Region: Regional Conflicts," http://www.eia.doe.gov/emeu/casp/caspconf.html; Michael P. Croissant and Bülent Aras, eds., *Oil and Geopolitics in the Caspian Sea Region* (Westport, CT: Praeger, 1999); Adam N. Stulberg, *Well-Oiled Diplomacy: Strategic Manipulation and Russia's Energy Statecraft in Eurasia* (Albany: State University of New York Press, 2007): 133–76; and U.S. Congress, Senate Committee on Foreign Relations, *Oil, Oligarchs, and Opportunity: Energy from Central Asia to Europe* (Washington, DC: Government Printing Office, 2008), http://purl.access.gpo.gov/GPO/LPS108989.

14. See Olga Oliker, *U.S. Interests in Central Asia: Policy Priorities and Military Roles* (Santa Monica, CA: RAND, 2005); Stephen Blank, *Challenges and Opportunities for the Obama Administration in Central Asia* (Carlisle, PA: U.S. Army War College, Strategic Studies Institute, 2009), http://purl.access.gpo.gov/GPO/LPS114399; Elizabeth Wishnick, *Russia, China, and the United States in Central Asia: Prospects for Great Power Competition and Cooperation in the Shadow of the Georgia Crisis* (Carlisle, PA: U.S. Army War College, Strategic Studies Institute, 2009); U.S. Congress, Senate Committee on Foreign Relations, Subcommittee on Near Eastern and South and Central Asian Affairs, *Reevaluating U.S. Policy in Central Asia* (Washington, DC: Government Printing Office, 2010); and Anita Sengupta, *Heartlands of Eurasia: The Geopolitics of Political Space* (Lanham, MD: Lexington Books, 2009).

15. Andrew E. Kramer, "Following Kyrgyz Vote a Victory Is Declared," *New York Times*, June 28, 2010: A7; and Central Intelligence Agency (CIA), "World Factbook 2010," https://www.cia.gov/library/publications/the-world-factbook/geos/kg.html.

16. See U.S. Department of State, "Background Notes," http://www.state.gov/r/pa/ei/bgn/, for updates on U.S. foreign policy toward these countries; Havva Kok, "China and the Geopolitics of Oil in East Turkestan," *Turkish Review of Eurasian Studies*, vol. 4 (2004): 55–72; Michael Clarke, "China Strategy in Xinjiang and Central Asia: Toward Chinese Hegemony in the 'Geographical Pivot of History,'" *Issues and Studies*, 41 (2)(2005): 75–118; Charles Hawkins and Robert Love, eds., *The New Great Game: Chinese Views on Central Asia: Central Asia Regional Security Issues, Economic and Political Challenges* (Fort Leavenworth, KS: Foreign Military Studies Office, 2006), http://purl.access.gpo.gov/GPO/LPS111770; Hasan H. Karar, *The New Silk Road Diplomacy: China's Central Asian Foreign Policy since the Cold War* (Vancouver, BC: University of British Columbia Press, 2009); Stulberg, *Well-Oiled Diplomacy*, 93–132, 177–212; U.S. Congress, House Committee on International Relations, Subcommittee on the Middle East and Central Asia, *Assessing Energy and Security Issues*

in Central Asia (Washington, DC: Government Printing Office, 2006), http://purl.access.gpo.gov/GPO/LPS76182; and U.S. Congress, House Committee on Foreign Relations, Subcommittee on Asia, the Pacific, and the Global Environment, *Central Asia: An Overview* (Washington, DC: Government Printing Office, 2008), http://purl.access.gpo.gov/GPO/LPS106727.

17. See Michael T. Klare and Daniel Volman, "America, China, and the Scramble for Africa's Oil," *Review of African Political Economy*, 33 (108)(2006): 297–309; Donovan C. Chau, *Political Warfare in Sub-Saharan Africa: U.S. Capabilities and Chinese Operations in Ethiopia, Kenya, Nigeria, and South Africa* (Carlisle, PA: U.S. Army War College, Strategic Studies Institute, 2007); U.S. Congress, Senate Committee on Foreign Relations, Subcommittee on African Affairs, *China in Africa: Implications for U.S. Policy* (Washington, DC: Government Printing Office, 2008), http://purl.access.gpo.gov/GPO/LPS108660; Brent Bankus and Karen Hughes Butts, "China and Natural Resources Competition," in *Understanding Africa: A Geographic Approach*, ed. Amy Richmond Krakowa and Laurel J. Hummel (West Point, NY: U.S. Military Academy and U.S. Army War College, Center for Strategic Leadership, 2009): 349–82; and Bo Kong, *China's International Petroleum Policy* (Santa Barbara, CA: Praeger Security International, 2010): 121–25, 172–74, 187–89.

18. See Guillermo R. Delamer, Lyle J. Goldstein, Jorge Eduardo Malena, and Gabriela E. Porn, "Chinese Interests in Latin America," in *Latin American Security Challenges: A Collaborative Inquiry from North and South*, ed. Paul D. Taylor (Newport, CT: Naval War College Press, 2004): 79–102; Javier Santiso, ed., *Visible Hand of China in Latin America* (Paris: Organisation for Economic Cooperation and Development, 2007); Kong, *China's International Petroleum Policy*, 125–26, 178–79, 187–89; and U.S. Congress, House Committee on Foreign Relations, Subcommittee on the Western Hemisphere, *The New Challenge: China in the Western Hemisphere* (Washington, DC: Government Printing Office, 2008): 1, http://purl.access.gpo.gov/GPO/LPS98866.

19. See Christopher J. Pehrson, *String of Pearls: Meeting the Challenge of China's Rising Power across the Asian Littoral* (Carlisle, PA: U.S. Army War College, Strategic Studies Institute, 2006).

20. Ibid., 3.

21. See Lawrence Spinetta, "Cutting China's 'String of Pearls,'" *U.S. Naval Institute Proceedings*, 132 (10)(October 2006): 40–42; Andrew S. Erickson, "Can China Become a Maritime Power?"; Gabriel S. Collins, "An Oil Armada? The Commercial and Strategic Significance of China's Growing Tanker Fleet"; and Andrew C. Winner, "India as a Maritime Power?" in *Asia Looks Seaward: Power and Maritime Strategy*, ed. Toshi Yoshihara and James R. Holmes (Westport, CT: Praeger Security International, 2008): 70–110, 111–24, 125–45, resp.

22. U.S. Department of Defense, "Annual Report to Congress: Military Power of the People's Republic of China 2008," http://www.defense.gov/pubs/pdf/China_Military_Report_08.pdf.

23. Examples of this multifaceted literature include Richard Bernstein and Ross H. Munro, *The Coming Conflict with China* (New York: Alfred A. Knopf, 1997); U.S. Department of Defense, "Annual Report to Congress"; David L. Shambaugh, *Modernizing China's Military: Progress, Problems, and Prospects* (Berkeley: University of California Press, 2002); Toshi Yoshihara and James Holmes, "Command of the

Sea with Chinese Characteristics," *Orbis*, 49 (4)(Fall 2005): 677–94; U.S. Congress, House Committee on Armed Services, *Military Power of the People's Republic of China* (Washington, DC: Government Printing Office, 2007); Jinghao Zhou, "Does China Threaten the United States?" *Asian Perspective*, 32 (3)(2008): 171–82; James R. Holmes and Toshi Yoshihara, "China's Naval Ambitions in the Indian Ocean," *Journal of Strategic Studies*, 31 (3)(June 2008): 367–94; and Andrew Erickson and Lyle Goldstein, "Gunboats for China's New 'Grand Canals'? Probing the Intersection of Beijing's Naval and Oil Security Policies," *Naval War College*, 62 (2)(Spring 2009): 43–76.

24. See U.S. Congress, House Committee on International Relations, Subcommittee on Asia and the Pacific, *Crisis in the Taiwan Strait: Implications for U.S. Foreign Policy* (Washington, DC: Government Printing Office, 1996); Michael O'Hanlon, "Why China Cannot Conquer Taiwan," *International Security*, 25 (2)(Fall 2000): 51–86; U.S-China Economic and Security Review Commission, *Hearing on Military Modernization and Cross-Strait Balance* (Washington, DC: Government Printing Office, 2004); Yoshihara and Holmes, "Command of the Sea with Chinese Characteristics," 684–85; Murray Scot Tanner, *Chinese Economic Coercion against Taiwan: A Tricky Weapon to Use* (Santa Monica, CA: RAND, 2007); Shirley A. Kan, *China/Taiwan: Evolution of the "One China" Policy: Key Statements from Washington, Beijing, and Taipei* (Washington, DC: Library of Congress, Congressional Research Service, 2007); William S. Murray, "Revisiting Taiwan's Defense Strategy," *Naval War College Review*, 61 (3)(Summer 2008): 13–38; Paul J. Smith, "China-Japan Relations and the Future Geopolitics of East Asia," *Asian Affairs: An American Review*, 35 (4)(Winter 2009): 237–40; Nancy Bernkopf Tucker, *Strait Talk: United States-Taiwan Relations and the Crisis with China* (Cambridge, MA: Harvard University Press, 2009); and U.S. Congress, House Committee on International Relations, Subcommittee on Asia, the Pacific, and the Global Environment, *Recognizing the 30th Anniversary of the Taiwan Relations Act* (Washington, DC: Government Printing Office, 2009).

25. The vast corpus of literature on this controversial subject includes Harm J. De Blij, *Why Geography Matters: Three Challenges Facing America: Climate Change, the Rise of China, and Global Terrorism* (New York: Oxford University Press, 2005); Bjørn Lomberg, *Cool It: The Skeptical Environmentalist's Guide to Global Warming* (New York: Alfred A. Knopf, 2007); Carolyn Pumphrey, ed., *Global Climate Change: National Security Implications* (Carlisle, PA: U.S. Army War College, Strategic Studies Institute, 2008); Nevelina I. Pachova, Mikiyasu Nakayama and Libor Jansky, eds., *International Water Security: Domestic Threats and Opportunities* (Tokyo: United Nations University Press, 2008); Australia Murray-Darling Basin Authority, "Murray-Darling Basin Authority," http://www.mdba.gov.au/; Felix Dodds, Andrew Higham, and Richard Sherman, eds., *Climate Change and Energy Insecurity: The Challenge for Peace, Security, and Development* (London: Earthscan, 2009); U.S. Congress, House Committee on Foreign Affairs, *Climate Change and the Arctic: New Frontiers of National Security* (Washington, DC: Government Printing Office, 2009), http://purl.access.gpo.gov/GPO/LPS113771; Rymn J. Parsons, *Taking Up the Security Challenge of Climate Change* (Carlisle, PA: U.S. Army War College, Strategic Studies Institute, 2009); and U.S. Congress, Senate Committee on Foreign Relations, *Climate Change and Global Secu-*

rity: Challenges, Threats, and Diplomatic Opportunities (Washington, DC: Government Printing Office, 2010), http://purl.access.gpo.gov/GPO/LPS119470.

26. United States Strategic Command, "Fact Sheets: U.S. Cyber Command," http://www.stratcom.mil/factsheets/cc/.

27. Examples of works on cyberwarfare include Timothy L. Thomas, *Dragon Bytes: Chinese Information-War Theory and Practice from 1995–2003* (Fort Leavenworth, KS: Foreign Military Studies Office, 2004); David C. Gompert, Irving Lachow, and Justin Perkins, *Battle-Wise: Seeking Time-Information Superiority in Networked Warfare* (Washington, DC: Center for Technology and National Security Policy, National Defense University Press, 2006); Janie Hulse, *China's Expansion into and U.S. Withdrawal from Argentina's Telecommunications and Space Industries and the Implications for U.S. National Securities* (Carlisle, PA: U.S. Army War College, Strategic Studies Institute, 2007), http://purl.access.gpo.gov/GPO/LPS86294; Christopher Paul, *Information Operations: Doctrine and Practice: A Reference Handbook* (Westport, CT: Praeger Security International, 2008); Martin C. Libicki, *Cyberdeterrence and Cyberwar* (Santa Monica, CA: RAND, 2009); U.S. Congress, House Committee on Armed Services, Subcommittee on Terrorism, Unconventional Threats, and Capabilities, *Strategic Communications and Countering Ideological Support for Terrorism* (Washington, DC: Government Printing Office, 2009); and Rich Mesic, *Air Force Cyber Command (Provisional) Decision Support* (Santa Monica, CA: RAND, 2010).

28. See the annually published U.S. Energy Information Administration, "International Energy Outlook," http://www.eia.doe.gov/oiaf/ieo/; U.S. Energy Information Administration, "Energy Security," http://www.eia.doe.gov/emeu/security/; Hugo McPherson, W. Duncan Wood, and Derek M. Robinson, eds., *Emerging Threats to Energy Security and Stability* (Dordrecht, Netherlands: Springer, 2005); U.S. Congress, Senate Committee on Foreign Relations, *Energy Trends in China and India: Implications for the United States* (Washington, DC: Government Printing Office, 2006); U.S. Congress, House Committee on Transportation and Infrastructure, *Administration Proposals on Climate Change and Energy Independence* (Washington, DC: Government Printing Office, 2007); National Academy of Engineering, Committee on America's Energy Future, *America's Energy Future: Technology and Transformation* (Washington, DC: National Academies Press, 2009); Patrick M. Cronin, ed., *Global Strategic Assessment 2009: America's Security Role in a Changing World* (Washington, DC: National Defense University Press, 2009); and Keith Crane, Andreas Goldthau, Michael Thoman, Thomas Light, Stuart E. Johnson, Alireza Nader, Angel Rabasa, and Harun Dogo, *Imported Oil and U.S. National Security* (Santa Monica, CA: RAND, 2009).

29. Global Policy Forum, "Failed States," http://globalpolicy.org/nations-a-states/failed-states.html.

30. "The Failed States Index," *Foreign Policy*, 173 (July/August 2009): 80–83.

31. See Elsina Wainwright, Quinton Clements, Mary-Louise O'Callaghan, and Greg Urwin, *Our Failing Neighbour: Australia and the Future of the Solomon Islands* (Barton, ACT: Australian Strategic Policy Institute, 2003); Aaron B. Frank, *Preconflict Management Tools: Winning the Peace* (Washington, DC: Center for Technology and Security Policy, National Defense University, 2005); Ashraf Ghani and Clare Lockhart, *Fixing Failed States: A Framework for Rebuilding a Fractured World* (New

York: Oxford University Press, 2008); Maria C. Haims, David C. Gompert, Gregory F. Treverton, and Brooke Stearns Lawson, *Breaking the Failed-State Cycle* (Santa Monica, CA: RAND, 2008); Robert H. Bates, *When Things Fall Apart: State Failure in Late-Century Africa* (New York: Cambridge University Press, 2008); Larry J. Woods and Timothy R. Reese, *Military Interventions in Sierra Leone: Lessons from a Failed State* (Fort Leavenworth, KS: Combat Studies Institute Press, U.S. Army Combined Arms Center, 2008); and Tiffiany Howard, *The Tragedy of Failure: Evaluating State Failure and Its Impact on the Spread of Refugees, Terrorism, and War* (Santa Barbara, CA: Praeger Security International, 2010).

32. Arizona state information resources on this legislation can be found at Arizona Governor, "Arizona Border Security Information Center," http://www.azgovernor.gov/AZBorderSecurity.asp. See U.S. Department of Justice, "Citing Conflict with Federal Law, Department of Justice Challenges Arizona Immigration Law," http://www.justice.gov/opa/pr/2010/July/10-opa-776.html, for the text of the U.S. government's lawsuit against Arizona's law and related documentation.

33. See Martin Tsamenyi and Chris Rahman, eds., *Protecting Australia's Maritime Borders: The MV Tampa and Beyond* (Wollongong, NSW: Centre for Maritime Policy, University of Wollongong, 2002); David Marr and Marian Wilkinson, *Dark Victory: The Tampa and the Military Campaign to Re-elect the Prime Minister* (Crows Nest, NSW: Allen and Unwin, 2003); and Paul Kelly, *The March of Patriots: The Struggle for Modern Australia* (Carlton, VIC: Melbourne University Press, 2009): 541–65.

34. See Niklaus Steiner, *Arguing about Asylum: The Complexity of Refugee Debates in Europe* (New York: St. Martin's Press, 2000); U.S. Congress, House Committee on International Relations, Subcommittee on International Terrorism and Nonproliferation, *Border Vulnerabilities and International Terrorism* (Washington, DC: Government Printing Office, 2006); Gordon H. Hanson, *The Economic Logic of Illegal Immigration* (New York: Council on Foreign Relations, 2007); Edward H. Alden, *The Closing of the American Border: Terrorism, Immigration, and Security since 9/11* (New York: Harper, 2008); and Ariane Chebel d'Appollonia and Simon Reich, eds., *Immigration, Integration, and Security: America and Europe in Comparative Perspective* (Pittsburgh, PA: University of Pittsburgh Press, 2008).

35. See Emma Rothschild, *The Last Empire: Security and Globalization in Historical Perspective* (Newport, RI: U.S. Naval War College, 2003); Vaughan Higgins and Geoffrey Lawrence, eds., *Agricultural Governance: Globalization and the New Politics of Regulation* (London: Routledge, 2005); Jürgen Osterhammel and Niels P. Petersson, *Globalization: A Short History* (Princeton, NJ: Princeton University Press, 2005); and Stephen M. Streeter, John C. Weaver, and William D. Coleman, eds., *Empires and Autonomy: Moments in the History of Globalization* (Vancouver, BC: University of British Columbia Press, 2009).

36. See U.S. Centers for Disease Control, "Emerging Infectious Diseases," http://www.cdc.gov/ncidod/EID/; U.S. Congress, House Committee on International Relations, *Infectious Diseases: A Growing Threat to America's Health and Security* (Washington, DC: Government Printing Office, 2000); CIA, *Global Infectious Disease Threat and Its Implications for the United States* (Washington, DC: CIA, 2000); Executive Office of the President, President's Council of Advisors on Science and Technology, *Report to the President on U.S. Preparations for 2009-H1N1 Influenza* (Washington, DC:

President's Council of Advisors on Science and Technology, 2009); U.S. Congress, Senate Committee on Health, Education, Labor, and Pensions, *Meeting the Global Challenge of AIDS, TB, and Malaria* (Washington, DC: Government Printing Office, 2009); Gerald T. Keusch, Marguerite Pappaioanou, Mila C. González, Kimberly Scott, and Peggy Tsai, eds., *Sustaining Global Surveillance and Response to Emerging Zoonotic Diseases* (Washington, DC: National Academies Press, 2009); and U.S. Congress, Senate Committee on Homeland Security and Governmental Affairs, Subcommittee on Oversight of Government Management, the Federal Workforce, and the District of Columbia, *Protecting Our Employees: Pandemic Influenza Preparedness and the Federal Workforce* (Washington, DC: Government Printing Office, 2010).

37. See Waheguru Pal Singh Sudhu and Jing-dong Yuan, *China and India: Cooperation or Conflict?* (Boulder, CO: Lynne Rienner, 2003); David van Praagh, *The Greater Game: India's Race with Destiny and China* (Montreal, QC: McGill-Queen's University Press, 2003); Stephen F. Burgess, *India's Emerging Security Strategy, Missile Defense, and Arms Control* (Colorado Springs, CO: U.S. Air Force Academy Institute for National Security Studies, 2004); Zhang Guihong, "U.S.-India Strategic Partnership: Implications for China," *International Studies*, 42 (3–4)(2005): 277–93; Stephen J. Blank, *Natural Allies? Regional Security in Asia and Prospects for Indo-American Strategic Cooperation* (Carlisle, PA: U.S. Army War College, Strategic Studies Institute, 2005); *Gauging U.S.-Indian Strategic Cooperation*, ed. Henry Sokolski (Carlisle, PA: U.S. Army War College, Strategic Studies Institute, 2007); Andrew C. Winner, "India as a Maritime Power," in Yoshihara and Holmes, *Asia Looks Seaward: Power and Maritime Strategy*; James R. Holmes and Toshi Yoshihara, "Strongman, Constable, or Free-Rider? India's 'Monroe-Doctrine' and Indian Naval Strategy," *Comparative Strategy*, 28 (4)(April–June 2009): 332–48; David Brewster, "India's Security Partnership with Singapore," *Pacific Review*, 22 (5)(December 2009): 597–618; and Robert D. Kaplan, *Monsoon: The Indian Ocean and the Future of American Power* (New York: Random House, 2010).

38. See Devin T. Hagerty, *The Consequences of Nuclear Proliferation: Lessons from South Asia* (Cambridge, MA: MIT Press, 1998); George Perkovich, *India's Nuclear Bomb: The Impact on Global Proliferation* (Berkeley: University of California Press, 1999); Graham P. Chapman, *The Geopolitics of South Asia: From Early Empires to the Nuclear Age*, 2nd ed. (Burlington, VT: Ashgate, 2002): 263–65, 267–68; Kanishkan Sathasivam, *Uneasy Neighbors: India, Pakistan and U.S. Foreign Policy* (Burlington, VT: Ashgate, 2005); P.R. Chari and Hasan Askari Rizvi, *Making Borders Irrelevant in Kashmir* (Washington, DC: U.S. Institute of Peace, 2008); Peter Lyon, *Conflict between India and Pakistan: An Encyclopedia* (Santa Barbara, CA: ABC-CLIO, 2008); and Jayshree Bajoria, "The U.S.-India Nuclear Deal," http://www.cfr.org/publication/9663/usindia_nuclear_deal.html.

39. See Judith Share Yaphe and Charles D. Lutes, *Reassessing the Implications of a Nuclear-Armed Iran* (Washington, DC: National Defense University, Institute of Strategic Studies, 2005); Kenneth Katzman, *Iran's Influence in Iraq* (Washington, DC: Library of Congress, Congressional Research Service, 2010); U.S. Congress, House Committee on Armed Services, *Iran: Assessing Geopolitical Dynamics and U.S. Policy Options* (Washington, DC: Government Printing Office, 2007); Yonah Alexander and Milton Hoenig, *The New Iranian Leadership: Ahmadinejad, Nuclear Ambition, and*

the Middle East (Westport, CT: Praeger Security International, 2008); Anthony H. Cordesman and Adam Seitz, *Iranian Weapons of Mass Destruction: The Birth of a Regional Arms Race?* (Santa Barbara, CA: Praeger Security International and Center for Strategic and International Studies, 2009); U.S. Department of State, "Country Reports on Terrorism: Western Hemisphere Overview 2008," http://www.state.gov/s/ct/rls/crt/2008/122435.htm; and U.S. Congress, House Committee on Foreign Affairs, Subcommittees on the Western Hemisphere, Middle East and South Asia, and Terrorism, Nonproliferation, and Trade, *Iran in the Western Hemisphere* (Washington, DC: Government Printing Office, 2009).

40. See U.S. Department of Defense, *Report to Congress: Measuring Stability and Security in Iraq* (Washington, DC: Government Printing Office, 2005–present); U.S. Congress, House Committee on Government Reform, Subcommittee on National Security, Emerging Threats, and International Relations, *The Evolving National Strategy for Victory in Iraq* (Washington, DC: Government Printing Office, 2007); Steven Metz, *Iraq and the Evolution of American Strategy* (Washington, DC: Potomac Books, 2008); Najim Abed Al-Jabouri, *Iraqi Security Forces after U.S. Troop Withdrawal: An Iraqi Perspective* (Washington, DC: National Defense University, Institute for National Strategic Studies, 2009); and U.S. Congress, House Committee on Armed Services, *Effective Counterinsurgency: How the Use and Misuse of Reconstruction Funding Affects the War Effort in Iraq and Afghanistan* (Washington, DC: Government Printing Office, 2010).

41. See Robert Marquand, "In Land of Few Burqas, France Debates a Ban," *Christian Science Monitor*, July 6, 2010; Anna Marij van der Meulen, "Far Right Surges in Dutch Election," *Wall Street Journal*, June 11, 2010; "The Swiss Minaret Ban," *The Economist*, November 30, 2009; Melanie Phillips, *Londonistan* (New York: Encounter Books, 2006); Ayaan Hirsi Ali, *Infidel* (New York: Free Press, 2007); Michael Emerson et al., eds., *Islamist Radicalisation: The Challenge for Euro-Mediterranean Relations* (Brussels: Center for European Policy Studies, 2009); Christopher Caldwell, *Reflections on the Revolution in Europe: Immigration, Islam, and the West* (New York: Doubleday, 2009); Amr Elshobaki and Gema Martin Muñoz, *Why Europe Must Engage with Political Islam* (Paris: European Institute for Security Studies and European Institute of the Mediterranean, 2010); and Phillip R. Cuccia, *Implications of a Changing NATO* (Carlisle, PA: U.S. Army War College, Strategic Studies Institute, 2010): 9.

42. See U.S. Congress, Senate Committee on Foreign Relations, *Israel's Disengagement from Gaza and Several West Bank Settlements: Staff Trip Report* (Washington, DC: 2005); Joel Beinein and Rebecca L. Stein, eds., *The Struggle for Sovereignty: Palestine and Israel, 1993–2005* (Stanford, CA: Stanford University Press, 2006); U.S. Congress, House Committee on Foreign Affairs, Subcommittee on Middle East and South Asia, *853 Days: From Gaza Disengagement to De Facto Power* (Washington, DC: Government Printing Office, 2008); Kenneth Katzman, *Iran: U.S. Concerns and Policy Responses* (Washington, DC: Library of Congress, Congressional Research Service, 2009): 30–31; James Kitfield, "Gaza Flotilla: Strategic Blunder or Unavoidable Confrontation," *National Journal Expert Blog: National Security*, June 7, 2010: 1–13, http://security.nationaljournal.com/2010/06/gaza-flotilla-strategic-blunde.php; Asad Ghanen, *Palestinean Politics after Arafat: A Failed National Movement* (Bloomington:

Indiana University Press, 2010); and Efraim Karsh, *Palestine Betrayed* (New Haven, CT: Yale University Press, 2010).

43. See Philip Kelly, *Checkerboards and Shatterbelts: The Geopolitics of South America* (Austin: University of Texas Press, 1997); Arie M. Kacowicz, "Geopolitics and Territorial Issues: Relevance for South America," *Geopolitics*, 5 (1)(Summer 2000): 81–100; Leslie W. Hepple, "South American Heartland: The Charcas, Latin American Geopolitics, and Global Strategies," *Geographical Journal*, 170 (4)(December 2004): 359–67; Gabriela Marcela, *American Grand Strategy for Latin America in the Age of Resentment* (Carlisle, PA: U.S. Army War College, Strategic Studies Institute, 2007); Jaime Suchlicki, *The Cuba-Venezuela Challenge to Hemispheric Security: Implications for the United States* (Coral Gables, FL: University of Miami Center for Hemispheric Policy, 2009), http://www6.miami.edu/hemispheric-policy/VenCubaSecurityChallenges.pdf; and Hal Brands, *Dealing with Political Ferment in Latin America: The Populist Revival, the Emergence of the Center, and Implications for U.S. Policy* (Carlisle, PA: U.S. Army War College, Strategic Studies Institute, 2009).

44. U.S. Congress, House of Representatives, *United States Mariner and Vessel Protection Act of 2009: Report to Accompany H.R. 3376*, H. Rpt. 111-386, pt. 1 (Washington, DC: Government Printing Office): 1–2.

45. Australia, Office of the Inspector of Transport Security, *International Robbery and Armed Piracy at Sea Security Inquiry Report* (Canberra: Office of the Inspector of Transport Security, 2010): 3.

46. See Graham Gerard Ong-Web, ed., *Piracy, Maritime Terrorism, and Securing the Malacca Straits* (Singapore: Institute of Southeast Asian Studies and International Institute for Asian Studies, 2006); Andrew Forbes, ed., *Asian Energy Security: Regional Cooperation in the Malacca Strait* (Canberra: Sea Power Centre-Australia, 2008); U.S. Department of Homeland Security, *Small Vessel Security Strategy* (Washington, DC: Department of Homeland Security, 2008); Wu Shicun and Zou Keyuan, eds., *Maritime Security in the South China Sea: Regional Implications and International Cooperation* (Farnham, UK: Ashgate, 2009); U.S. Congress, Senate Committee on Armed Services, *Ongoing Efforts to Combat Piracy on the High Seas* (Washington, DC: Government Printing Office, 2009); U.S. Congress, House Committee on Foreign Affairs, Subcommittee on International Organizations, Human Rights, and Oversight, *International Efforts to Combat Maritime Piracy* (Washington, DC: Government Printing Office, 2009); and Andrew S. Erickson, "Chinese Sea Power in Action: The Counterpiracy Mission in the Gulf of Aden and Beyond," in *The PLA at Home and Abroad: Assessing the Operational Capabilities of China's Military*, ed. Roy Kamphausen, David Lai, and Andrew Scobell, (Carlisle, PA: U.S. Army War College, Strategic Studies Institute, 2010): 295–376.

47. Max G. Manwaring, *A Contemporary Challenge to State Sovereignty: Gangs and Other Illicit Transnational Criminal Organizations in Central America, El Salvador, Mexico, Jamaica, and Brazil* (Carlisle, PA: U.S. Army War College, Strategic Studies Institute, 2007): vii.

48. See Howard Campbell, *Drug War Zone: Frontline Dispatches from the Streets of El Paso and Juárez* (Austin: University of Texas Press, 2009); U.S. Congress, House Committee on the Judiciary, Subcommittee on Crime, Terrorism, and Homeland Security, *Escalating Violence in Mexico and the Southwest Border as a Result of the Illicit*

Drug Trade (Washington, DC: Government Printing Office, 2009); U.S. National Drug Intelligence Center, *National Gang Threat Assessment* (Johnstown, PA: National Drug Intelligence Center, 2009); U.S. Congress, House Committee on Homeland Security, Subcommittee on Border, Maritime, and Global Counterterrorism, *Border Violence: An Examination of DHS Strategies and Resources* (Washington, DC: Government Printing Office, 2010); Evan Brown and Dallas D. Owens, *Drug Trafficking, Violence, and Instability in Mexico, Colombia, and the Caribbean: Implications for U.S. National Security* (Carlisle, PA: U.S. Army War College, Strategic Studies Institute, 2010); and Hal Brands, *Crime, Violence, and the Crisis in Guatemala: A Case Study in the Erosion of the State* (Carlisle, PA: U.S. Army War College, Strategic Studies Institute, 2010).

49. See U.S. Congress, House Committee on International Relations, Subcommittee on Africa, Global Human Rights, and International Operations, *Nigeria's Struggle with Corruption* (Washington, DC: Government Printing Office, 2006); A. T. Simbine, *Security in the Niger Delta* (Ibadan: Nigerian Institute of Social and Economic Research, 2008); Judith Burdin Asuni, *Blood Oil in the Niger Delta* (Washington, DC: U.S. Institute of Peace, 2009); and U.S. Energy Information Administration, "Country Analysis Briefs: Nigeria," http://www.eia.doe.gov/emeu/cabs/Nigeria/pdf.pdf.

50. Edward Bruner, *North Korean Crisis: Possible Military Options* (Washington, DC: Library of Congress, Congressional Research Service, 2003): 1–3.

51. Choe Sang-Hun, "South Korea to Accuse North Korea of Sinking Ship, Officials Say," *New York Times*, May 19, 2010: 4.

52. See Daniel J. Orcutt, *Carrot, Stick, or Sledgehammer: U.S. Policy Options for North Korean Nuclear Weapons* (Colorado Springs, CO: USAF Institute for National Security Studies, 2004); David J. Bishop, *Dismantling North Korea's Nuclear Weapons Program* (Carlisle, PA: U.S. Army War College, Strategic Studies Institute, 2005); U.S. Congress, House Committee on International Relations, Subcommittee on Asia and the Pacific, *North Korean Brinksmanship: Is U.S. Policy Up to the Challenge?* (Washington, DC: Government Printing Office, 2006); Jacques L. Fuqua Jr., *Nuclear Endgame: The Need for Engagement with North Korea* (Westport, CT: Praeger Security International, 2007); Kuk-Sin Kim, *Transformation of the Japan-U.S. Alliance and South Korea's Security Strategy* (Seoul: Korean Institute for National Unification, 2008); Bruce W. Bennett, *Uncertainties in the North Korean Nuclear Threat* (Santa Monica, CA: RAND, 2010); and U.S. Congress, Senate Committee on Foreign Relations, *North Korea Back at the Brink* (Washington, DC: Government Printing Office, 2010).

53. See Gawdat Bahgat, *American Oil Diplomacy in the Persian Gulf and the Caspian Sea* (Gainesville: University Press of Florida, 2003); Jon B. Alterman, *Iraq and the Gulf States: The Balance of Fear* (Washington, DC: U.S. Institute of Peace, 2007); U.S. Energy Information Administration, "World Oil Transit Chokepoints," http://www.eia.doe.gov/emeu/cabs/World_Oil_Transit_Chokepoints/pdf.pdf; and Jeffrey R. Macris, *The Politics and Security of the Gulf: Anglo-American Hegemony and the Shaping of a Region* (London: Routledge, 2010).

54. European Commission, Directorate General for Energy, *Europe's Energy Position Markets and Supply* (Luxembourg: European Union, 2010): 21–22.

55. See Robert L. Larsson, *Russia's Energy Policy: Security Dimensions and Russia's Reliability as an Energy Supplier* (Stockholm: FOI Swedish Defence Research Agency, 2006); Robert Winchester, *European Energy Security: Wrestling the Russian Bear for Caspian Natural Gas* (Carlisle, PA: U.S. Army War College, 2007); Stulberg, *Well-Oiled Diplomacy*; U.S. Congress, Senate Committee on Foreign Relations, *Oil, Oligarchs, and Opportunity: Energy from Central Asia to Europe* (Washington, DC: Government Printing Office, 2008); Marshall I. Goldman, *Petrostate: Putin, Power, and the New Russia* (New York: Oxford University Press, 2010); and Keith C. Smith, *Russia-Europe Energy Relations: Implications for U.S. Policy* (Washington, DC: Center for Strategic and International Studies, 2010): 1.

56. See David D. Laitin, *Identity in Formation: The Russian-Speaking Populations in the Near Abroad* (Ithaca, NY: Cornell University Press, 1998); Kaare Dahl Martinsen, *The Russian-Belarussian Union and the Near Abroad* (Oslo: Norwegian Institute for Defense Studies, 2002); Janusz Bugasjki, *Cold Peace: Russia's New Imperialism* (Westport, CT: Praeger and Center for Strategic and International Studies, 2004); Stephen M. Saideman, *For Kin or Country: Xenophobia, Nationalism, and War* (New York: Columbia University Press, 2008); and Peter B. Humphrey, "The State of Play in Russia's Near Abroad," *Joint Force Quarterly*, 55 (2009): 41–46.

57. Paul J. D'Anieri, *Economic Interdependence in Ukranian-Russian Relations* (Albany: State University of New York Press, 1999); Herman Pirchner, *Reviving Greater Russia? The Future of Russia's Borders with Belarus, Georgia, Kazakhstan, Moldova, and Ukraine* (Washington, DC: American Foreign Policy Council and University Press of America, 2005); Kestitutis Paulauskas, *The Baltics: From Nation States to Member States* (Carlisle, PA: U.S. Army War College, Strategic Studies Institute, 2006); Christoph Zürcher, *The Post-Soviet War: Rebellion, Ethnic Conflict, and Nationhood in the Caucasus* (New York: New York University Press, 2007); Ruth Deyermond, *Security and Sovereignty in the Former Soviet Union* (Boulder, CO: Lynne Rienner, 2008); Wishnick, *Russia, China, and the United States in Central Asia*; U.S. Congress, Senate Committee on Foreign Relations, Subcommittee on European Affairs, *Georgia: One Year after the August War* (Washington, DC: Government Printing Office, 2010); and Ronald D. Asmus, *A Little War That Shook the World: Georgia, Russia, and the Future of the West* (New York: Palgrave Macmillan, 2010).

58. See Allan Shephard, *Seeking Spratly Solutions: Maritime Tensions in the South China Sea* (Canberra: Australia Parliamentary Library, 1993); Lai Tao Lee, *China and the South China Sea Dialogues* (Westport, CT: Praeger, 1999); U.S. Congress, Senate Committee on Foreign Relations, Subcommittee on East Asian and Pacific Affairs, *Maritime Disputes and Sovereignty Issues in East Asia* (Washington, DC: Government Printing Office, 2009); and Justin Corfield, "South China Sea," in *Seas and Waterways of the World: An Encyclopedia of History, Uses, and Issues*, ed. John Zumerchik and Steven L. Danver (Santa Barbara, CA: ABC-CLIO, 2010): 245–47.

59. See Jim Cooney and Donald B. Freeman, *The Straits of Malacca: Gateway or Gauntlet?* (Montreal, QC: McGill-Queens University Press, 2003); *Chinese Oil Dependency: Opportunities and Challenges* (Carlisle, PA: U.S. Army War College, 2005); Bronson Percival, *Indonesia and the United States: Shared Interests in Maritime Security* (Washington, DC: United States-Indonesia Society, 2005); Graham Gerard

Ong-Webb, ed., *Piracy, Maritime Terrorism, and Securing the Malacca Straits* (Leiden, Netherlands: International Institute of Asian Studies and Institute of Southeast Asian Studies, 2006); Pehrson, *String of Pearls*, 4; Yun Yun Teo, "Target Malacca Straits: Maritime Terrorism in Southeast Asia," *Studies in Conflict and Terrorism*, 30 (6)(2007): 541–61; and U.S. Energy Information Administration, "World Oil Transit Chokepoints," 2–4.

60. BusinessDictionary.com, s.v. "sovereign debt," http://www.businessdictionary.com/definition/sovereign-debt.html.

61. See Thomas Melito, *Developing Countries: U.S. Financing for Multilateral Debt Reduction Initiative Experiencing a Shortfall* (Washington, DC: Government Accountability Office, 2008); U.S. Congress, Senate Committee on Foreign Relations, *Building on International Debt Relief Initiatives* (Washington, DC: Government Printing Office, 2008); Peter Costello, with Peter Coleman, *The Costello Memoirs: The Age of Prosperity* (Carlton, VIC: Melbourne University Press, 2008): 168–87; U.S. Department of the Treasury, "The Debt to the Penny and Who Holds It," *Treasury Direct*, http://www.treasurydirect.gov/NP/BDPLogin?application=np, for daily and recent historical quantification of U.S. sovereign debt; and United Kingdom, Office for National Statistics, "Economy: Public Sector," http://www.statistics.gov.uk/cci/nugget.asp?id=206.

62. See Paolo Manasse, Nouriel Roubini, and Axel Schimmelpfenning, *Predicting Sovereign Debt Crises* (Geneva, Switzerland: International Monetary Fund, 2003); Michael L. Levin, *The Next Great Clash: China and Russia versus the United States* (Westport, CT: Praeger Security International, 2008); Wayne M. Morrison and Marc Labonte, *China's Holdings of U.S. Securities: Implications for the U.S. Economy* (Washington, DC: Library of Congress, Congressional Research Service, 2008); Gordon Platt, "Greek Debt Crisis Morphing into Euro Problem," *Global Finance*, 24 (6) (June 2010): 85–86; Gavin Finch and John Glover, "Europe's Banks Face a Funding Squeeze," *Bloomberg Businessweek*, 4184 (June 21, 2010): 51–52; U.S.-China Economic and Security Review Commission, "U.S. Debt to China: Implications and Repercussions," http://www.uscc.gov/hearings/2010hearings/hr10_02_25.php.

63. See U.S. Department of State, Office of the Coordinator for Counterterrorism, "Country Reports on Terrorism," http://www.state.gov/s/ct/rls/crt/, for these annual reports documenting terrorist incidents; U.S. National Counterterrorism Center, "Worldwide Incidents Tracking System," http://www.nctc.gov/wits/witsnextgen.html; and resources produced by the Memorial Institute for the Prevention of Terrorism, Lawson Library, http://www.mipt.org/library, for access to terrorist incident chronologies and other resources on terrorism.

64. See Joshua H. Goldstein, *The Real Price of War: How You Pay for the War on Terror* (New York: New York University Press, 2004); U.S. Congress, House Committee on Government Reform, Subcommittee on National Security, Emerging Threats, and International Relations, *Progress since September 11th: Protecting Health and Safety of the Responders and Residents* (Washington, DC: Government Printing Office, 2007); Robert Mandel, *Global Threat: Target-Centered Assessment and Management* (Westport, CT: Praeger Security International, 2008); Bruce Clements, *Disasters and Public Health: Planning and Response* (Amsterdam: Butterworth-Heinemann/Elsevier, 2009); U.S. Congress, House Committee on Homeland Security, Subcommittee on

Intelligence, Information Sharing, and Terrorist Risk Assessment, *Assessing and Addressing the Threat: Defining the Role of a National Commission on the Prevention of Violent Radicalization and Homegrown Terrorism* (Washington, DC: Government Printing Office, 2009); U.S. Congress, House Committee on Homeland Security, Subcommittee on Intelligence, Information Sharing, and Terrorist Risk Assessment, *Using the Web as a Weapon: The Internet as a Tool for Violent Radicalization and Homegrown Terrorism* (Washington, DC: Government Printing Office, 2009); President of the United States, *Summary of the White House Review of the Details of the December 25, 2009 Attempted Terrorist Attack* (Washington, DC: White House, 2010); and U.S. Congress, Senate Committee on the Judiciary, Subcommittee on Terrorism, Technology, and Homeland Security, *Protecting National Security and Civil Liberties: Strategies for Terrorism Information Sharing* (Washington, DC: Government Printing Office, 2010).

65. U.S. Energy Information Administration, "World Oil Transit Chokepoints," 2, 7–9.

66. See Stephen J. Blank, Stephen Pelletiere, and William Thomas Johnson, *Turkey's Strategic Position at the Crossroads of World Affairs* (Carlisle, PA: U.S. Army War College, Strategic Studies Institute, 1993); U.S. Congress, House Committee on Foreign Affairs, Subcommittee on Europe, *U.S.-Turkish Relations and the Challenges Ahead* (Washington, DC: Government Printing Office, 2007); F. Stephen Larrabee, *Turkey as a U.S. Security Partner* (Santa Monica, CA: RAND Project Air Force, 2008); and U.S. Department of State, "Background Note: Turkey," http://www.state.gov/r/pa/ei/bgn/3432.htm.

67. See Graham E. Fuller, *The New Turkish Republic: Turkey as a Pivotal State in the Muslim World* (Washington, DC: U.S. Institute of Peace, 2009); Bulent Aliriza, *Turkey's Evolving Dynamics: Strategic Choices for U.S. Turkey-Relations: Final Report of the CSIS U.S.-Turkey Strategic Initiative* (Washington, DC: CSIS, 2009); Jeffrey Fleishman, "Turkey Holds Funeral for Gaza Flotilla Activists," *Los Angeles Times*, June 4, 2010: A1; and F. Stephen Larrabee, *Troubled Partnership: U.S.-Turkish Relations in an Era of Global Geopolitical Change* (Santa Monica, CA: RAND Project Air Force, 2010).

68. Larrabee, *Troubled Partnership*, 111–17.

69. See U.S. Congress, House Committee on Armed Services, *Attack on the U.S.S. Cole* (Washington, DC: Government Printing Office, 2001); and U.S. Energy Information Administration, "World Oil Transit Chokepoints," 2, 6.

70. See Christopher Boucek, "Collision Course: Yemen's Converging Crises," *Jane's Intelligence Review*, 21 (10)(October 2009): 34–37; Jack Freeman, "The al Houthi Insurgency in the North of Yemen: An Analysis of the Shabab al Moumineen," *Studies in Conflict and Terrorism*, 32 (11)(November 2009): 1008–19; U.S. Department of State, "Background Note: Yemen," http://www.state.gov/r/pa/ei/bgn/35836.htm; U.S. Department of State, "Travel Warning: Yemen," http://www.travel.state.gov/travel/cis_pa_tw/tw/tw_936.html; Barak A. Salmoni, Bryce Loidolt, and Madeleine Wells, *Regime and Periphery in Northern Yemen: The Huthi Phenomenon* (Santa Monica, CA: RAND, 2010); and U.S. Congress, House Committee on Foreign Affairs, *Yemen on the Brink: Implications for U.S. Policy* (Washington, DC: Government Printing Office, 2010).

CHAPTER 4

U.S., Foreign, and International Government Organization Geopolitical Information Resources

Any examination of geopolitics as a scholarly research venue and as an interdisciplinary factor for analyzing international political, economic, and security trends needs to recognize the important role government and military agencies play in formulating these continually evolving policies. Such examination must include close scrutiny of the information resources produced by numerous national and international government organizations, including energy or natural resources departments, foreign ministries, intelligence agencies, military agencies and professional military educational institutions, and international economic policy–oriented agencies. Fortunately, a wide variety of geopolitical information resources produced by national and international government organizations are Internet accessible to most users, and many of these are available in English.

This chapter intends to introduce readers to the global array of geopolitical information produced by governmental agencies. Naturally, this information will reflect prevailing and continually evolving government assessments of their national geopolitical interests, depending on the nature and policies of the government in power at the moment in time when these documents were produced. It seeks to be global in coverage scope and present a wide array of perspectives representing multiple agencies.

African Union

The African Union was established in 1999 to accelerate the process of continental integration and to address social, economic, and political problems it sees as being caused by globalization. It is located in Addis Ababa, Ethiopia, and also seeks to promote unity among African countries and safeguard the sovereignty and territorial integrity of member states.[1] Its Web site, http://www.africa-union.org/, contains information about organizational activities, including the texts of documentary decisions, articles from the journal *African Integration Review* (2007 to present), and reports such as *Meeting the Challenge of Conflict Prevention in Africa—Towards the Operationalization of the Continental Early Warning System* (2006).

Argentina National Defense School

Argentina's National Defense School was established on December 29, 1950, as National Defense College, began offering its first higher educational courses in 1952, received its present name on December 24, 1973, and is located in Buenos Aires. Its missions include preparing military officers and public officials for anticipating, evaluating, and resolving war scenarios that might affect Argentina and seeking to examine and resolve international problems Argentina might face.[2] Its Web site, http://www.mindef.gov.ar/edn.htm, provides information about its curricular and research programs and support facilities such as the library and translations of some publications such as *South American Geopolitics* (2001), *Geopolitics Bases for Argentina* (2001), and Spanish-language works such as *La Cuenca del Plata: Aproximatión Geopolítica a Su Realidad* (2007), which analyzes the Plata river basin's geopolitical realities.

Australia

Australian Defence College

The Australian Defence College (ADC) was initially established in 1967 in Canberra and sought to unify existing armed service staff branches; its first courses began in 1970. Subsequent reorganizations have given ADC the mission of promoting the growth and learning of leaders and managers interested in national and international defense and security issues through organizational components such as the Centre for Defence and Strategic Studies, Australian Command and Staff College, and Australian Defence Force Academy.[3]

ADC's Web site, http://www.defence.gov.au/jetwc/, provides information about this institution's educational and research programs, with many of them examining geopolitical matters, including *Australian Defence Force Journal* (1976 to present); *Piracy, Maritime Terror, and Regional Interests* (2005); and *Is the Expansion of the Chinese Military a Threat to the Western Pacific?* (2009).

Australian Security Intelligence Organisation

The Australian Security Intelligence Organisation (ASIO) was established in 1949 and is responsible for identifying security threats, including attacks on Australian defense systems and foreign threats, and is located in Russell, Australian Capital Territory.[4] ASIO's Web site, http://www.asio.gov.au/, provides additional information on its activities, including selected publications such as its *Annual Report to Parliament* and *Counter-terrorism White Paper: Securing Australia, Protecting Our Community* (2010).

Australian Security Intelligence Service

The Australian Security Intelligence Service (ASIS) was established in 1952 and serves as Australia's overseas human intelligence agency, emphasizing the Asia-Pacific region.[5] ASIS's Web site, http://www.asis.gov.au/, contains information about its history, its governance, and its oversight, which includes being part of the Department of Foreign Affairs and reporting to a parliamentary joint committee.

Department of Defence

Australia's Department of Defence is responsible for implementing military aspects of Australian foreign and national security policy. Its origins date from the Australian federation's beginning in 1901 and it and Australia's armed forces has evolved over the subsequent century to try to meet the country's military requirements.[6] Its Web site, http://www.defence.gov.au/, provides access to a variety of information resources on Australian geopolitical interests and national security strategy including A *History of Australian Strategic Policy Since 1945* (2009) featuring Australian strategic policy documents from 1946–1976 and the Defence White Paper *Defending Australia in the Asia-Pacific Century: Force 2030* (2009).

Air Power Development Centre

The Royal Australian Air Force's Air Power Development Centre (APDC) is responsible for enhancing the effectiveness of Australian air and space power which transcends training and doctrine by providing timely and strategic advice and historical analysis to assist civilian and military policy makers.[7] APDC's Web site, http://airpower.airforce.gov.au/, features a variety of works analyzing geopolitical aspects of aerospace power, including *Air Power for Australia's Security: More Than the Three Block War* (2007), *Offensive Air Power in Counter-insurgency Operations: Putting Theory into Practice* (2008), and *Seven Perennial Challenges to Air Forces* (2009).

Sea Power Centre

The Royal Australian Navy's Sea Power Centre (SPC) was established to engage in activities promoting awareness, discussion, and study of maritime issues and strategies within the military and civilian communities. It also aspires to promote understanding of sea power and its application to Australian national interests, developing maritime concepts, force structures decisions, and strategies and to make informed recommendations on maritime defense issues.[8] SPC's Web site, http://www.navy.gov.au/spc/, provides information about center operations and numerous publications including those dealing with maritime geopolitical strategy, including *The Enforcement Aspects of Australia's Ocean's Policy* (2003); *Asian Energy Security: Regional Cooperation in the Malacca Strait* (2008); *Presence, Power Projection, and Sea Control: The RAN in the Gulf, 1990–2009* (2009); *Japanese Sea Power: A Maritime Nation's Struggle for Identity* (2009); and *Maritime Policy: The Australian Jurisdiction* (2010).

Department of Foreign Affairs and Trade

Australia's Department of Foreign Affairs and Trade (DFAT) is responsible for providing foreign policy and trade advice to the government, advancing the interests of Australian security, and promoting Australian economic prosperity.[9] DFAT's Web site, http://www.dfat.gov.au/, contains a variety of information resources describing current and historical Australian foreign policy and foreign economic policy along with information produced by departmental component organizations such as the Australian Safeguards and Non-proliferation Office (http://www.dfat.gov.au/asno/). Examples of these materials include *Potential for Production of Proliferation Sensitive Materials in Research Reactors* (2008), *India: A Trade Partner of Growing Importance* (2008), and selected volumes from the documentary series *Documents on Australian Foreign Policy*.

Office of National Assessments

The Office of National Assessments (ONA) was established in 1977 as an independent organization accountable to the prime minister. It provides all source assessments on international economic, political, and strategic developments for the National Security Committee of the Cabinet. Its assessments are based on governmental and open source resources, and these assessments seek to focus on emerging international and long-term issues of particular interest to the government as well as evaluating the effectiveness and funding of Australian foreign intelligence operations.[10] ONA's Web site, http://

www.ona.gov.au/, provides some information about organizational activities, including director-general speeches and budget information.

Brazil

Ministry of Defense, Virtual Library

This Ministry of Defense resource provides access to technical and scholarly works on security and defense by Brazilian researchers.[11] Its Web site, http://www.defesa.gov.br/espaco_academico/index.php?page=biblioteca_virtual, provides access to theses, dissertations, articles, and book-length studies on geopolitical and security issues. Although the text of these documents is in Portuguese, it is possible to automatically translate their titles into English. Examples of these works include *Sovereignty and Interference in the Brazilian Amazon* (2003); *Geopolitical Background and Employment of the Armed Forces in South America* (2004); and *India, Brazil, and South Africa: Prospects for Co-operation on Security* (2006).

Ministry of Foreign Relations

Brazil's Foreign Ministry dates its postindependence organization from 1822 and is responsible for conducting Brazilian foreign policy and seeking to advance that country's international interests.[12] The ministry's Web site, http://www.mre.gov.br/, provides information about the geopolitical thinking and foreign policy objectives of South America's preeminent nation and an emerging global power. It will feature information about Brazilian bilateral relations with various countries and multilateral relations with international organizations such as the South American free trade organization Mercosur, Brazilian views on international sea and environmental policy, earth observation, G20 country finance, space policy, and terrorism.

Superior War College

Brazil's Superior War College (Escuela Superior De Guerra, ESG) is Brazil's leading professional military educational institution and was founded in 1949. Its mission is preparing civilian and military officials for performing national security policy making and for enhancing the sophistication of this policy making by civilian leaders.[13] ESG's Web site, http://www.esg.br/, is primarily in Portuguese, but you can find information about its curriculum, the work of its Center for Strategic Studies, the text of its *Notebooks for Strategic Studies*, and articles from its scholarly journal *Revista* from 1996 to 2006.

Canada

Canadian Forces College Papers

Located in suburban Toronto, Canadian Forces College (CFC) is Canada's premier professional military educational institution. Its missions include preparing senior military and civilian leaders to meet the future's complex security challenges by educating them about war, peace, and security.[14] A particularly useful information resource on this Web site are the research papers prepared by CFC students, which are accessible from 1998 to present at http://www.cfc.forces.gc.ca/en/cfcpapers/. Examples of these papers include *Climate Change and the Impact on the Northwest Passage: A Challenge to Canadian (Arctic) Sovereignty* (2006); *Developing a Coherent Plan to Deal with Canada's Conundrum in the Northwest Passage* (2007); *NATO Enlargement and Russia: The Need for a Dual Track Policy* (2008); *China's Role in Africa: Reconsidering the Facts in Sierra Leone, the Democratic Republic of the Congo and Sudan* (2008); and *The Effects of Climate Change on the Arctic: Implication and Challenge for the Canadian Defence Strategy* (2009).

Department of National Defence

Canada's Department of Defence (DND) and the Canadian Forces (Canada's military) are responsible for advising the government and implementing government decisions on defending Canadian interests domestically and internationally.[15] DND's Web site, http://www.dnd.ca/, contains a variety of geopolitical and security-related information resources, including descriptions of Canada-U.S. defense relations, reports such as the current *Defense White Paper*, a database with descriptions of Canadian military force operations since 1945, information on the activities of Canadian force service branches, and publications such as *Canadian Military Journal* (2000 to present) and *Canadian Air Force Journal* (2008 to present).

Foreign Affairs and International Trade Canada

This agency serves as Canada's foreign policy and international trade promotion agency, and its beginnings date from its 1909 establishment.[16] The department's Web site, http://international.gc.ca/, features a variety of information resources about Canadian foreign policy, including information on Canadian activities in Afghanistan, its efforts to exercise national sovereignty in the Arctic region, explaining Canada's global international economic interests, and the text of many reports, including its official documentary series *Documents on Canadian External Relations*.

Natural Resources Canada

Natural Resources Canada (NRCAN) was established in 1842 as the Geological Survey of Canada. NRCAN is Canada's primary agency seeking to enhance the responsible development and use of Canadian natural resources and the competitiveness of its natural resource products, including its extensive natural gas and oil assets.[17] NRCAN's Web site, http://www.nrcan.gc.ca/, provides information about Canadian energy resources and natural resources policy, including reports such as *Canadian Refining and Oil Security* (2008) and *Canadian Natural Gas: Review of 2007/08 and Outlook to 2020* (2008), and information about its controversial Alberta tar sands industry.

China

Central Military Commission

The Central Military Commission (CMC) is China's central military organization responsible for commanding that country's armed forces and serves as its top military decision-making entity. Its organizational components include General Staff Headquarters, General Political Department, General Logistics Department, General Armament Department, the Ministry of Defense, headquarters offices for various armed forces branches, and regional military commands.[18] A limited amount of information can be found on CMC's English-language Web site, http://www.gov.cn/english/links/cmc.htm, including descriptions of center activities and the names of current members (http://english.gov.cn/2008–03/content_921750.htm).

Ministry of Commerce

The Ministry of Commerce is responsible for implementing various domestic and international economic activities, including promoting foreign trade and international economic cooperation and handling a broad spectrum of bilateral and multilateral economic matters, including export control, technology transfer, and trade.[19] The ministry's English-language Web site, http://english.mofcom.gov.cn/, provides selective information and statistics about China's foreign trade, foreign economic assistance, foreign investment policies, news releases, and relationship with the World Trade Organization (WTO).

Ministry of National Defence

This ministry (MND) is responsible for implementing Chinese military policy through its armed services, including the multiple branches of the

People's Liberation Army (PLA).[20] MND's English-language Web site, http://eng.mod.gov.cn/, features the text of defense white papers from 1995–2008, brief biographies of 36 individuals designated by the CMC as "Military Strategists of the PLA," listings but not the text of defense laws and regulations, materials on defense technology programs, what MND contends are military spending statistics, and news about domestic and international military security developments.

People's Liberation Army National Defense University

This institution (PLANDU) serves as China's premier professional military educational institution and is located in Changping, near Beijing. It was founded in 1985 by combining the Political Academy, Military Academy, and Logistics Academy. This event represented the first time in PLA history that there was an all-service academy seeking to stress joint operations within the Chinese military. PLANDU features five study tracks or courses, including National Defense Research, Basic Studies, Advanced Studies, Graduate Research, and Instructor Training. The National Defense Research course is also considered the capstone course and is responsible for preparing the most senior officers and civilians for leading roles in future Chinese defense and national security policy making.[21]

Besides graduating nearly 1,000 Chinese officers annually, PLANDU also conducts a growing educational program for foreign military officers, which graduated 500 of these individuals in 2007, with many of these graduates coming from Latin America, South America, and Southeast Asian countries such as Thailand.[22] A Singaporean analyst of PLANDU's emergence maintains that China's investment in training and educating foreign officers is an attempt to influence the leaders of countries where it has interests, to build contacts in countries for potential future arms sales, and to counterbalance American preeminence. This assessment also asserts that defense and military education are critical components of a Chinese strategy of building its soft power globally; that its increasing prosperity will give it additional resources to spend on foreign military education and training; that China is carving a niche in such pedagogy, even though the United States, Australia, and the United Kingdom remain the first choice for foreign militaries to educate and train their officers; and that this generally overlooked aspect of Chinese power should not be underestimated.[23]

PLANDU does not have an accessible English-language Web site as of May 2010, but it is likely to be a key producer of the individuals and writings that will influence China's geopolitical aspirations and strategies in the years ahead.

European Union

Common Foreign and Security Policy

The European Union (EU) Common Foreign and Security Policy (CFSP) seeks to have member states cooperate in developing collaborative foreign and security policies. CFSP components include identifying terrorism, weapons of mass destruction, regional conflicts, failed states, and organized crime and major threats and conflict prevention, rapid response, and assistance in all stages of crisis situations.[24]

CFSP's Web site, http://ec.europa.eu/external_relations/cfsp/, provides information about its activities, descriptions of its relations with various global regions, and selected publications, including *EU-India: Global Partners Tackling Global Challenges* (2009) and *The European and Ukraine: Towards Political Association and Economic Cooperation* (2010).

Energy Policy

EU energy policy has significant economic and geopolitical import because more than 50 percent of member countries energy resources comes from nonmember countries, and that percentage is growing. Russia is the leading energy supplier of EU countries, and there are often transit disputes between these countries that have caused supply disruptions. Consequently, the EU has become interested in looking for alternative energy suppliers, with particular emphasis on the Caspian Sea region.[25] Information on EU energy policy activities can be found at http://europa.eu/pol/index_en.htm. These resources include the text of legislation, policy development overviews, and statistics and publications such as *Panorama of Energy: Energy Statistics to Support EU Policies and Solutions* (2009) and *Europe's Energy Position: Markets and Supply* (2010).

Institute of Security Studies

The EU's Institute of Security Studies was established in 2001, is located in Paris, and is a think tank researching security issues and conducting debate on these topics.[26] Its Web site, http://www.iss.europa.eu/, provides a number of useful geopolitical analyses, including its Chaillot Papers and Occasional Papers monographic series, featuring works such as *From Suez to Shanghai: The European Union and Eurasian Maritime Security* (2009) and *The Gas Crisis and the Financial Crisis: The Impact on EU–Central Asia Relations in the Energy Sphere* (2009).

France

Collegè Interarmées de Defénse

This organization (CID) serves as France's premier professional military educational institution; its name can be translated as the Joint Defense College. It was originally founded on January 18, 1751, by Louis XV and assumed its current organizational structure on September 1, 1993. Its mission is preparing military officers to assume command staff and leadership positions to execute national defense policy. CID's four primary curricular and research emphases are European and global geopolitical analysis, strategy and the art of war, Ministry of Defense interactions with other government departments, and defense acquisition and management.[27] CID's Web site, http://www.college.interarmees.defense.gouv.fr/, although primarily in French, provides a number of English-language resources about institutional activities and research analysis of geopolitical and security matters. Examples of these, comprising translated titles, include *How to Find the Path of European Strategic Autonomy in the Choice of Sea Power?* (2008), *Strategic Surprises: Southeast Asia and the Contemporary World* (2008), *After the French Nuclear Testing in the South Pacific: The Bomb to Bounce* (2010), and *The Decline of Modern Societies: Ideal for Strategic or Tragic?* (2010).

Germany

Foreign Ministry

Germany's Foreign Ministry is responsible for conducting German foreign policy. It began with Germany's 1871 establishment, has gone through numerous political and ideological changes, moved to Bonn in 1951, and returned to Berlin in 1999.[28] The Foreign Ministry Web site, http://www.auswaertiges-amt.de/, provides details on Germany's multilateral foreign policy with organizations like the EU, United Nations, and NATO; information on its bilateral relations with countries around the world such as Afghanistan, where German military forces are involved as part of NATO's International Security Assistance Force; and information on how it approaches various international issues such as energy, environmental protection, the Greek financial crisis, globalization, human rights, nonproliferation, and terrorism.

India

Ministry of Defence

India's Ministry of Defence (IMOD) is responsible for defending this country and is responsible for implementing governmental defense policies.

IMOD's modern organization began with national independence in August 1947 and has gone through various organizational evolutions in the subsequent six decades.[29] Its Web site, http://mod.nic.in/, features information about India's armed forces and *Annual Reports* (1999–2000 to present).

India National Defence College

The India National Defence College (INDC) is located in New Delhi and serves as that country's leading professional military educational institution. It was established in 1960 as part of the IMOD to provide joint training and instruction to senior military and civilian officers. Its curriculum and research involves economic, industrial, political, scientific, and strategic aspects of national defense.[30] Its Web site, http://ndc.viburnix.com/, features information about the university's curriculum, faculty, lists of articles from *NDC Journal* (2000–2007), and the text of student theses from 2001 to 2006, with examples including *Conflicts in the South China Sea and Its Impacts on Regional Security* (2001); *China's Growing Influence in International Relations: Impact on India's National Security* (2005); *Pakistan in the Coming Decade: Issues and Options* (2006); and *India's Energy Security* (2006). It is hoped that INDC will soon add more recent and historical student theses to its Web site.

International Atomic Energy Agency

The International Atomic Energy Agency (IAEA) is affiliated with the United Nations, is located in Vienna, and was founded in 1957. Its purposes include working for the safe, secure, and peaceful uses of nuclear science and technology while attempting to verify that safeguarded nuclear materials and activities are not used for military purposes.[31] IAEA's Web site, http://www.iaea.org/, contains information about its programmatic activities in the areas of nuclear energy, safeguards, safety, and technical cooperation, along with publications such as the annual periodicals *Nuclear Safety Review* and *Safeguards Implementation Summary*.

International Energy Agency

The International Energy Agency (IEA) is a Paris-based intergovernmental organization that is part of the Organization for Economic Cooperation and Development and that was established in 1974. IEA serves as an energy policy advisor to 28 member countries and seeks to ensure affordable, clean, and reliable energy for these countries citizens; coordinate relief measures during oil supply emergencies; and promote energy security, economic development, environmental protection, and technology collaboration.[32] IEA's

Web site, http://www.iea.org/, provides information about organizational structure and activities, including some free information resources such as *Energy Security and Climate Policy: Assessing Interactions* (2007), *Medium-Term Oil Market Report* (2009), and *Key World Energy Statistics* (2009).

International Maritime Organization

The International Maritime Organization (IMO) is an intergovernmental organization established in 1948 and located in London. Its responsibilities include taking measures to improve the safety and security of international shipping, preventing marine pollution from ships, and facilitating international maritime traffic.[33] IMO's Web site, http://www.imo.org/, features a variety of resources about this organization's structure and global activities. Examples of freely accessible publications include the monthlies *Current Awareness Bulletin* (2008 to present), featuring news stories on important maritime developments, and *Reports on Acts of Piracy and Armed Robbery against Ships*, the annual *International Shipping and World Trade: Facts and Figures* (2009), and *Information Resources on Climate Change and the Maritime Industry* (2010).

Israel

Israel Defense Force

The Israel Defense Force (IDF) is that country's military services and is responsible for defending Israel against conventional and unconventional military.[34] IDF's English-language Web site, http://dover.idf.il/, provides information about recent news stories involving the IDF, including its controversial interception of a Turkish ship carrying supplies to Gaza.

Ministry of Defense

Israel's Ministry of Defense (IMOD) is responsible for directing Israeli national security activities.[35] IMOD's Web site, http://www.mod.gov.il/, features some English-language information, including press releases, details about national export control policy, and defense budget information.

Ministry of Foreign Affairs

Israel's Ministry of Foreign Affairs (MFA) is responsible for formulating, implementing, and presenting Israel's foreign policy to foreign governments and international government organizations.[36] MFA's Web site, http://www.mfa.gov.il/, provides a wide variety of information resources on Israeli foreign policy, including its antiterrorism efforts, concerns over Iran, and the text of its official foreign policy documentary series *Israel's Foreign Relations: Selected Documents*, dated from 1947 to 2001.

Japan

Japan Maritime Self-Defense Force

Japan's Maritime Self-Defense Force (MSDF) is responsible for defending Japan by sea since that country is dependent on the ocean for over 90 percent of the raw materials essential to its economic development and growth.[37] The MSDF Web site, http://www.mod.go.jp/msdf/, features information about this force's capabilities and how it will respond to threats from ballistic missile attacks and guerilla operations and will conduct warning and surveillance in adjoining sea areas and airspace to prevent invasion of Japanese islands.

Ministry of Foreign Affairs

Japan's Ministry of Foreign Affairs (MOFA) is responsible for conducting Japanese foreign policy and its bilateral and multilateral relations with foreign governments and international government organizations.[38] MOFA's Web site, http://www.mofa.go.jp/, contains information on and documents about Japanese foreign policy in areas such as climate change, conflict prevention, maritime affairs, and piracy, along with its bilateral and multilateral relationships with other countries and international government organizations.

North Atlantic Treaty Organization

The North Atlantic Treaty Organization (NATO) was established in 1949 and is an international security organization involving North American and European countries seeking to advance their national security interests and international security interests. Article 5 of the treaty establishing NATO says that an armed attack against any member country is considered an attack against all member countries, permitting these countries to individually or collectively defend themselves.[39] NATO's Web site, http://www.nato.int/, provides additional information about the alliance, including news releases, reports on various activities, and information on alliance operations in Kosovo and Afghanistan.

NATO Defense College

The NATO Defense College (NDC) is located in Rome and was established in 1951; its responsibilities include enhancing alliance cohesion and effectiveness by fostering strategic-level thinking on political-military matters, preparing selected officers and officials for important NATO and

NATO-related multinational appointments, conducting academic studies and research supporting wider alliance goals, and supporting an active outreach program with other educational institutions.[40] NDC's Web site, http://www.ndc.nato.int/, provides further information about its curricular and research activities. Examples of accessible NDC geopolitically related publications include *NATO and Energy Security after the Strasbourg-Kehl Summit* (2009), *Security Prospects in the High North: Geostrategic Thaw or Freeze?* (2009), *Piracy: Threat or Nuisance* (2010), and *NATO: Peacekeeping in the Holy Land? A Feasibility Study* (2010).

Pakistan

National Defence University

Pakistan's National Defense University (PNDU) serves as that country's premier professional military educational institution and strives to be a center of academic and research excellence on national and international security in close consultation with the Pakistan government and military and defense universities in allied countries.[41] PNDU's Web site, http://www.ndu.edu.pk/, provides information on university research activities, including the table of contents for *NDU Journal* (2001–2008) and the Margalla Papers monographic series (2001–2008).

Romania

National Defense University "Carol I," Centre for Defense and Security Strategic Studies

The Centre for Defense and Security Strategic Studies (CDSSS) at National Defence University "Carol I" was founded in 2000 as a research institution for the Romanian military's general staff. Its responsibilities include developing expertise for Romanian political-military institutions, investigating military-strategic environmental changes affecting Romanian interests, studying national societal developments influencing the military, and enhancing national security through international cooperation.[42] CDSSS's Web site, http://cssas.unap.ro/, includes articles from the journal *Strategic Impact* (2002 to present) and the text of Romanian-language reports whose translated titles include *European Environmental Dynamics Security* (2007) and *Outlook for Security and Defence in Europe* (2009).

Russia

Foreign Intelligence Service

The Russian Federation's Foreign Intelligence Service (SVR) was established on December 18, 1991, after going through various names and functions during the Soviet era of Russian history. SVR serves as part of Russia's security forces, and its mission is protecting Russia against external threats.[43] SVR's Web site, http://www.svr.gov.ru/, includes some translated public relations–oriented English-language resources. These include press releases from 2000 to present and descriptions of historical documentary collections on Soviet intelligence operations.

Gazprom

Gazprom is a Russian joint stock company created in 1993 by the Russian government and privatized in 1998. It serves as a major natural gas– and petroleum-producing and distribution company that is heavily influenced by the Russian government and delivers these commodities to Russian, European, and other international customers.[44] Gazprom's Web site, http://www.gazprom.ru/, contains some English-language material on its operations, including production financial statistics, shareholder news, and press releases from 2008 to the present. However, more detailed information, such as annual reports, are in Russian and are dated from 1998 to the present.

Ministry of Defense

The Russian Federation's Ministry of Defense is responsible for executing national defense activities, as directed by the Federation president, and seeks to exert its influence and these policies in a variety of geographic regions.[45] Its Web site, http://www.mil.ru/, provides some English-language resource on Russian ministry and military activities, including biographical information on the defense minister, press releases, a military encyclopedia of selected facts and figures, selected recent articles from *Red Star* military newspaper, and Russian-language issues of the magazine *Russian Military Review* (2006 to present).

Ministry of Foreign Affairs

Russia's Ministry of Foreign Affairs is responsible for administering and executing Russian Federation foreign policy objectives.[46] Its Web site, http://www.mid.ru/, features English-language descriptions of Russian foreign policy viewpoints, national security documents such as *Maritime Doctrine of the Russian Federation until 2020* (2001), and descriptions of Russia's relations with Commonwealth of Independent States nations and other countries and international government organizations.

Security Council Russian Federation

Russia's Security Council (SCRF) is the executive organization constitutionally responsible for carrying out presidential national security decisions. It was established in 1992, and its multiple responsibilities include preparing an annual report for the president on national security and foreign policy matters; developing proposals to protect constitutional order, sovereignty, and territorial integrity; and addressing and meeting current and emerging needs in areas such as information security, energy security, antiterrorism, and various foreign policy objectives.[47] SCRF's Web site, http://www.scrf.ru/, contains information about council activities, membership, policy-making processes, and press releases from 2005 to the present.

Singapore

Ministry of Defence

Singapore's Ministry of Defence (SMOD) and the country's armed forces are responsible for enhancing national peace and security through deterrence and diplomacy and achieving swift and decisive victory over aggressors if military conflict occurs.[48] SMOD's Web site, http://www.mindef.gov.sg/, provides information about the ministry's organizational structure and leadership and the text of policy documents such as *Defending Singapore in the 21st Century* (2008) and the scholarly journal *Pointer*.

South Africa

Department of Defence

South Africa's Department of Defence is responsible for defending and advancing that country's national security interests.[49] The department's Web site, http://www.dod.mil.za/, features the text of departmental *Annual Reports* (2002 to present), the text of relevant statutory laws, historic defense white papers, and the news magazine *SA Soldier* (2007 to present).

Department of International Relations and Cooperation

South Africa's Department of International Relations and Cooperation seeks to enhance South African national interests, enhancing the quality of its bilateral and multilateral relationships, protecting territorial integrity and sovereignty, and monitoring international developments and advising the government on relevant foreign policy and domestic matters.[50] The ministry's Web site, http://www.dfa.gov.za/, provides information and statistics about multiple aspects of South African foreign policy and foreign economic relations.

Military Academy

South Africa's military academy is located in Stellenbosch at Stellenbosch University. Established in 1950, it serves as the South African National Defence Force's training unit, providing military education and professional military development for career officers.[51] The academy's Web site, http://science.sun.ac.za/, features information about its curriculum and research programs and the text of articles from its scholarly journal *Scientis Militaria: South African Journal of Military Studies* from 2008 to present at http://www.ajol.info/index.php/smsajms.

South African Secret Service

The South African Secret Service (SASS) provides intelligence management to help the national government strategically manage its economic, political, and national security interests. Its modern organizational structure dates from 1995, when various apartheid-era governmental and insurgency intelligence gathering activities were combined.[52] SASS's Web site, http://www.sass.gov.za/, features information about its history, the text of relevant laws governing its activities, and selected press releases and reports.

South Korea

Korea Institute for National Unification

The Korean Institute for National Unification (KINU) is a South Korean government agency established in 1990 to advise governmental policy makers, develop a national political consensus for Korean Peninsula unification, and conduct research promoting peace and prosperity in this geographic region.[53] KINU's Web site, http://www.kinu.or.kr/, features information about institute activities and the text of numerous reports and analyses, including the journal *International Journal of Korean Unification Studies* (1992 to present), *Internal and External Perceptions of the North Korean Army* (2008), *The US-ROK Alliance in the 21st Century* (2009), and *Kim Jong Il's China Visit and China's Strategic Diplomacy* (2010).

Korean National Defense University

Located in Seoul, the Korean National Defense University (KNDU) was established in 1955 and serves as South Korea's leading national security affairs educational and research institution. Its major organizational components include a Graduate School for National Security, Graduate School for Defense Management, Joint Staff College, and Research Institute for

National Security Affairs.[54] KNDU's Web site, http://www.kndu.ac.kr/, features information on student enrollment and the number of faculty personnel, succinct course descriptions, and descriptions of English-language publications such as *Korean Journal of Security Affairs* and *Annual Report of Strategic Assessment on the Korean Peninsula*.

National Intelligence Service

South Korea's National Intelligence Service (NIS) was established in 1961 as the Korea Central Intelligence Agency and received its current name in 1999. Its purpose is collecting, coordinating, and distributing information on national security and strategy.[55] NIS's English-language Web site, http://eng.nis.go.kr/, features an organizational historical chronology, information on selected instances of North Korean infiltration, testimonials by North Korean defectors, and news translations of North Korean media reports from May 2008 to the present.

Taiwan

Mainland Affairs Council

Taiwan's Mainland Affairs Council (MAC) is a governmental agency established in 1988 to enhance peaceful political and economic contacts between Taiwan and China, coordinate Taiwanese government policy toward Beijing, and seek to resolve differences between these two countries through dialogue.[56] MAC's Web site, http://www.mac.gov.tw/, provides statistics on economic and cultural exchanges between these two countries, the text of laws governing Taiwanese relations with China and that country's Special Administrative Regions of Hong Kong and Macau, and the text of policy documents such as *Easing Restrictions on Cross-Strait Securities Investments* (2008).

National Defense University

Taiwan's National Defense University (TNDU) was originally established on the mainland in 1911, was relocated to Taiwan in 1949, and received its current name in 2000. Its civilian and military colleges train middle and high-ranking officers for military service and are responsible for meeting the educational needs of a modern and professional military establishment.[57] TNDU's Web site, http://www.ndu.edu.tw/, provides information about organizational components such as its War College and armed service branch command and staff colleges and listings of university publications.

United Kingdom

Cabinet Office Intelligence, Security, and Resilience Committee

The British Cabinet Office Intelligence, Security, and Resilience Committee directs cross-governmental work to advise the prime minister and other senior ministers on intelligence, security, and resilience preparedness and response.[58] This office's Web site, http://www.cabinetoffice.gov.uk/intelligence-security-resilience.aspx, provides information on British intelligence and national security policy planning and documents such as *HMG Security Policy Framework* (2009) and their most recent *Annual Report to Parliament* (2009–2010).

Defence Academy Research and Assessment Group

The Defense Academy Research and Assessment Group (ARAG) is located in Shrivenham and seeks to harvest and utilize defense and security ideas from a variety of British government agencies to the military's defense academy, the Ministry of Defence, and other British government agencies.[59] ARAG's Web site, http://www.da.mod.uk/colleges/arag, provides information about its research activities and the text of many geopolitical reports, including *Russian Oil and Gas Projects and Investments in Central Asia* (2008), *Russia and Latin America: Competition in Washington's "Near Abroad"* (2009), *The Greek Minority in Albania: Current Tensions* (2010), and *The Strategic Challenge of Chinese Organizations* (2010).

Foreign and Commonwealth Office

The Foreign and Commonwealth Office (FCO) is responsible for promoting British international interests and supporting its businesses and citizens globally.[60] Its Web site, http://www.fco.gov.uk/, provides access to a variety of contemporary and historic resources on British foreign policy and geopolitical issues, including weapons proliferation, Afghanistan, and antipiracy initiatives.

Ministry of Defence

The Ministry of Defence (MOD) is responsible for carrying out British national security and military policies, and its activities cover areas such as air, land, and maritime operations and assorted personnel and security matters.[61] MOD's Web site, http://www.mod.uk/, features a variety of information resources on British national security and geopolitical interests, including government defense white papers such as *The Future of the United Kingdom's Nuclear Deterrent* (2006); *Strategic Environmental Appraisal of the Strategic Defence Review* (2007); and papers written by Royal College of Defence Studies students, including *Assess the Influence of Brazil with Its Neighbours in Terms of Hard and Soft Power* (2010) and *Assess the Influence of China in Sub-Saharan Africa* (2010).

Parliament House of Commons Defence Committee

This committee is responsible for examining MOD's expenditure, administration, and policy and that of its associated organizations.[62] The committee's Web site, http://www.parliament.uk/business/committees/committees-a-z/commons-select/defence-committee/, features listings of committee members, committee hearing minutes, and transcripts of committee reports and government responses from 1997 to the present such as *Scrutiny of Arms Export Controls (2010): UK Strategic Export Controls Annual Report 2008, Quarterly Reports for 2009, Licensing Policy and Review of Export Control Legislation* (2010).

Parliament House of Commons Foreign Affairs Committee

This committee is responsible for monitoring the administration, policy, and expenditures of the Foreign and Commonwealth Office and associated public organizations such as the British Council and BBC World Service.[63] The committee's Web site, http://www.parliament.uk/business/committees/committees-a-z/commons-select/foreign-affairs-committee/, features a variety of information resources on British foreign policy from 1997 to the present, including committee members, news releases, hearing transcripts, and reports and government responses, including *Global Security: Afghanistan and Pakistan* (2009) and *Global Security: UK-US Relations* (2010).

Royal Air Force Centre for Air Power Studies

This organization seeks to strengthen collaboration between academe and the Royal Air Force to stimulate air power thought and enhance the operational success of current and future British aerospace operations.[64] The center's Web site, http://www.airpowerstudies.co.uk/, provides access to articles from its scholarly journal *Air Power Review* (2000 to present) and geopolitically oriented airpower application studies, including *Air Power UAVS: The Wider Context* (2009) and *Air Power, Insurgency and the "War on Terror"* (2009).

Secret Intelligence Service (MI6)

Britain's Secret Intelligence Service (SIS), commonly known as MI6, is responsible for collecting Britain's foreign intelligence and possesses a global covert capability to defend British national security and economic prosperity.[65] Its Web site, http://www.mi6.gov.uk/, provides some historical background information, career information, and the text of the *Intelligence Services Act* (1994) and *Regulation of Investigatory Powers Act* (2000), which govern its operations.

United Nations Division for Oceans and Law of the Sea

The United Nations Division for Oceans and Law of the Sea (UNDOLS) is the United Nations organization responsible for regulating and enforcing the United Nations Convention on the Law of the Sea (UNCLOS) established in 1982 after several years of policy formulation. UNCLOS regulates national oceanic territorial sea limits, navigational rights, economic jurisdiction, the legal status of seabed resources beyond national territorial waters, marine resource conservation, and legal procedures for settling disputes between states.[66] UNDOLS's Web site, http://www.un.org/depts/los/, features a variety of information resources, including the text of UNCLOS, scientific studies of oceanic policy, documents on international oceanic law, and links to Web sites of subsidiary organizations UNDOLS has established, including the Commission on the Limits of the Continental Shelf and International Seabed Authority.

United States

Department of Commerce Bureau of Industry and Security

The Bureau of Industry and Security (BIS) was most recently reorganized in 2002, though it existed prior to that as the Bureau of Export Administration and under other names. BIS seeks to advance U.S. national security, foreign policy, and economic objectives by developing an effective export control and treaty compliance system, effectively regulating the export of sensitive U.S. goods and technology, and ensuring that the U.S. industrial base can fulfill U.S. national and homeland security requirements.[67] BIS's Web site, http://www.bis.doc.gov/, features information about the regulations it enforces, including the Export Administration Regulations, details of its enforcement activities, and publications such as its most recent *Annual Report* and *Annual Report on Foreign Policy–Based Export Controls*.

Department of Defense

The U.S. Department of Defense (DOD) was established in 1949 and is responsible for providing the military forces necessary to deter war and protect the United States.[68] The DOD Web site, http://www.defense.gov/, provides information about departmental activities and policies and links to various geopolitical information produced by organizational components and armed services branches, which will now be described.

Air University (U.S. Air Force Counterproliferation Center)

The U.S. Air Force Counterproliferation Center (CPC) is located at Air University in Maxwell Air Force Base, Alabama, which serves as this armed service's professional military educational institution. CPC's mission is assisting Air Force counterproliferation research and educational efforts, including assessing nuclear, biological, chemical, and missile proliferation threats and recommending appropriate diplomatic and military strategies for countering these threats.[69] CPC's Web site, http://cpc.au.af.mil/, provides information about center activities, course syllabi, and links to bibliographic citations on counterproliferation topics prepared by Air University Library, along with publications such as *Federal Response to a Domestic Nuclear Attack* (2009).

Army War College Strategic Studies Institute

The Army War College Strategic Studies Institute (SSI) serves as the army's geostrategic and national security research and analysis institute. It conducts strategic research and analysis to support Army War College curricula, provides direct analysis for army and DOD leadership, and interacts with the wider strategic studies community.[70] SSI's Web site, http://www.strategicstudiesinstitute.army.mil/, provides access to a tremendous variety of resources on geopolitical and geostrategic military analysis, with representative reports including *Russian Elite Image of Iran: From the Late Soviet Era to the Present* (2009), *Endgame for the West in Afghanistan? Explaining the Decline in Support for the War in Afghanistan in the United States, Great Britain, Canada, Australia, France, and Germany* (2010), *Sufism in Northern Nigeria: A Force for Counter-radicalization?* (2010), and *Transnational Insurgencies and the Escalation of Regional Conflict: Lessons for Iraq and Afghanistan* (2010).

Asia-Pacific Center for Security Studies

The Asia-Pacific Center for Security Studies (APCSS) is a DOD academic institution established in 1995. APCSS addresses regional and global security issues involving U.S. and Asian-Pacific countries military and civilian personnel while also supporting U.S. Pacific Command's objectives of developing professional and personal ties among regional national security establishments.[71] Its Web site, http://www.apcss.org/, features information about center faculty and their research interests, course descriptions, and the text of reports on Asia-Pacific geopolitics, including *Russia, America, and Security in the Asia-Pacific* (2007), *India-China Relations* (2009), and *Governance in China in 2010* (2009).

Assistant Secretary of Defense, International Security Affairs

This official (ISA) serves as the principal advisor to the secretary of defense and undersecretary of defense for policy on international security strategy and DOD policy issues relating to European nations and international government organizations such as NATO, Middle East and African governments, and defense establishments and oversees military cooperation and weapons sales programs in these regions.[72] ISA's Web site, http://policy.defense.gov/sections/policy_offices/isa/, lists the names of individuals holding this position from 1947 to the present, gives relevant DOD news releases, and provides links to selected military publications.

Central Intelligence Agency

The Central Intelligence Agency (CIA) was established by the 1947 National Security Act and is responsible for collecting, evaluating, and disseminating critical economic, political, military, scientific, and other information to safeguard national security. It also carries out other related responsibilities as directed by the president and director of national intelligence.[73] The CIA's Web site, https://www.cia.gov/, provides general descriptions of organizational activities; the text of regularly updated reference and periodical sources such as *Chiefs of State and Cabinet Members of Foreign Governments*, *World Factbook*, and *Studies in Intelligence*; and historic national intelligence estimates (NIEs) and operational histories through its Freedom of Information Act Web site and Center for the Study of Intelligence.

Defense Intelligence Agency, National Defense Intelligence College

NDIC is an educational institution within the Defense Intelligence Agency that was established in 1962 and received its current name in December 2006 as part of DOD Instruction 3305.01. NDIC is a premier intelligence education and research institute whose enrollment exceeds 700 federal civilian and military officials holding top secret security clearances. It is authorized by Congress to award bachelor of science degrees in intelligence and master of science degrees in strategic intelligence.[74] NDIC's Web site, http://www.dia.mil/college/, lists admission requirements and descriptions of organizational entities such as the Center for Strategic Intelligence Research and Center for Science and Technology Intelligence. A Web site highlight is access to National Intelligence College Press publications, including *Intelligence Professionalism in the Americas* (2004), *A Muslim Archipelago: Islam and Politics in Southeast Asia* (2007), and *Registering the Human Terrain: A Valuation of Cadastre* (2008).

Defense Security Cooperation Agency

The Defense Security Cooperation Agency (DSCA) is a DOD agency that collaborates with the State Department to provide financial and technical assistance, transfer defense material, train and provide military services to friendly countries and allies, and promote military-to-military contacts with these countries and their militaries.[75] DSCA's Web site, http://www.dsca.mil/, features an organization chart, press releases from 2001 to the present, and documents such as *Excess Defense Articles Database* (1993 to present), *Security Assistance Management Manual* (2004 to present), *Historical Facts Book* (2008), and the agency's *2009–2014 Strategic Plan* (2009).

Defense Threat Reduction Agency

The Defense Threat Reduction Agency (DTRA) is DOD's official combat support agency for countering weapons of mass destruction, and its globally dispersed personnel are experts in biological, chemical, nuclear, radiological, and high-yield explosive threats. DTRA and its personnel seek to anticipate and mitigate future threats to the United States and its allies long before they emerge.[76] Its Web site, http://www.dtra.mil/, provides information about agency programmatic activities covering the Nunn-Lugar Global Cooperation Initiative, nuclear detection and forensics, arms control verification, chemical and biological defense, and consequence management programs if a weapon of mass destruction incident occurs.

National Defense University, Institute for National Strategic Studies

Located in Washington, D.C., National Defense University (NDU) serves as the United States' premier joint professional military educational institution and contains a number of geopolitically oriented research centers within its organization. The Institute for National Strategic Studies (INSS) conducts strategic studies for the secretary of defense, Joint Chiefs of Staff, and unified combatant commands to support the national strategic components of NDU academic programs while reaching out to other U.S. government agencies and the wider national security community.[77] INSS's Web site, http://www.ndu.edu/inss/, provides information about additional institute research components such as the Center for Strategic Research and Center for Technology and National Security Policy as well as access to publications such as *"Oil for the Lamps of China": Beijing's 21st Century Search for Energy* (2003), *Reassessing the Implications of a Nuclear Armed Iran* (2005), *Global Strategic Assessment 2009: America's Security Role in a Changing World* (2009), and *Assessing Chinese Military Transparency* (2010).

Africa Center for Strategic Studies

The Africa Center for Strategic Studies (ACSS) is an NDU component organization established in 1999 and relocated to NDU in 2005. ACSS conducts security studies, research, and outreach in Africa while academically engaging African state partners and institutions to meet their security challenges, promote civil-military relations, respect democratic values, and safeguard human rights.[78] Its Web site, http://africacenter.org/, provides information about center programs and regional offices, listings of its subject specialists, and publications such as *Navies versus Coast Guards: Defining the Roles of African Maritime Security Forces* (2009) and *Misinterpreting Ethnic Conflicts in Africa* (2010).

Center for Hemispheric Defense Studies

NDU's Center for Hemispheric Defense Studies (CHDS) promotes security studies in the Americas and cooperates with military personnel and civilian policy makers in this region on mutual security challenges.[79] CHDS's Web site, http://www.ndu.edu/chds/, provides information about its academic programs and courses such as the Caribbean Defense and Security Course, the journal *Security and Defense Studies Review* (2001 to present), and publications such as *New Regionalism and Security Leadership in Brazilian Security and Defense Policy* (2009) and *CHDS and Brookings Institution Host Conference on China's Evolving Relationship with Latin America* (2010).

Center for the Study of the Chinese Military Affairs

The Center for the Study of Chinese Military Affairs is responsible for conducting multidisciplinary research and exchange on China's national strategic goals and posture and its ability to develop effective military power to support its national security objectives.[80] Its Web site, http://www.ndu.edu/inss/index.cfm?secID=83&pageID=4&type=section, provides information about its mission, experts, and publications such as *Managing Strategic Competition with China* (2009).

George C. Marshall European Center for Security Studies

The Marshall Center was established by DOD Directive 5200.34 in November 1992 and is located in Garmish, Germany; its missions include creating a more stable security environment by advancing democratic institutions and relationships in defense and security cooperation areas and building enduring partnerships among North American, European, and Eurasian nations.[81] Its Web site, http://www.marshallcenter.org/, features admission requirements, course descriptions, faculty biographies, and a wide variety of publications, including *What Roles and Missions for Europe's Military and Security Forces in the 21st Century?* (2005), *Europe's Dependence on Russian Natural Gas: Perspectives and Recommendations for a Long-Term Strategy* (2008), and *NATO Enlargement: Approaching a Standstill* (2009).

Near East South Asia Center for Strategic Studies

This NDU entity analyzes security issues in a region ranging from the western end of North Africa to Bangladesh and seeks to enhance security in this region by building mutually beneficial relationships, promoting regional security cooperation, and encouraging effective communications on these issues in an academic setting.[82] Its Web site, http://nesa-center.org/, provides information about its pedagogical programs, faculty biographies and résumés, and research expertise and the text of publications such as *Winning in Afghanistan* (2009) and *Uzbek Reactions to Holbrooke Visit and US Regional Interests* (2010).

Naval War College

The Naval War College (NWC) is located in Newport, Rhode Island, and was established in 1884. It serves as the navy's professional military educational institution and seeks to provide rigorous and relevant programs on navy roles and missions; support naval combat readiness; and strengthen maritime security cooperation for U.S. military officers, civilian U.S. government employees, nongovernmental organizations, and international military officers.[83] NWC's Web site, http://www.usnwc.edu/, provides detailed information about the college and its extensive and ongoing record of geopolitical research and analysis. Resources on its Web site include details on its academic programs, research and gaming activities, and its extensive publications corpus produced by the Naval War College Press. Examples of these publications include the scholarly journal *Naval War College Review* (spring 2001 to present) and monographic works such as *Perspectives on Strategy: Essays from the Americas* (2008), *Somalia . . . From the Sea* (2009), and *Piracy and Maritime Crime: Historical and Modern Case Studies* (2010). NWC publications are essential reading for those interested in maritime aspects of geopolitics.

China Maritime Studies Institute

The China Maritime Studies Institute (CMSI) is an NWC component established in 2006 to increase knowledge and understanding of China's maritime rise. Its research specialties include energy, global commerce, law of the sea, maritime technologies, merchant marine, naval development and diplomacy, and shipbuilding.[84] CMSI's Web site, http://www.usnwc.edu/Research—Gaming/China-Maritime-Studies-Institute.aspx, features a faculty roster; citations to books written by institute faculty for commercial publishers; the text of reports such as *Comprehensive Survey of China's Dynamic Shipbuilding Industry: Commercial Development and Strategic Implications* (2008), *Chinese Mine Warfare: A PLA "Assassinations Mace" Capability* (2009), and *Five Dragons Stirring Up the Sea: Challenge and Opportunity in China's Improving Maritime Enforcement Capabilities* (2010); and a video webcast of the April 15, 2010, lecture "The South China Sea: Symbolic Conflicts, Common Interests." CMSI-produced publications are valuable resources for understanding China's increasing geopolitical importance and how the U.S.-Chinese maritime relationship is becoming increasingly important in 21st-century international relations.

Office of Assistant Secretary of Defense for Acquisition–Industrial Policy

This office (IP) is responsible for ensuring DOD's industrial base is capable of meeting U.S. military requirements, is cost-effective, and is dependable. It also seeks to monitor defense industry readiness, competitiveness, innovation capabilities, and financial stability; leverage DOD research and development, acquisition, and logistics decisions to enhance national security; and lead efforts to promote transparency and increase public-private defense partnerships.[85] IP's Web site, http://www.acq.osd.mil/ip/, features an organizational chart, the text of defense supply security agreements with countries such as the United Kingdom, the text of presentations such as "Ground Vehicle Sector Industrial Assessment" (2009) and "Verifying Trust for Defense Use Commercial Semiconductors" (2010), and reports such as *Annual Industrial Capabilities Report to Congress* (2004 to present), *Global Shipbuilding Industrial Base Benchmarking Study–Part 1: Major Shipyards* (2006), and *Fortresses and Icebergs: The Evolution of the Trans-Atlantic Defense Market and the Implications for U.S. National Security Policy* (2009).

Office of Net Assessment

The Office of Net Assessment (ONA) was initially established in 1971 and is authorized by DOD Directive 5111.11, which defines net assessment as

> the comparative analysis of military, technological, political, economic, and other factors governing the relative military capability of nations. Its purpose is to identify problems and opportunities that deserve the attention of senior defense officials.[86]

During its nearly four decades, ONA has examined topics such as competitive environments between the United States and former Soviet Union and topics of geopolitical interest such as the revolution in military affairs, terrorism, and U.S. national security policy. Since its inception, it has been directed by Andrew Marshall, who is a highly secretive individual, as is this office due to the absence of a publicly accessible Web site. This secrecy, regrettably, makes Marshall and ONA the subject of considerable traditional print and Internet speculation and conspiracy theorizing, although some credible information is available on this individual and office.[87]

U.S. Department of Energy

The Department of Energy (DOE) was established in 1977, and its missions include fostering a secure and reliable energy system that is environmentally sound and economically sustainable, stewarding the national nuclear weapons arsenal, and advancing energy-related scientific research.[88] DOE's Web site, http://www.energy.gov/, provides information on DOE programs and research, the text of numerous scientific and energy policy–related reports, and information on departmental components producing geopolitically relevant information, which will now be profiled.

Energy Information Administration

The Energy Information Administration (EIA) is DOE's statistical and analytical agency whose responsibilities include collecting and disseminating impartial energy information to enhance policy-making quality. EIA collects and produces information on domestic U.S. and international energy resources, supplies, and strategic trends.[89] Its Web site, http://www.eia.doe.gov/, features numerous studies on international energy geopolitics, including the annual *International Energy Outlook*, *International Petroleum Monthly* (1996 to present); the Country Energy Profile and Country Analysis Brief series, documenting energy resource and policy developments in individual countries; and specialized reports such as *World Oil Transit Chokepoints* (2008).

National Nuclear Security Administration

The National Nuclear Security Administration (NNSA) is responsible for managing and securing the United States' nuclear weapons arsenal, securing U.S. nuclear nonproliferation and naval nuclear reactor programs, responding to nuclear emergencies in the United States and overseas, and providing safe and secure transportation for nuclear weapons and components.[90] NNSA's Web site, http://www.nnsa.doe.gov/, features numerous information resources about its multifaceted missions. These include press releases, congressional testimony, a monthly newsletter (2003 to present), and factsheets such as *Global Threat Reduction Initiative (GTRI): Reducing Nuclear Threats* (2009), *NNSA: Working to Prevent Nuclear Terrorism* (2009), and *NNSA's Second Line of Defense Program* (2010).

Office of Policy and International Affairs

DOE's Office of Policy and International Affairs (PI) advises the secretary of energy on domestic and international energy policy analysis, development, and implementation. It represents the United States in international energy policy and strategy discussions and promoting clean energy technology exports and departmental climate change initiatives.[91] Its Web site, http://www.pi.energy.gov/, features information on office program initiatives such as the Energy and Climate Partnership of the Americas, congressional testimony and speeches by office personnel, and reports such as *National Security Review of International Energy Requirements* (2006) and *World Biofuels Production Potential* (2008).

U.S. Department of the Interior, U.S. Geological Survey Mineral Resources Program

The U.S. Geological Survey (USGS) Mineral Resources Program provides scientific information to produce objective resource assessments and research results on mineral potential, production, consumption, and environmental effects. These analyses cover domestic U.S. and international mineral resources.[92] The program Web site, http://minerals.usgs.gov/, features detailed information about mineral resources, including mineral industry trends, commodity summaries, and industry surveys. The flagship information resource is the annual *Minerals Yearbook,* which is available online (1994 to present). This resource is broken up into three volumes: *Metals and Minerals*, *Area Reports: Domestic*, and *Area Reports: International*. The international volume provides detailed analysis and statistics on mineral resource production, trade, legal, and governmental policy-making developments affecting these resources and industries within individual countries as well as projections of future trends.

Office of the Director of National Intelligence

The Office of the Director of National Intelligence (ODNI) was established by the 2004 Terrorism Prevention Act. Its responsibilities include serving as the president's principal intelligence advisor and coordinating intelligence community activities; ensuring intelligence community information sharing; and determining the National Intelligence Program budget and directing spending of those funds.[93] ODNI's Web site, http://www.dni.gov/, provides information about its organizational components, including the National Counterproliferation Center and National Counterterrorism Center, its open source program initiatives, video webcasts, and documents such as *The National Intelligence Strategy of the United States of America* (2009), annual unclassified reports for Congress on weapons of mass destruction and advanced conventional munitions technology acquisition (2005 to present), the *Annual Report to Congress on Foreign Economic Collection and Industrial Espionage* (1995 to present), and *Terrorist Identities Datamart Environment* (2010).

National Intelligence Council

The National Intelligence Council (NIC) is an ODNI component that serves as the U.S. intelligence community's center for medium- and long-term strategic thinking. Its responsibilities include supporting the director of national intelligence in his or her leadership role; reaching out to nongovernment experts in academe and the private sector to expand intelligence community perspectives; and leading intelligence community efforts to produce NIEs to assist policy makers' needs.[94] NIC's Web site, http://www.dni.gov/nic/, is a rich resource of historical and contemporary intelligence assessments on geopolitical matters facing the United States. These include *Nonstate Actors: Impact on International Relations and Implications for the United States* (2007), *Strategic Implications of Global Health* (2008), *Global Trends 2025: A Transformed World* (2008), and *The Impact of Climate Change to 2030: Commissioned Research and Conference Reports* (2009–2010), with representative samples of these reports including *Southeast Asia: The Impact of Climate Change to 2030: Geopolitical Implications* and *North Africa: The Impact of Climate Change to 2030*.

NIC's Web site also provides access to numerous declassified NIEs and document collections produced by the intelligence community for U.S. policy makers. Representative samples include *Baptism by Fire: CIA Analysis of the Korean War* (1950–1954), *Strategic Warning and the Role of Intelligence: Lessons Learned from the 1968 Soviet Invasion of Czechoslovakia*, and *Selected China NIEs, 1948–1976*.

U.S.-China Economic and Security Review Commission

The U.S.-China Economic and Security Review Commission (USCC) was established in 2000 by the 2001 National Defense Spending Authorization Act. USCC consists of 12 commissioners, serving two-year terms, who are selected by the congressional leadership and supported by a professional staff with expertise in trade, economics, weapons proliferation, and Sino-U.S. relations. Its objectives include monitoring, investigating, and submitting an annual report to Congress on the national security implications of the bilateral trade and economic relationship between these countries; proliferation practices; economic transfers; energy; U.S. capital markets; and regional economic and security impacts.[95] The commission's Web site, http://www.

uscc.gov/, features commissioner biographies and congressional testimony. Accessible publications include the text of its annual reports (2002 to present); hearing transcripts (2001 to present), including *U.S. Debt to China: Implications and Repercussions* (2010) and *Taiwan-China: Recent Economic, Political, and Military Developments across the Strait, and Implications for the United States* (2010); and USCC commissioned reports, including *China's Overseas Investments in Oil and Gas Production* (2006), *Capability of the People's Republic of China to Conduct Cyber Warfare and Computer Network Exploitation* (2009), and *China's Defense Industry on the Path of Reform* (2009).

U.S. Department of State

The Department of State was established in 1789 and is responsible for advising the president in formulating and executing U.S. foreign policy and in promoting long-range national security and prosperity.[96] Its Web site, http://www.state.gov/, provides access to numerous resources about historical and current U.S. foreign diplomatic policy and foreign economic policy from the following organizational components.

Directorate of Defense Trade Controls

The Directorate of Defense Trade Controls (DDTC) is responsible for controlling the export and temporary import of defense articles and services covered by the U.S. Munitions List documented in Title 22, Part 121 of the Code of Federal Regulations.[97] DDTC's Web site, http://www.pmddtc.state.gov/, provides access to its export licensing system D-Trade, information on defense export licensing requirements, the text of laws and regulations it enforces such as the Arms Export Control Act and International Traffic in Arms Regulations, license processing statistics, and individual country policy and embargo announcements.

Examples of accessible reports include congressional notification letters about selected individual arms sales (2001 to present), *End-Use Monitoring of Defense Articles and Defense Services: Commercial Exports* (2001 to present), and *Section 655 Annual Military Assistance Reports* (2001 to present), which list the aggregate dollar value and quantity of defense articles and services authorized as direct sales to individual foreign countries.

Office of the Historian

The State Department's Office of the Historian (OH) is responsible for preparing and publishing *Foreign Relations of the United States* (FRUS), which is the official U.S. historical foreign policy documentary record. OH also researches and publishes other historical studies on U.S. foreign policy for State Department policy makers, officials in other government agencies, and the general public.[98] Their Web site, http://www.history.state.gov/, features the text of FRUS volumes from the Kennedy to the Nixon-Ford administrations, with representative examples including *Foreign Relations of the United States, 1969–1976: Volume XXXIX, European Security* (2008) and *Foreign Relations of the United States, 1969–1976: Volume XIX, Korea Part 1, 1969–1972* (2010). This site also features historical information about U.S. diplomatic relations with individual countries and reference works such as *Chiefs of Missions*, which lists U.S. ambassadors to various countries.

Undersecretary for Arms Control and International Security

The Undersecretary for Arms Control & International Security serves as the President and Secretary of State's senior advisor on arms control, nonproliferation, and disarmament. This official also manages U.S. global security policy in these areas along with regional security and defense relations and security assistance.[99] Its Web site, http://www.state.gov/t/, includes the text of speeches given by this official, the video webcast of an April 30, 2010 briefing on the Nonproliferation Treaty Review Conference, and the text of a proposed 2010 strategic nuclear arms reduction treaty between the U.S. and Russian Federation.

Undersecretary for Democracy and Global Affairs

The undersecretary for democracy and global affairs is responsible for coordinating U.S. foreign relations on global issues such as democracy, labor, human rights, oceans, environment, health and science, refugees, migration, and trafficking in persons.[100] Its Web site, http://www.state.gov/d/, contains information about office organizational components such as the Office of Science and Technology Advisor and publications including *Seeds of a Perfect Storm: Genetically Modified Crops and the Global Food Security Crisis* (2008); *The United States of America National Report: Transport, Chemicals, Waste Management, Mining, and Sustainable Consumption and Production* (2010); *U.S. Climate Action Report* (2010); and the annual *Trafficking in Persons* (2001 to present).

Undersecretary for Economics, Energy, and Agricultural Affairs

The undersecretary for economics, energy, and agricultural affairs serves as the State Department's senior economic official advising the secretary of state on international economic policy, trade, agriculture, aviation, and bilateral economic relations with other countries.[101] Its Web site, http://www.state.gov/e/, provides access to multiple resources on U.S. foreign economic policy, including information on organizational components such as the Office of Terrorism Finance and Economic Sanctions policy; publications, including *U.S. Annual Report to the Kimberley Process* (2009) on conflict diamonds; and links to international economic and trade resources produced by the Foreign Agricultural Service (http://www.fas.usda.gov/) and the International Trade Administration (http://www.ita.doc.gov/).

Undersecretary for Political Affairs

The undersecretary for political affairs serves as the department's third-ranking official and senior career diplomat. This official serves as the day-to-day manager of overall regional and bilateral foreign policy issues, including State Department bureaus such as Africa, East Asia, and the Pacific, International Organizations, International Narcotics, and Law Enforcement.[102] Its Web site, http://www.state.gov/p/, features speeches by this official (2009 to present) and regional and functional bureau Web sites such as the Bureau of Western Hemisphere Affairs. Examples of publications accessible through this office Web site include the annuals *International Narcotics Control Strategy Report* (1996 to present), *Voting Practices in the United Nations* (2000 to present), *Foreign Operations Appropriated Assistance: Kyrgyz Republic* (2009), and *Weekly Iraq Status Reports* (2009 to present).

U.S. Department of the Treasury

The U.S. Department of the Treasury was established in 1789 and is responsible for formulating domestic and international economic and tax policy for the United States, including managing U.S. public debt.[103] The department's Web site, http://www.treas.gov/, has a variety of information resources on its domestic and international economics, which can affect global geopolitics, including the ongoing global recession, as well as links to its multifaceted offices and bureaus, which will now be described.

Office of International Affairs

The Office of International Affairs (OIA) strives to protect and support U.S. economic prosperity by enhancing the external environment for U.S. growth, preventing and reducing global financial instability, and managing important global challenges.[104] OIA's Web site, http://www.treas.gov/offices/international-affairs/, includes press releases, information about its regional and functional offices covering areas such as Africa, the Committee on Foreign Investment in the United States (CFIUS), Development Policy and Debt, and the U.S.-China Strategic and Economic Dialogue. Accessible information resources include *Semiannual Report on International Economic and Exchange Rate Policies* (2005 to present), *CFIUS Annual Report* (2008 to present), and *Implementation of Certain Legislative Provisions Relating to the International Monetary Fund* (2004 to present).

Office of Terrorism and Financial Intelligence

The Office of Terrorism and Financial Intelligence (OTFI) organizes the Treasury Department's intelligence and enforcement functions to protect the financial system against illegal use and fighting rogue nations, terrorist facilitators, weapons of mass destruction proliferators, money launderers, drug kingpins, and other national security threats.[105] OTFI's Web site, http://www.treas.gov/offices/enforcement/, contains information about the activities of its organizational components, including the Office of Terrorist Financing and Financial Crimes; the Office of Intelligence and Analysis; the Office of Foreign Assets Control, which enforces U.S. economic sanctions against targeted countries, organizations, and individuals;[106] and the Financial Crimes Enforcement Network.

Information resources provided by OTFI include the current *Specially Designated Nationals and Blocked Persons List*, featuring individuals and organizations against whom the United States has imposed economic sanctions; *North Korea: What You Need to Know about Sanctions* (2008); and *Terrorism: What You Need to Know about U.S. Sanctions* (2010).

U.S. Trade Representative

The Office of the U.S. Trade Representative (USTR) was created in 1963 and became part of the Executive Office of the President in 1974. USTR is responsible for setting and administering overall U.S. international trade policy, and its responsibilities include negotiating bilateral and multilateral trade agreements with other countries and international government organizations, overcoming barriers to these agreements, and interacting with the WTO in trade disputes.[107]

USTR's Web site provides multiple information resources concerning its activities on bilateral and multilateral U.S. international trade agreements. It also provides analytical and statistical information about U.S. trade relations with various regions, such as the Americas, and with individual countries within these regions, including the U.S. trade balance; topical details about U.S. trade in areas such as agricultural, environment, intellectual property, and textiles and apparel; and reports such as the annual *National Trade Estimate Report on Foreign Trade Barriers* (2001 to present), *Trade Policy Agenda and Annual Report of the President of the United States on the Trade Agreements Program* (2001 to present), and *2008 Report on China's WTO Compliance* (2008).

House Armed Services Committee

Numerous congressional committees have constitutional oversight over federal agencies conducting geopolitical activities involving the military services, U.S. foreign policy, intelligence operations, and U.S. international trade and also mandate preparation of reports by the agencies and offices they oversee.[108] The House Armed Services Committee (HASC) is responsible for considering the defense budget and DOE national security programs and various operational aspects of U.S. military and international security policy, which it has done since separate War and Navy Department oversight committees were consolidated in 1947.[109]

HASC's Web site, http://armedservices.house.gov/, features listings of committee and subcommittee members, the text of its biennial congressional session oversight plans, news releases (September 2006 to present), hearing schedule information, witness statements and partial transcripts, audio webcasts, and links to minority party viewpoints. Recent examples of hearings accessible here include *Developments in Afghanistan* (2010), *Security and Stability in Pakistan: Developments in U.S. Policy and Funding* (2010), and *Private Sector Perspectives on Department of Defense Information Technology and Cybersecurity Activities* (2010).

House Foreign Affairs Committee

The House Foreign Affairs Committee dates back to 1775, when it was established by the Continental Congress to correspond with the revolution's allies in other parts of the world.[110] Its jurisdictional activities include oversight and funding of State Department operations, U.S. foreign policy, U.S. foreign assistance programs, the deployment and use of U.S. military forces, relations with international government organizations, and other related topics.[111] Its Web site, http://foreignaffairs.house.gov/, lists committee rules, members, and the names of its geographically and functionally oriented subcommittees such as those on Africa and Global Health, Terrorism, Nonproliferation, and Trade, and Middle East and south Asia. A variety of hearings, transcripts, and video webcasts are available, including *U.S.-Greece Relations and Regional Issues* (2007), *A Strategic and Economic Review of Aerospace Exports* (2009), *Horn of Africa: Current Conditions and U.S. Policy* (2010), and *Thailand: The Path toward Reconciliation* (2010).

House Select Intelligence Committee

The House Select Intelligence Committee was established in 1977 to oversee U.S. government intelligence and intelligence-related activities and submit appropriate legislative proposals and reports to this chamber on intelligence and intelligence-related programs.[112] The committee's Web site, http://intelligence.house.gov/, lists the names of committee members, the names of its subcommittees on Terrorism, Human Intelligence (HUMINT), Analysis, and Counterintelligence; Technical and Tactical Intelligence; Intelligence Community Management; and Oversight and Investigations.

Although many materials reviewed by this committee are not published, a number of resources are, including annual Intelligence Authorization Act reports (1998 to present) and selected public hearings, including the *Annual Worldwide Threat Assessment* (2008 and 2010), *Cyber Security* (2008), and *Assessing the Fight against al Qaida* (2008).

House Ways and Means Committee

The House Ways and Means Committee has existed since 1789 and is responsible for administering, overseeing, and funding taxes; raising money; and administering various social assistance programs such as Social Security. Where geopolitics is concerned, its jurisdictional activities also cover international trade, including U.S. Trade Representative office oversight, existing and proposed free trade agreements with other countries and international government organizations, dispute settlement with the WTO, and oversight of U.S. enforcement of national rights under the WTO.[113] The committee's Web site, http://waysandmeans.house.gov/, serves as a conduit to further information about this committee's multifaceted responsibilities, including those dealing with international trade. Examples of accessible trade-related hearings conducted by this committee include *Hearing on Trade Aspects of Climate Change Legislation* (2009), *Hearing on U.S.-Cuba Policy* (2010), and *Hearing on Customs Trade Facilitation and Enforcement in a Secure Environment* (2010).

Senate Armed Services Committee

The Senate Armed Services Committee is responsible for conducting oversight of DOD- and DOE-related defense activities and confirmation of major defense policy-making officials and military officers.[114] The committee's Web site, http://armed-services.senate.gov/, includes the names of committee members and lists of subcommittees such as those covering emerging threats and capabilities and sea power, press releases (1999 to present), and reports on annual defense spending legislation. The Web site also features live video and some archived webcasts of current committee hearings and statements and transcripts of these hearings from 1999 to present, with representative samples including *Hearing to Continue to Receive Testimony on Afghanistan* (2009), *Hearing to Receive a Briefing on Operation Moshtarak in Helmand Province, Afghanistan* (2010), *Hearing to Receive Testimony on U.S. Threats to Counter Violent Extremism* (2010), and *Hearing to Receive Testimony on the New START and Implications for National Security* (2010).

Senate Finance Committee

The Senate Finance Committee has oversight responsibilities for taxes; U.S. bonded debt; customs; ports of entry and delivery; reciprocal trade agreements; tariff and import quotas; and various domestic social assistance programs, including Medicare.[115] Its Web site, http://finance.senate.gov/, lists the names of committee members and information about subcommittee activities, including the Subcommittee on International Trade, Customs, and Global Competitiveness. Access to committee reports and hearings on international trade (including some video webcasts) is also provided. Representative samples include *Trade Promotion Authority Annotated* (2007), *Iran Counter-proliferation Act of 2007* (2008), *Doubling U.S. Exports: Are U.S. Sea Ports Ready for the Challenge?* (2010), and *The U.S.-China Trade Relationship Relationships: Finding a New Path Forward* (2010).

Senate Foreign Relations Committee

The Senate Foreign Relations Committee was established in 1816 and is responsible for developing and influencing U.S. foreign policy. It does this by overseeing foreign policy programs, ratifying or denying treaties with foreign countries, confirming important policy-making officials such as secretaries of state or U.S. ambassadors to foreign countries, and grappling with the president on determining who arbitrates U.S. foreign policy.[116] Its Web site, http://foreign.senate.gov/, features information about treaties the committee is reviewing, legislative reports, press releases, and testimony from hearings from 2003 to present. Examples of these hearings include "Finding Common Ground with a Rising China" (2010), "The Historical and Modern Context for U.S.-Russian Arms Control" (2010), "Assessing the Strength of Hezbollah" (2010), and "Iran Policy in the Aftermath of UN Sanctions" (2010).

Senate Select Intelligence Committee

The Senate Select Intelligence Committee was established in 1976 to oversee and study U.S. government intelligence activities and programs, craft legislation to improve these programs, and ensure that intelligence community entities provide timely notification to Congress and the executive branch to make sound decisions on U.S. national security.[117] Its Web site, http://intelligence.senate.gov/, provides information on committee rules and its policies on the public release of official nomination documents, roster of members, the text of legislation it has passed such as the most recent annual Intelligence Authorization Act, and the text of relevant statutes such as the Intelligence Reform and Terrorism Prevention Act of 2004 and Foreign Intelligence Surveillance Act of 1978 Amendments Act of 2008. It also provides access to some hearing transcripts and related publications, including *Nomination of Dennis C. Blair to Be Director of National Intelligence* (2009), *Unclassified Executive Summary of the Committee Report on the Attempted Terrorist Attack on Northwest Airlines Flight 253* (2010), and *Current and Projected Threats to the United States* (2010).

World Trade Organization

The WTO is a global organization of 153 countries based in Geneva. It was established in 1995 from its predecessor, the General Agreement on Tariffs and Trade. WTO seeks to reduce or eliminate obstacles to international trade such as import tariffs; agree on rules governing international trade conduct; administer various trade rules, including intellectual property rights; monitor and review members' trade policies and ensure bilateral and regional trade agreements are transparent; settle member country trade agreement disputes; help countries desirous of joining WTO; conduct economic research and collect and disseminate international trade information; and educate the public about institutional mission activities.[118]

WTO's Web site, http://www.wto.org/, lists member countries, contains press releases from 1998 to present, and describes its activities in areas such as dispute settlements, civil aircraft, competition policy, development, electronic commerce, the environment, government procurement, and investment. Examples of the multiplicity of documents and reports on the Web site include *Committee on Anti-dumping Practices: Semi-annual Report under Article 16.4 of the Agreement South Africa* (2009), *Committee on Import Licensing: Brazil's Non-automatic Import Licensing Procedures: Replies by Brazil to China* (2010), and *Report on G20 Trade and Investment Measures (September 2009 to February 2010)* (2010).

Notes

1. See African Union, "African Union in a Nutshell," http://www.africa-union.org/root/au/AboutAu/au_in_a_nutshell_en.htm; U.S. Congress, Senate Committee on Foreign Relations, Subcommittee on African Affairs, *African Organizations and Institutions: Cross-Continental Progress* (Washington, DC: Government Printing Office, 2007); and Timothy Murithi, *The African Union: Pan-Africanism, Peacebuilding, and Development* (Burlington, VT: Ashgate, 2005).

2. Republic of Argentina, Ministry of Defense, National Defense School, "Background," http://www.mindef.gov.ar/edna/antecedents.htm.

3. *A History of the Australian Defence College* (Canberra: Australian Defence College, 2008): 1–3, http://www.defence.gov.au/adc/docs/ADC/History%20of%20the%20ADC.pdf.

4. See Australian Security Intelligence Organisation, "About ASIO Overview," http://www.asio.gov.au/About-ASIO/Overview.html; and Frank Cain, *Terrorism and Intelligence in Australia: A History of ASIO and National Surveillance* (North Melbourne: Australian Scholarly Publishing, 2008).

5. See Australian Security Intelligence Service, "About Us–History," http://www.asis.gov.au/history.html; Australian government, *Report of the Inquiry into Australian Intelligence Agencies (Flood Report)* (Canberra: Department of the Prime Minister and Cabinet, 2004): 146–52, http://www.dpmc.gov.au/publications/intelligence_inquiry/.

6. Eric Andrews, *The Department of Defence* (Melbourne: Oxford University Press, 2001).

7. See Royal Australian Air Force, Air Power Development Centre, "About the Air Power Development Centre," http://airpower.airforce.gov.au/Contents/About-APDC/2/About-APDC.aspx; and Alan Stephens, *The Royal Australian Air Force* (South Melbourne: Oxford University Press, 2001).

8. See Royal Australian Navy, Sea Power Centre, "Sea Power Centre Australia Mission," http://www.navy.gov.au/Sea_Power_Centre_Australia_Mission; David Stephens, ed., *The Royal Australian Navy* (South Melbourne: Oxford University, 2001); and David Stevens and John Reeve, eds., *Southern Trident: Strategy, History, and the Rise of Australian Naval Power* (Crows Nest, NSW: Allen and Unwin, 2001).

9. See Australia, Department of Foreign Affairs and Trade, "About Us," http://www.dfat.gov.au/dept/; Rod Lyon, *Australia's Strategic Fundamentals* (Barton, ACT: Australian Strategic Policy Institute, 2007); and Coral Bell, *Living with Giants: Australian Policy Making in a Changing International Landscape* (Barton, ACT: Australian Strategic Policy Institute, 2005).

10. See Australia, Office of National Assessments, "About Us," http://www.ona.gov.au/aboutus.htm; and Australia Office of National Assessments, *The Australian Intelligence Community: Agencies, Functions, Accountability and Oversight* (Canberra: Commonwealth of Australia, 2005): 8–9, http://pandora.nla.gov.au/tep/67797.

11. Eliezer Rizzo de Oliveira, *Democracy and National Defense: The Creation of the Ministry of Defense in the Presidency of Fernando Henrique de Cardoso* (Barueri, Brazil: Manole, 2005).

12. See Brazil, Ministério das Relações Exteriores, "The Role of the Foreign Ministry," http://www.mre.gov.br/index.php?option=com_content&task=view&id=6&Itemid=342; and Ronald M. Schneider, *Brazil: Foreign Policy of a Future World Power* (Boulder, CO: Westview Press, 1976).

13. Riordan Rhett, *Brazil: Politics in a Patrimonial Society*, 5th ed. (Westport, CT: Praeger, 1999): 110–11.

14. Canadian Forces College, "Vision and Mission of the Canadian Forces College," http://www.cfc.forces.gc.ca/263-eng.html.

15. See Canada, Department of National Defence, "About DND: What Is the Relationship between DND and the Canadian Forces?," http://www.forces.gc.ca/site/about-notresujet/index-eng.asp; Vernon J. Kronenberg, *All Together Now: The Organization of the Department of National Defence in Canada, 1964–1972* (Toronto, ON: Canadian Institute of International Affairs, 1973); and Andrew Richter, *The Evolution and Development of Strategic Thinking at the Canadian Department of National Defence, 1950–1963*, PhD diss., York University, 1998.

16. See Foreign Affairs and International Trade Canada, "'*Punching above Our Weight': A History of the Department of Foreign Affairs and International Trade*," http://www.international.gc.ca/history-histoire/department-ministere/index.aspx?lang=eng; John Hilliker, *Canada's Department of External Affairs*, vol. I, *The Early Years, 1909–1946* (Kingston, QC: McGill-Queen's University Press, 1990); and John Hilliker and Donald Barry, *Canada's Department of External Affairs*, vol. II, *Coming of Age, 1946–1968* (Kingston, QC: McGill-Queen's University Press, 1995).

17. See Natural Resources Canada, "NRCan: First and Fascinating Facts from Its Illustrious Past," http://www.nrcan-rncan.gc.ca/com/deptmini/histhist/facfai-eng.php; and G. Bruce Doern and Jeffrey S. Kinder, *Strategic Science in the Public Interest: Canada's Government Laboratories and Science-Based Agencies* (Toronto, ON: University of Toronto Press, 2007).

18. See China Central Military Commission, "The Central Military Commission," http://www.gov.cn/english/links/cmc.htm; China Central Military Commission, "Organizations of the Central Military Commission," http://english.gov.cn/20095–09/02/content_28477.htm; John Hill, "China Reshuffles Central Military Commission," *Jane's Intelligence Review*, 16 (12)(December 2004): 42–45; and Li Nan and Christopher Weuve, "China's Aircraft Carrier Ambitions," *Naval War College Review*, 63 (1) (Winter 2010): 12–31.

19. See China, Ministry of Commerce, "Main Mandate of the Ministry of Commerce," http://english.mofcom.gov.cn/mission.shtml; James Kynge, *China Shakes the World: A Titan's Rise and Troubled Future—and the Challenge for America* (Boston: Houghton Mifflin, 2006); and Stefan A. Halper, *The Beijing Consensus: How China's Authoritarian Model Will Dominate the Twenty-first Century* (New York: Basic Books, 2010).

20. *The "People" in the PLA: Recruitment, Training, and Education in China's Military*, ed. Roy Kamphausen, Andrew Scobell, and Travis Tanner (Carlisle, PA: U.S. Army War College, Strategic Studies Institute, 2008).

21. See Thomas J. Bickford, "Trends in Education and Training, 1924–2007: From Whampoa to Nanjing Polytechnic," in Kamphausen et al., *The "People" in the PLA*, 33; and Paul H. B. Godwin, "The Cradle of Generals: Strategists, Commanders, and the PLA-National Defense University," in Kamphausen et al., *The "People" in the PLA*, 327.

22. Loro Horta, "China's National Defense University: A Case Study," *Australian Defence Force Journal*, 181 (2010): 52–53, 57.

23. Ibid., 56, 59.

24. See European Commission, "Why: Key Challenges and EU Obligations," http://ec.europa.eu/external_relations/peace_security/why_en.htm; Edward G. Gunning, *The Common European Security and Defense Policy (ESDP)* (Colorado Springs, CO: USAF Institute for National Security Studies, 2001); and Daniel S. Hamilton, ed., *The New Frontiers of Europe: The Enlargement of the European Union: Implications and Consequences* (Washington, DC: Center for Transatlantic Relations, Paul H. Nitze School of Advanced International Studies, Johns Hopkins University, 2005).

25. See European Union, "Activities of the European Union: Energy," http://europa.eu/pol/ener/index_en.htm; Nicole Gnesotto and Giovanni Grevi, *The New Global Puzzle: What World for the EU in 2025?* (Paris: European Union Institute for Security Studies, 2006): 53–74; and Paul Belkin, *The European Union's Security Challenges* (Washington, DC: Library of Congress, Congressional Research Service, 2007), http://handle.dtic.mil/100.2/ADA471184.

26. European Union Institute of Security Studies, "About Us," http://www.iss.europa.eu/about-us/.

27. See France, College of Joint Defense, "The Center of Excellence for Military Education Higher French," http://www.college.interarmees.defense.gouv.fr/spip.

php?rubrique4; France, College of Joint Defense, "Four Areas of Education," http://www.college.interarmees.defense.gouv.fr/spip.php?article856; and Henri Boré, "Complex Operations in Africa: Operational Culture Training in the French Military," *Military Review*, 89 (2)(March/April 2009): 65–71.

28. See Germany, Foreign Ministry, "The History of the Foreign Ministry," http://www.auswaertiges-amt.de/diplo/de/AAmt/Geschichte/Uebersicht.html; and David Wetzel and Theodore S. Hamerow, eds. *Imperial Politics and German History: The Past Informs the Present* (Westport, CT: Praeger, 1997).

29. India, Ministry of Defence, "About the Ministry," http://mod.nic.in/aboutus/welcome.html; Stephen F. Burgess, *India's Emerging Security Strategy, Missile Defense, and Arms Control* (Colorado Springs, CO: U.S. Air Force Academy Institute for National Security Studies, 2004); and Stephen Blank, *Natural Allies? Regional Security in Asia and Prospects for Indo-American Strategic Cooperation* (Carlisle, PA: U.S. Army War College, Strategic Studies Institute, 2005).

30. See India, National Defence College, "History: Early Days," http://ndc.viburnix.com/contents/index/12; and Rajiv Shastri, *A Historical Perspective: National Defence College and Raksha Bavan* (New Delhi: National Defence College, 1995), http://ndc.viburnix.com/uploads/static_pdf/dhistory.pdf.

31. See International Atomic Energy Agency, "Our Work: Pillars of Nuclear Cooperation," http://www.iaea.org/OurWork/; Henry Sokolsi, ed. *Falling Behind: International Scrutiny of the Peaceful Atom* (Carlisle, PA: Strategic Studies Institute, U.S. Army War College, 2008); and David Fischer, *History of the International Atomic Energy Agency: The First Forty Years* (Vienna, Austria: IAEA, 1997).

32. See International Energy Agency, "About the IEA," http://www.iea.org/about/docs/iea2008.pdf; and Richard Scott, *History of the International Energy Agency, 1974–1994: IEA, the First 20 Years*, vol. I, *Origins and Structure* (Paris: OECD/IEA, 1994).

33. See International Maritime Organization, "Frequently Asked Questions," http://www.imo.org/About/mainframe.asp?topic_id=774#1; U.S. Congress, House Committee on Transportation and Infrastructure, Subcommittee on Coast Guard and Marine Transportation, *Oversight of the U.S. Role in the International Maritime Organization* (Washington, DC: Government Printing Office, 1998); and Kenneth R. Simmonds, *The International Maritime Organization* (London: Simmonds and Hill, 1994).

34. See Martin Van Creveld, *The Sword and the Olive: A Critical History of the Israeli Defense Force* (New York: Public Affairs, 1998); Yoram Peri, *The Israeli Military and Israel's Palestinian Policy: From Oslo to the al Aqsa Intifada* (Washington, DC: U.S. Institute of Peace, 2002); and David E. Johnson, *Military Capabilities for Hybrid War: Insights from the Israel Defense Forces in Lebanon and Gaza* (Santa Monica, CA: RAND, 2010).

35. See Israel Levite, *Offense and Defense in Israeli Military Doctrine* (Boulder, CO: Westview Press, 1990); Uri Bar-Joseph, ed., *Israel's National Security toward the 21st Century* (London: Frank Cass, 2001); and Martin Van Creveld, *Defending Israel: A Controversial Plan toward Peace* (New York: Thomas Dunne Books/St. Martin's Press, 2004).

36. See Israel, Ministry of Foreign Affairs, "Functions and Structure," http://www.mfa.gov.il/MFA/MFAArchive/2000_2009/2003/10/Ministry+of+Foreign+Affairs.

htm; and Jonathan Adams, *The Rise of Israel: A History of a Revolutionary State* (New York: Routledge, 2008).

37. See Japan, Maritime Self Defense Force, "Mission of JMSDF," http://www.mod.go.jp/msdf/formal/english/; James E. Auer, *The Postwar Rearmament of Japanese Maritime Forces, 1945–1971* (New York: Praeger, 1973); and Naolo Sajima and Kyoichi Tachikawa, *Japanese Sea Power: A Maritime Nation's Struggle for Identity* (Canberra: Australia Department of Defense, Sea Power Centre, 2009).

38. See Ministry of Foreign Affairs of Japan, "About the Ministry," http://www.mofa.go.jp/about/hq/org.html; Reinhard Drifte, *Japan's Foreign Policy for the 21st Century: From Economic Superpower to What Power?* 2nd ed. (New York: St. Martin's Press, 1998); and Kazuhiko Tōgō, *Japan's Foreign Policy, 1945–2009: The Quest for a Proactive Policy*, 3rd ed. (Boston: Brill, 2010).

39. Bert Chapman, *Military Doctrine: A Reference Handbook* (Santa Barbara, CA: Praeger Security International, 2009): 124.

40. NATO Defense College, "NATO Defense College Mission," http://www.ndc.nato.int/about/statement.php?code=23.

41. See National Defence University, "About NDU," http://www.ndu.edu.pk/about_msnvsn.htm; and Hassan Abbas, ed. *Pakistan's Troubled Frontier* (Washington, DC: Jamestown Foundation, 2009).

42. Romania, Centre for Defense and Security Strategic Studies, "History," http://cssas.unap.ro/.

43. See Russia, Foreign Intelligence Service, "The Names of Intelligence in Different Periods of Activity," http://www.svr.gov.ru/history/history.htm; Russia, Foreign Intelligence Service, "Aims Service," http://www.svr.gov.ru/svr_today/celi.htm; Vladimir Plugin, *Russian Intelligence Services* (New York: Algora, 2000); and Richard F. Staar and Corliss A. Tacosa, "Russia's Security Services," *Mediterranean Quarterly*, 15 (1) (Winter 2004): 39–57.

44. See "Gazprom: 15 Years of Joint Stock Company 'Gazprom,'" http://www.gazpromquestions.ru/index.php?id=41; and Jonathan P. Stern, *The Future of Russian Gas and Gazprom* (New York: Oxford University Press, 2005).

45. See Russian Federation, Ministry of Defense, http://www.mil.ru/847/index.shtml; Stephen Rosefiede, *Russia in the 21st Century: The Prodigal Superpower* (New York: Cambridge University Press, 2005); U.S. Congress, House Committee on Foreign Affairs, *Russia: Rebuilding the Iron Curtain* (Washington, DC: Government Printing Office, 2007); Svante E. Cornell and S. Frederick Starr, eds. *The Guns of August 2008: Russia's War in Georgia* (Armonk, NY: M.E. Sharpe, 2009); and Elana Wilson Rowe, ed. *Russia and the North* (Ottawa, ON: University of Ottawa Press, 2009).

46. See Janusz Bugajski, *Cold Peace: Russia's New Imperialism* (Westport, CT: Praeger and Center for Strategic and International Studies, 2004); Bugajski, *Expanding Eurasia: Russia's European Ambitions* (Washington, DC: CSIS Press, 2008); Jeffrey Mankoff, *Russian Foreign Policy: The Return of Great Power Politics* (Lanham, MD: Rowland and Littlefield, 2009); and Marshall I. Goldman, *Petrostate: Putin, Power, and the New Russia* (New York: Oxford University Press, 2010).

47. Security Council Russian Federation, "History, Legal Status, Structure, and Main Directions," http://www.scrf.gov.ru/documents/15.html.

48. See Singapore, Ministry of Defence, "Mission," http://www.mindef.gov.sg/mindef/about_us/mission.shtml; and Tim Huxley, *Defending the Lion City: The Armed Forces of Singapore* (St. Leonard's, NSW: Allen and Unwin, 2000).

49. Deane-Peter Baker, *New Partnerships for a New Era: Enhancing the South African Army's Stabilization Role in Africa* (Carlisle, PA: U.S. Army War College, Strategic Studies Institute, 2009), http://purl.access.gpo.gov/Government Printing Office/LPS114370.

50. See South Africa, Department of International Relations and Cooperation, "About the Department," http://www.dfa.gov.za/department/; F. H. Toase and E. J. Yorke, *The New South Africa: Prospects for Domestic and International Security* (New York: St. Martin's Press, 1998); and James J. Hentz, *South Africa and the Logic of Regional Cooperation* (Bloomington: Indiana University Press, 2005).

51. Military Academy South Africa, *A Brief History of the South African Military Academy, 1950–2007*, http://sun.ac.za/milscience/history.htm.

52. See South African Secret Service, "Historical Perspective of SASS," http://www.sass.gov.za/; and Kevin O'Brien, *The South African Intelligence Services: From Apartheid to Democracy, 1948–2005* (New York: Routledge, 2010).

53. See Korean Institute for National Unification, "Mission and History," http://www.kinu.or.kr/eng/about/about_02_01.asp; Edward A. Olsen, *Korea: The Divided Nation* (Westport, CT: Praeger Security International, 2005); and Donald Kirk, *Korea Betrayed: Kim Dae Jung and Sunshine* (New York: Palgrave Macmillan, 2009).

54. Korea National Defense University, "A Message from the President," http://www.kndu.ac.kr/eng/.

55. See South Korea, National Intelligence Service, "About NIS: History," http://eng.nis.go.kr/docs/about/history.html; and Byungki Kim, "The Role of State Institutions, Organizational Culture, and Policy Perception in South Korea's International Security Policymaking Process: 1998–Present," *International Journal of Korean Unification Studies*, 15 (1)(2006): 106–131.

56. See Taiwan, Mainland Affairs Council, "About Us," http://www.mac.gov.tw/ct.asp?xItem=55898&CtNode=5901%mp=3; and Nancy Bernkopf Tucker, ed., *Dangerous Strait: The U.S.–Taiwan–China Crisis* (New York: Columbia University Press, 2005).

57. Taiwan, National Defense University, "History," http://www.ndu.edu.tw/eng/history.html.

58. See Michael S. Goodman, *The Anvil of Discussion: The Official History of the Joint Intelligence Committee*, (Forthcoming 2011); and United Kingdom, Cabinet Office, "Intelligence, Security, and Resilience: Our Work," http://www.cabinetoffice.gov.uk/intelligence-security-resilience.aspx.

59. United Kingdom, Defence Academy, "Research and Assessment Branch," http://www.da.mod.uk/colleges/arag.

60. See Great Britain, Foreign and Commonwealth Office, "What Is the FCO?" http://www.fco.gov.uk/en/about-us/what-is-the-fco/; and Great Britain, Foreign and Commonwealth Office, *The FCO: Policies, People and Places, 1782–2000*, 6th ed. (London: Historical Branch, Foreign and Commonwealth Office Library and Records Department, 2000).

61. See Great Britain, Ministry of Defence, "What We Do: MOD's Responsibilities and Main Organisations," http://www.mod.uk/DefenceInternet/AboutDefence/

WhatWeDo/; Sir Ewen Broadbent, *The Military and Government: From Macmillan to Heseltine* (Basingstoke, UK: Macmillan, 1988); and Paul Smith, ed., *Government and the Armed Forces in Britain, 1856–1990* (London: Hambledon, 1996).

62. See Great Britain, Parliament, House of Commons Defence Committee, "Commons Select Committee-Defence Committee," http://www.parliament.uk/business/committees/committees-a-z/commons-select/defence-committee/; and Oonagh McDonald, *The Defence Select Committee, 1979–1992* (London: Brassey's for the Centre for Defence Studies, 1993).

63. Great Britain, Parliament, House of Commons Foreign Affairs Committee, "Foreign Affairs Committee-Role," http://www.parliament.uk/business/committees/committees-a-z/commons-select/foreign-affairs-committee/role/.

64. United Kingdom, Royal Air Force Centre for Airpower Studies, homepage, http://www.airpowerstudies.co.uk/.

65. See Great Britain, Secret Intelligence Service, "About Us," http://www.mi6.gov.uk/output/about-us.html; Great Britain Cabinet Office, *National Intelligence Machinery*, 3rd ed. (London: Stationery Office, 2005); Gordon Corera, "UK Makes Changes to Secret Intelligence Service," *Jane's Intelligence Review*, 17 (2)(February 2005): 48–51; and Keith Jeffrey, *The Secret History of MI6* (New York: Penguin Press, 2010).

66. See United Nations, Division for Ocean Affairs and Law of the Sea, "The United Nations Convention on the Law of the Sea: A Historical Perspective," http://www.un.org/depts/los/convention_agreements/convention_historical_perspective.htm; United States, National Intelligence Council, "Law of the Sea: The Endgame," http://purl.access.gpo.gov/Government Printing Office/LPS53876; Suzette V. Suarez, *The Outer Limits of the Continental Shelf: Legal Aspects of Their Establishment* (Berlin: Springer, 2008); and Scott Gerald Borgerson, *National Interest and the Law of the Sea* (New York: Council on Foreign Relations, 2009).

67. See U.S. National Archives and Records Administration, *United States Government Manual, 2009–2010* (Washington, DC: Government Printing Office, 2009): 132; Ian F. Fergusson, *The Export Administration Act: Evolutions, Provisions, and Debate* (Washington, DC: Library of Congress, Congressional Research Service, 2009); and U.S. Congress, House Committee on Foreign Affairs, Subcommittee on Terrorism, Nonproliferation, and Trade, *The Export Administration Act: A Review of Outstanding Policy Considerations* (Washington, DC: Government Printing Office, 2009).

68. U.S. National Archives and Records Administration, *United States Government Manual, 2009–2010* (Washington, DC: Government Printing Office, 2009): 147.

69. See U.S. Air Force Counterproliferation Center, "About This Center," http://cpc.au.af.mil/about.htm; and Charles R. Heflebower, Laura J. Le Gallo, John P. Lawrence, and Bert A. Cline, *Counter WMD Concepts of Operations at U.S. and Allied Air Bases* (Maxwell Air Force Base, AL: USAF Counterproliferation Center, 2005), http://purl.access.gpo.gov/Government Printing Office/LPS66908.

70. U.S. Army War College, Strategic Studies Institute, "About the Strategic Studies Institute," http://www.strategicstudiesinstitute.army.mil/about/strategic-studies-institute.cfm.

71. Asia Pacific Center for Security Studies, "About APCSS," http://www.apcss.org/text/text_about.htm.

72. See United States, Department of Defense, International Security Affairs Office of the Undersecretary of Defense for Policy, "Responsibilities and Functions," http://policy.defense.gov/sections/policy_offices/isa.html; Chester J. Pach, *Arming the Free World: The Origins of the United States Military Assistance Program, 1945–1950* (Chapel Hill: University of North Carolina Press, 1991); and Kendall D. Gott, managing ed., *Security Assistance: U.S. and International Historical Perspectives: The Proceedings of the Combat Studies Institute 2006 Military History Symposium* (Fort Leavenworth, KS: Combat Studies Institute Press, 2006).

73. National Archives and Records Administration, *United States Government Manual, 2009–2010* (Washington, DC: Government Printing Office, 2009): 355–56.

74. U.S. National Defense Intelligence College, "Welcome to the National Defense Intelligence College," http://www.dia.mil/college/#.

75. See U.S. Defense Security Cooperation Agency, "Welcome to DSCA: Strength through Cooperation," http://www.dsca.mil/briefing_slides/dsca1001/overview_web_final_1001.ppt; and United States, General Accounting Office, *Nonproliferation: Improvements Needed to Better Control Technology Exports for Cruise Missiles and Unmanned Aerial Vehicles* (Washington, DC: Government Accountability Office, 2004).

76. See U.S. Defense Threat Reduction Agency, "About Us," http://www.dtra.mil/About/AboutHome.aspx; and United States, Defense Threat Reduction Agency, Department of Defense, *Defense's Nuclear Agency, 1947–1997* (Washington, DC: Defense Threat Reduction Agency, U.S. Department of Defense, 2002).

77. Institute for National Strategic Studies, "About INSS," http://www.ndu.edu/inss/index.cfm?pageID=2&type=page.

78. See Africa Center for Strategic Studies, "History," http://africacenter.org/about/history/; and Africa Center for Strategic Studies, "About Us," http://africacenter.org/about/.

79. Center for Hemispheric Defense Studies, "CHDS Strategic Program Overview," http://www.ndu.edu/chds/index.cfm?ID=265&pageID=91&type=section.

80. Center for the Study of Chinese Military Affairs, "Mission Statement," http://www.ndu.edu/inss/index.cfm?secID=83&pageID=4&type=section.

81. George C. Marshall European Center for Security Studies, "The Marshall Center Mission," http://www.marshallcenter.org/mcpublicweb/en/nav-mc-about-mission.html.

82. Near East South Asia Center for Strategic Studies, "Mission & Vision," http://nesa-center.org/en/missionandvision.

83. See U.S. Naval War College, "Mission/Vision," http://www.usnwc.edu/About/MissionVision.aspx; Ronald H. Spector, *Professors of War: The Naval War College and the Development of the Naval Profession* (Newport, RI: Naval War College Press, 1977); and John B. Hattendorf, B. Mitchell Simpson, and John R. Wadleigh, *Scholars and Professors: The Centennial History of the U.S. Naval War College* (Newport, RI: Naval War College Press, 1984).

84. China Maritime Studies Institute, "About CMSI," http://www.usnwc.edu/Research—Gaming/China-Maritime-Studies-Institute.aspx.

85. U.S. Office of the Assistant Secretary of Defense for Acquisition-Industrial Policy, "Our Mission," http://www.acq.osd.mil/ip/about.shtml.

86. See James Carafano, Frank Ciluffo, Richard Weitz, and Jan Lane, *Stopping Surprise Attacks: Thinking Smarter about Homeland Security* (Washington, DC: Heritage Foundation, 2007): 2; and U.S. Department of Defense, Directive 5111.11 (2009): 1, http://www.dtic.mil/whs/directives/corres/pdf/511111p.pdf.

87. See Carafano et al., *Stopping Surprise Attacks*, 2–3; and Paul Bracken, "Net Assessment: A Practical Guide," *Parameters*, 36 (1)(Spring 2006): 90–100. For information on Andrew Marshall, see also Jay Winik, "Secret Weapon," *Washingtonian*, 34 (7)(April 1999): 45–55; and Thomas E. Ricks, "Pentagon Study May Bring Big Shakeup: Unconventional Defense Thinker Conducting Review," *Washington Post*, February 9, 2001: A01. For an example of Marshall's writing, see the foreword to Zalmay Khalilzad, John P. White, and Andrew M. Marshall, eds., *Strategic Appraisal: The Changing Role of Information in Warfare* (Santa Monica, CA: RAND, 1999): 1–6.

88. See U.S. National Archives and Records Administration, *U.S. Government Manual 2009/2010* (Washington, DC: National Archives and Records Administration, 2009), 204; and Terrence R. Fehner and Jack M. Holl, *Department of Energy, 1977–1994: A Summary History* (Washington, DC: U.S. Department of Energy, 1994).

89. U.S. Energy Information Administration, "About EIA: Mission and Overview," http://www.eia.doe.gov/abouteia/mission_overview.cfm.

90. See National Nuclear Security Administration, "Our Mission," http://www.nnsaenergy.gov/ourmission; and U.S. Government Accountability Office, *Nuclear Weapons: NNSA and DOD Need to More Effectively Manage the Stockpile Life Extension Program* (Washington, DC: Government Accountability Office, 2009), http://purl.access.gpo.gov/Government Printing Office/LPS113415.

91. U.S. Department of Energy, Office of Policy and International Affairs, "About Us," http://www.pi.energy.gov/about_us.htm.

92. See U.S. Geological Survey, "Mineral Resources Program," http://minerals.usgs.gov/; and Susan J. Kropschot, *USGS Mineral Resources Program—Supporting Stewardship of America's Natural Resources* (Reston, VA: U.S. Geological Survey, 2006), http://pubs.usgs.gov/circ/2006/1289/.

93. See *U.S. Government Manual, 2009/2010*, 476–78; and U.S. Congress, Senate Select Committee on Intelligence, *Statutory Authorities of the Director of National Intelligence* (Washington, DC: Government Printing Office, 2009), http://purl.access.gpo.gov/Government Printing Office/LPS114665.

94. See U.S. National Intelligence Council, "NIC Mission," http://www.dni.gov/nic/NIC_about.html.

95. U.S.-China Economic and Security Review Commission, "Overview," http://www.uscc.gov/about/overview.php.

96. See *U.S. Government Manual, 2009/2010* (Washington, DC: National Archives and Records Administration, 2009): 291; and Elmer Plischke, *United States Department of State: A Reference History* (Westport, CT: Greenwood Press, 1999).

97. See U.S. Directorate of Defense Trade Controls, "Mission," http://www.pmddtc.state.gov/; and "Directorate of Defense Trade Controls and the Defense Trade Function," *DISAM Journal of International Security Assistance Management*, 30 (2) (Summer 2008): 138–41.

98. U.S. Department of State, Office of the Historian, "About Us," http://www.history.state.gov/about/.

99. U.S. Department of State, Office of the Historian, "Undersecretary for Arms Control and International Security," http://www.state.gov/t/.

100. U.S. Department of State, Office of the Historian, "Undersecretary for Democracy and Global Affairs," http://www.state.gov/g/.

101. See U.S. Department of State, Office of the Historian, "Undersecretary of State for Economics, Energy, and Agricultural Affairs," http://www.state.gov/e/; Cynthia Hody, *The Politics of Trade: American Political Development and Foreign Economic Policy* (Hanover, NH: University Press of New England, 1996); Ira Katznelson and Martin Shefter, eds., *Shaped by War and Trade: International Influences in American Political Development* (Princeton, NJ: Princeton University Press, 2002).

102. U.S. Department of State, Undersecretary of Political Affairs, "Under Secretary for Political Affairs," http://www.state.gov/p/.

103. See *U.S. Government Manual, 2009/2010*, 331; and Esther Rogoff Taus, *The Role of the U.S. Treasury in Stabilizing the Economy, 1941–1946* (Washington, DC: University Press of America, 1981).

104. U.S. Department of the Treasury, Office of International Affairs, "Mission," http://www.treas.gov/offices/international-affairs/.

105. See U.S. Department of the Treasury, Office of International Affairs, Terrorism and Financial Intelligence, "Mission," http://www.treas.gov/offices/enforcement/; U.S. Government Accountability Office, *International Financial Crime: Treasury's Roles and Responsibilities Relating to Selected Provisions of the USA PATRIOT Act* (Washington, DC: Government Accountability Office, 2006), http://purl.access.gpo.gov/Government Printing Office/LPS78858.

106. U.S. Department of the Treasury, Office of Foreign Assets Control, "About," http://www.treas.gov/offices/enforcement/ofac/.

107. See *U.S. Government Manual, 2009/2010*, 99; U.S. Congress, Senate Committee on Governmental Affairs, Subcommittee on Oversight of Government Management, the Federal Workforce, and the District of Columbia, *Pirates of the 21st Century: The Curse of the Black Market* (Washington, DC: Government Printing Office, 2004); and Steve Dryden, *Trade Warriors: USTR and the American Crusade for Free Trade* (New York: Oxford University Press, 1995).

108. See U.S. Constitution, Article 1 Section 8, for an example of constitutional authorization of congressional prerogatives on this subject.

109. U.S. Congress, House Armed Services Committee, "110th Congress Oversight Plan," http://armedservices.house.gov/oversight110.shtml.

110. U.S. Congress, House Committee on Foreign Affairs, "History of the Committee," http://foreignaffairs.house.gov/about.asp?sec=history.

111. U.S. Congress, House Committee on Foreign Affairs, "Jurisdiction of the Committee for the 111th Congress," http://foreignaffairs.house.gov/about.asp?section=jurisdiction.

112. See Bert Chapman, *Researching National Security and Intelligence Policy* (Washington, DC: CQ Press, 2004): 23–24; and Frank John Smist, *Congress Oversees the United States Intelligence Community, 1947–1989* (Knoxville: University of Tennessee Press, 1990).

113. See Donald R. Kennon, *The Committee on Ways and Means: A Bicentennial History, 1789–1989* (Washington, DC: Government Printing Office, 1989?); and U.S. Congress, House Committee on Ways and Means, "Oversight Plan," http://waysandmeans.house.gov/media/pdf/111/Oversight_111.pdf.

114. See U.S. Congress, Senate Committee on Armed Services, "Committee Jurisdiction," http://armed-services.senate.gov/about.htm.

115. U.S. Congress, Senate Committee on Finance, "Jurisdiction," http://finance.senate.gov/about/jurisdiction/.

116. See U.S. Congress, Senate Committee on Foreign Relations, *Committee on Foreign Relations, 1816–2000* (Washington, DC: Government Printing Office, 2000); and U.S. Congress, Senate Committee on Foreign Relations, "History of the Committee," http://foreign.senate.gov/about/history/.

117. See Chapman, *Researching National Security*, 242; and U.S. Congress, Senate Select Committee on Intelligence, "Jurisdiction Overview," http://intelligence.senate.gov/jurisdiction.html.

118. See World Trade Organization, "About the WTO—A Statement by the Director-General," http://www.wto.org/english/thewto_e/whatis_e/wto_dg_stat_e.htm; Kevin Buterbaugh and Richard Fulton, *The WTO Primer: Tracing Trade's Visible Hand through Case Studies* (New York: Palgrave Macmillan, 2008); and Kyle Bagwell and Robert W. Staiger, *The Economics of the World Trading System* (Cambridge, MA: MIT Press, 2002).

CHAPTER 5

Monographic Scholarly Literature

The monographic scholarly literature of geopolitics is multifaceted and interdisciplinary, representing a variety of perspectives, including classical and critical geopolitics covering many global areas. Classical geopolitics can be defined as emphasizing realist political science theory and traditional political and geographic factors such as economic, military, and political power; competition for natural resources; and the desire of countries to control territory and keep other countries or groups of countries from restricting national access to territory or resources.[1]

Critical geopolitics seeks to challenge conventional geopolitical understandings. Heavily influenced by various intellectual deconstructionist movements, it challenges what it regards as state-centric, ethnocentric, and determinist traits in classical geopolitical writings. It places acute emphasis on examining and manipulating geopolitical and strategic rhetoric and to fit a leftist ideological worldview that is harshly critical of what it claims is Western imperialism and militarism.[2]

This chapter will examine and annotate works representing these two strands of thought in geopolitical literature from the 1980s to the present. Works represented here will cover a variety of historical, recent, and emerging geopolitical issues and give readers an in-depth guide to the multifaceted scholarly monographic literature produced on geopolitics and the issues debated and analyzed by practitioners in this interdisciplinary field.

Entries will include standard bibliographic citations, listings of publishers' monographic series that the entries may be a part of, the entries' International Standard Bibliographic Numbers (ISBNs) to facilitate purchasing or ordering through Interlibrary Loan services, and Web URLs if these resources are freely available on the Internet.

Ahrari, M. Esahan. *Jihadi Groups, Nuclear Pakistan, and the New Great Game*. Carlisle, PA: Strategic Studies Institute, U.S. Army War College, 2001. ISBN: 9781584870609. http://purl.access.gpo.gov/GPO/LPS14542.

This work describes the role played by Jihadist groups in Pakistan who seek to wage "holy war" against what they see as non-Islamic influences within that country as they aspire to establish their vision of an Islamic state. Ahrari makes this assessment with a "great game" framework for seeking influence in central Asia involving a number of states. This could lead to increased violence if outside states such as the United States were pulled into this conflict. Since the work was published a month prior to the 9/11 terrorist attacks, the author's prediction of increased violence has been vividly vindicated, as ongoing conflicts in Afghanistan and Pakistan demonstrate.

Anderson, Ewan W. *Global Political Flashpoints: An Atlas of Conflict*. Chicago: Fitzroy Dearborn Publishers, 2000. ISBN: 1-57958-137-4.

This atlas provides succinct overviews of over 120 international political flash points or hot spots. These areas may be bilateral or multilateral sources of contentiousness due to their possession of coveted natural resources, disputes over boundary demarcations, problems serving as points of contention between nations and transnational organizations, being located in geographically and economically critical transit areas, and for other reasons. Examples of flash points profiled in this work include the Basque Country, the Black Sea, Croatia, Golan Heights, Strait of Hormuz, North Korea, Nigeria, South Lebanon, and the Spratly Islands.

Descriptive entries for each of these flash points feature an introductory overview describing the issues causing these regions to be geopolitically contentious, a map of the affected region(s), the situation's status at the time this book was published, and bibliographic references. A global map depicting the location each of these hot spots is also a valuable asset of this atlas.

Black, Jeremy. *Maps and History: Constructing Images of the Past*. New Haven: Yale University Press, 1997. ISBN: 0-300-06976-6.

Historical study of the political and other roles played by historical atlases in European and international history from the 16th century to the present. These atlases have influenced educational portrayals of national and international territory, popular perceptions of international political issues, and sought to present varying political agendas by using cartographic resources to document diplomatic, economic, environmental, ethnographic, military, and political changes. Technological changes in map production are also covered from historical techniques used to produce various kinds of paper maps to then emerging electronic technologies such as CD-ROM and Geographic Information Systems (GIS).

Blouet, Brian W. *Halford Mackinder: A Biography*. College Station: Texas A&M University Press, 1987. ISBN: 0-89096-292-8.

Blouet presents a biographical portrait of one of the leading architects of what has become known as geopolitics. Halford Mackinder (1861–1947), a key

British proponent of what became known as the Heartland theory, lived a lengthy life, and his professional career involved founding Reading University, being a major figure in the Royal Geographical Society, serving as a director of the London School of Economics and a Conservative MP during the World War I era, being an enthusiastic promoter of imperial unity (including trading preferences) within the British Empire, and being an enthusiastic and prolific promoter of geography's importance in international relations and military strategy throughout his career.

Broeze, Frank. *Island Nation: A History of Australians and the Sea*. St. Leonards, NSW: Allen and Unwin, 1998. ISBN: 1-86448-424-1.

This work seeks to analyze the multifaceted roles played by the sea in sculpting Australia's cultural, diplomatic, economic, military, and political relationship with the world and within Australian society and culture. The first part of Brazee's work emphasizes how Australians have sought to use the sea to enhance their geopolitical interests, with particular emphasis on becoming self-reliant in their defense capabilities. A second part stresses the use of the sea as an international trade conduit to overcome geographic isolation and enhance the material living standards of Australians through robust international trade. The final part accentuates how Australians have used the sea to develop a distinct maritime culture and identity that has placed acute emphasis on and romanticized the roles played by maritime workers and their trade unions in building a unique Australian cultural identity.

Brzezinski, Zbigniew. *The Grand Chessboard: American Primacy and Its Geostrategic Imperatives*. New York: Basic Books, 1997. ISBN: 0-465-02725-3.

Written by the Carter administration's National Security Advisor and a prolific analyst of international affairs, *The Grand Chessboard* seeks to emphasize the traditional importance of Eurasia as a world power, the United States' emergence as the first truly global power, and the need for a "comprehensive and integrated Eurasian geostrategy" to ensure that no Eurasian challenger can emerge who will be capable of dominating Eurasia and challenging the United States.[3]

Brzezinksi describes how the Spanish-American War marked the U.S. emergence as a major power into the international geopolitical arena. He goes on to describe Eurasia's importance in international political, economic, and military affairs by noting that the world's six largest economies and military weaponry expenditures are by Eurasian nations,[4] while also noting the multiple geostrategic strengths and weaknesses of these countries. He also describes the geopolitical vacuum created in Eastern Europe, central Asia, and East Asia by the Soviet Union's collapse; the critical importance of the United States being involved in East Asian economic, political, and strategic affairs; and the need for the United States to effectively balance its multiple global interests to enhance its national interests and international stability.

Chapman, Graham P. *The Geopolitics of South Asia: From Early Empires to the Nuclear Age*. 2nd ed. Burlington, VT: Ashgate, 2002. ISBN: 0-7546-3442-6.

South Asia features the presence of India and Pakistan as nuclear weapons powers, and both of these countries also have unresolved political disputes in their bilateral relationship. The ongoing turmoil in Afghanistan involving non–south Asian powers such as the United States and the NATO's International Security Assistance Force further enhances the geopolitical importance of this region.

This work provides detailed historical overview and analysis of the multiple religious, political, and geographic factors that have sculpted the region's contemporary international political and security environment. The first section describes the Hindu and Islamic religious influences informing regional political ideologies. A second section describes the role played by the British and other colonial rivals such as the French in developing regional political and security institutions. A third section addresses geopolitical developments since India and Pakistan achieved independence from the United Kingdom in 1947.

This last section scrutinizes developments such as the 1971 creation of Bangladesh, regions such as Jammu and Kashmir that remain sources of Indo-Pakistani bilateral contentiousness, the role of hydropolitics in the Indus River basin, and the historical and ongoing contemporary strategic interests of countries such as the Soviet Union/Russia, United States, China, Pakistan, Afghanistan, Bangladesh, India, and the South Asian Association for Regional Cooperation in this increasingly important part of the world.

Child, Jack. *Geopolitics and Conflict in South America: Quarrels among Neighbors*. New York: Praeger, 1985. ISBN: 0-03-001453-0.

Treatise examining the multiple factors influencing geopolitical contentiousness in South America during the early 1980s. Divided into four broad sections, including an introductory overview, descriptions of the nature and impact of South American geopolitical thinking, case studies of geopolitics and conflict, and concluding observations. Examples of case studies profiled include Argentine and Chilean conflict over the Beagle Channel Islands, disputes between Chile, Bolivia, and Peru in the Central Andes, Argentine and Brazilian rivalry, Argentina's conflict with the United Kingdom over the Falklands Islands, contentiousness between various powers over control of the South Atlantic and Antarctica, and disputes between South American and Caribbean countries over islands such as that between Nicaragua and Columbia over the San Andres and Providencia islands.

The author concludes that geopolitical thinking has been most concentrated in countries, such as Argentina, Brazil, and Chile, that have large and sophisticated military establishments and recent histories of military rule repressing political opposition and that South American geopolitical thinking has been influenced by similar thinking in the United States and northern Europe, particularly Germany, during the Third Reich.[5]

Collins, John M. *Military Geography for Professionals and the Public*. Washington, DC: National Defense University Press, 1998. ISBN: 1-57906-002-1. https://digitalndulibrary.ndu.edu/cdm4/document.php?CISOROOT=/ndupress&CISOPTR=37236&REC=4.

Detailed overview documenting the importance of geography in military planning and decision making. This work is broken up into four broad sections covering physical geography, cultural geography, political-military geography, and area analyses. Topics addressed in the physical geography section include spatial relationships, lay of the land including geology and soils, oceans and seashores including marine topography, earth's atmosphere, regional peculiarities such as mountainous regions, inner and outer space, and natural resources and raw materials.

The cultural geography section addresses demography, urbanization, and lines of communication such as railroads, seaports, harbors, and military bases. Examples of political-military geography include diversified viewpoints on security issues along with territorial limits, strategic friction, and theater and tactical areas of responsibility. Area analyses emphasize the need for geographical databases to assist in planning and executing military operations and descriptions and analyses of how geography influenced military operations during the Vietnam War.

Dalby, Simon. *Continent Adrift: The Changing Geostrategic Parameters of Australian Discourse*. Working Paper 35. Canberra: Australian Defence Studies Centre, 1995. ISBN: 0-7317-0340-5.

Dalby presents an dissident ideologically leftist perspective on Australian geopolitical or geostrategic interests. He believes Australian interests are best served by emphasizing regional concerns and defense issues emphasizing Australia's role as a continental power geographically adjacent to Asia's south instead of as a North Atlantic power.

He contends that Australian academic analyses of international politics and strategy have been influenced by Anglo-American approaches and produced by institutions such as Australian National University, which has a close relationship with the Australian government. Dalby pays particular attention to criticisms of the Australian–New Zealander–U.S. alliance, which he and other dissident critics believe was motivated by guilt over European colonization and its alleged racist foundations, the World War II failure of Britain to defend the region after naval defeat at Singapore, and continuing Australian fears of a resurgent Japan after World War II.

The author also criticizes the role of U.S. defense bases in Australia and the extent of U.S.-Australian intelligence cooperation. He goes on to mention how dissident critics advocated Australia pursuing a policy of armed neutrality in regional security matters, contending that Australia has been a greater security threat to its neighbors than its neighbors, such as Indonesia, are to Australia, and he ultimately believes that countries recognizing mutual vulnerabilities to military, environmental, and economic factors should become preeminent factors in formulating Australian strategic thinking.

Dekmejian, R. Hrair, and Hovann H. Simonian. *Troubled Waters: The Geopolitics of the Caspian Region*. London: I. B. Tauris, 2003. ISBN: 1-86064-922-X.

The Caspian Sea has become an increasingly important arena of geopolitical interest since the cold war due to its considerable oil and natural gas resources. These interests affect adjacent countries such as Russia, Iran, Azerbaijan, Kazakhstan, and Turkemenistan. The 9/11 terrorist attacks have also made the United States and other Western countries interested in this region's increasing strategic and economic importance as they seek to influence Caspian Sea countries to look favorably on their geopolitical aspirations and interests.

Essay topics within this work examine the Caspian's historical and contemporary roles in an increasingly globalized world, the Caspian's international legal and environmental status, estimates of its energy reserves, and the costs of developing and exploiting these assets; how adjacent states are reacting to the Caspian's increased importance in regional and international economics and foreign policy; how the United States, Europe, and various Asian countries are reacting to the Caspian's emergence as a source of international economic and strategic importance; and how nongovernmental organizations such as criminal groups, ethnonationalist entities such as separatist groups within adjacent countries, multinational corporations, and religious activists are seeking to utilize the Caspian's increased importance to advance and fulfill their own agendas.

Dodds, Klaus. *Geopolitics in Antarctica: Views from the Southern Oceanic Rim*. Polar Research Series. New York: John Wiley, in association with Scott Polar Research Institute, 1997. ISBN: 0-471-96992-3.

Dodds examines Antarctica's increasing geopolitical importance for international policy makers, scientists, and tourists due to the island continent's natural resource reserves and the interests of many countries in these reserves. He begins by describing various international agreements on Antarctica, including the 1959 Antarctic Treaty prohibiting military activities here and the 1982 Convention on the Conservation of Antarctic Marine Living Resources.

Subsequent chapters describe and analyze the economic, geopolitical, and scientific interest countries such as Argentina, Australia, Chile, India, New Zealand, and South Africa have in Antarctica and how these southern oceanic countries have worked or not worked with each other to maintain national objectives in Antarctica consistent with international agreements. The Antarctic interests of other major international powers such as the United States, European Union, Russia, and China must also be taken into consideration when discussing southern hemisphere geopolitical aspirations toward Antarctica.

Flint, Colin, ed. *Geography of War and Peace: From Death Camps to Diplomats*. New York: Oxford University Press, 2005. ISBN: 0-19-516209-9.

This collection of essays stresses how geography still has a significant impact in shaping global war and peace. It is broken up into three thematic sections focusing on theoretical foundations for understanding war and peace geographies, spatial geographies of war, and spatial geographies of peace. Examples of topics addressed within these sections include the political geography of conflict, the multifaceted roles played by soldiers in forging national territorial identity, how religion can influence wartime geographies, spatial challenges posed by terrorism, geographical implications of natural resource wars and drug trafficking, shifting terms of debate in maritime conflicts, how boundaries and borders impact contemporary ethnonational conflict, and the geographies of peace movements, diplomacy, NATO expansion, and postwar conflict recovery.

Grygiel, Jakub J. *Great Powers and Geopolitical Change*. Baltimore: Johns Hopkins University Press, 2006. ISBN: 0-8018-8480-2.

Grygiel's analysis examines geopolitics and geostrategy with particular emphasis on historical case studies of how Venice, the Ottoman Empire, and Ming China confronted these matters between the 11th and 16th centuries. Key thrusts of this analysis include asserting that geography needs to be included when studying international relations, that current foreign policy must reflect underlying geopolitics, and that current and emerging U.S. foreign policy can learn lessons from the historical case studies presented in this work.

Grygiel emphasizes that states can maintain and increase their power by pursuing a geostrategy emphasizing control of resources and communication lines and that the locations of natural resources and trade networks, along with the stability of national boundaries, play a critical role in the success or failure of historical and current national powers. He also emphasizes the critical importance of the United States maintaining its ability to project military power in East Asia given increasing Chinese ambitions and power projection in that region.

Kearns, Gerry. *Geopolitics and Empire: The Legacy of Halford Mackinder*. New York: Oxford University Press, 2009. ISBN: 978-0-19-923011-2.

This work presents an early-21st-century leftist ideological perspective on the how the influence of Halford Mackinder is shaping the current renaissance of geopolitics in international policy making. Kearns examines how Mackinder's theories influenced the British Empire's geopolitical aspirations. He also stresses what he sees as the importance of social Darwinism in shaping Western strategic policy making, how the United States has been a practitioner of imperial policy making since it replaced Britain as the West's preeminent power, and examples of what the author sees as conservative and progressive geopolitics in contemporary international politics.

Kelly, Phillip. *Checkerboards and Shatterbelts: The Geopolitics of South America*. Austin: University of Texas Press, 1997. ISBN: 0-292-74327-0.

Kelly presents his appraisal of South American geopolitics, with particular emphasis on the roles played by checkerboards and shatterbelts. The former concept refers to the neighboring states of individual countries being confederates or opponents, depending on regional political dynamics. The latter concept refers to military rivalries between external powers, such as the cold war–era rivalry between the United States and Soviet Union in this region, which influence local conditions and enhance the possibility of conflict escalation.[6]

Topics addressed by Kelly include an overview of South American geopolitics and how countries such as Argentina, Brazil, and Chile have adhered to different geopolitical theories incorporating concepts such as continental economic and security dependency on powers such as the United States, the importance of ocean cycles in shaping trade, the role of manifest destiny as modeled by the United States and adopted by Argentina, Brazil, and Chile, realpolitik, and the role of the Monroe Doctrine. He goes on to describe the writings of South American geopoliticans such as Brazilians Carlos de Meira Mattos (1913–2007) and Golbery do Couto e Silva (1911–1987), Argentine Enrique Guglialmelli (1922–1983), and Chilean Augusto Pinochet Ugarte (1915–2006).

Later chapters describe South American regional politics, including border disputes and conflicts between countries such as Argentina, Paraguay, and Uruguay; Chile and Peru; the Falklands/Malvinas conflict between Argentina and the United Kingdom; Bolivia's quest for an ocean outlet; and how South American relations with the United States have distinct geopolitical attributes in a continually shifting international multilateral political and strategic environments.

Krakowka, Amy Richmond, and Laurel J. Hummel, eds. *Understanding Africa: A Geographic Approach*. West Point, NY: U.S. Military Academy and Center for Strategic Leadership, U.S. Army War College, 2009. http://www.csl.army.mil/usacsl/publications/understanding_africa.pdf.

This collection of essays seeks to highlight the increasing importance of Africa in international political and strategic affairs, with emphasis on how important Africa is becoming to U.S. strategic interests. The first part of this compendium provides regional perspectives of Africa, focusing on cultural, economic, environmental, political, and strategic developments in north, east, central, west, and southern Africa.

A second section provides more detailed topical analysis on current African trends and developments with geopolitical implications. These include how maps of African countries were drawn by European colonial powers and do not reflect existing African ethnic and cultural identities, current African questions about the legitimacy of the U.S. military's newly created African Command, mineral resources and human security in Tanzania, the role of traditional African religions in current political development, how Africa's youthful population structures impact the continent's security environment, sub-Saharan Africa's urban geography, medical geography including the impact of AIDS, and China's increasing interest in acquiring Africa's abundant natural resources, including oil.

LeDonne, John P. *The Russian Empire and the World, 1700–1917: The Geopolitics of Expansion and Containment, 1700–1917*. New York: Oxford University Press, 1997. ISBN: 0-19-510926-0.

Historical review of Russian territorial expansion and international containment of this expansion spanning this time period and how geopolitical aspirations and ideology influenced this process. The first part of this work stresses how Russia sought to expand its geopolitical sphere of influence west into Europe with the 1772, 1793, and 1795 partitions of Poland, with Austria-Hungary and Prussia being particularly vivid demonstrations of such aggressiveness.

A second part examines Russian expansion to the south, with emphasis on its interactions with the Ottoman Empire and Persia. A third part focuses on Russian advances to the east and the conflicts this would produce with China and Japan. Part four looks at how Germanic powers sought to contain Russia, with particular emphasis on Bismarckian Germany. A concluding section stresses how coastal powers such as Great Britain sought to restrict Russian expansionism through conflicts such as the Crimean War and their vigorous resistance to Russian expansion in the Balkans as part of the Eastern Question in 19th-century European geopolitical skirmishing.

Lo, Bobo. *Axis of Convenience: Moscow, Beijing, and the New Geopolitics*. London: Chatham House and Brookings Institution Press, 2008. ISBN: 978-0-8157-5340-7.

Lo argues that the "strategic partnership" between China and Russia is based on mutual convenience and does not threaten international stability or Western vital interests. Topics examined in this assessment include the historical origins and development of Sino-Russian relations, Moscow's desire to use Beijing to counterbalance purported U.S. international hegemony, Beijing's desire to use Moscow to supplement its relationships with the United States and Europe, economic development in Russian Asia that favors China due to that country's geographic proximity and higher economic growth rate, and the increasing influence of energy resources in the economic, trade, and strategic interests of both countries. Lo ultimately sees the relationship between these countries as being a traditional great power interaction with the strengths and weaknesses of these relationships throughout history.[7]

Macris, Jeffrey R. *The Politics and Security of the Gulf: Anglo-American Hegemony and the Shaping of a Region*. London: Routledge, 2009. ISBN: 978-0-415-77871-8 (pbk).

Macris seeks to analyze British and American interests in the Persian Gulf region and how both of these powers have sought to ensure the free flow of petroleum and other commerce through this vital tributary. Topics covered within this work include Britain's legacy in the gulf, the World War II arrival of the United States as a strategic player in this region, how Egyptian president Gamal Nasser's rebellion against the British in the 1950s strengthened U.S. interests in having a strong security presence in this region, and the emergence and evolution of the United States' strategic hegemony in this region in recent decades.

Murphy, David Thomas. *The Heroic Earth: Geopolitical Thought in Weimar Germany, 1918–1933*. Kent, OH: Kent State University Press, 1997. ISBN: 0-8733-8564-0.

This study examines the development and evolution of German geopolitical thought in the period between the end of World War II and the rise of the Nazi regime. The emergence of geopolitics was reflected in the emergence of geographical institutes at German universities offering geopolitical lectures and seminars, through radio broadcasts issued by prominent advocates of geopolitics such as Karl Haushofer (1869–1946), and in the emergence of journals such as *Geopolitischer Typen-Atlas* (Atlas of Geopolitical Types) and *Geographische Grundlagen der Geschichte* (Geographic Foundations of History).

Specific chapters examine the emergence of German geopolitics in the quarter century before World War I, how this conflict transformed German geopoliticsm, the emergence of demography and the clamor for lebensraum (living space) becoming part of German political aspirations, the incorporation of geopolitics into German educational curricula, how geopolitics began influencing Germany's reaction to its World War I defeat and its subsequent response to this defeat in Weimarian foreign policy, and how Nazi abuse of geopolitics left this field with a poisoned and controversial legacy.

O'Loughlin, John, ed. *Dictionary of Geopolitics*. Westport, CT: Greenwood Press, 1994. ISBN: 0-313-26313-2.

This work represents the most authoritative dictionary of this subject, although it could use revision and updating. It begins with an introductory overview of geopolitic as an academic discipline, with particular emphasis on American and German influences. The main part of this work features 219 entries describing key concepts, individuals, institutions, and publications that have contributed to this subject's interdisciplinary development. Examples of these entries include American exceptionalism, Brazilian frontier policy, environmental security, geopolitical discourse, Colin Gray, Japanese geopolitics, Friedrich Ratzel, World Island, and *Zeitschrift für Geopolitik*.

Ó Tuathail, Gearóid. *Critical Geopolitics*. Borderlines Series. Minneapolis: University of Minnesota Press, 1996. ISBN: 0-8166-2603-0.

This is the most important work of the methodological perspective of critical geopolitics, which stresses that geography emphasizes power and that it represents a continually changing map of human struggle over borders, space, and authority. Critical geopolitics seeks to use literary terms such as *deconstruction* to skeptically examine and overturn established meanings of words to look for allegedly hidden interpretive nuances and meanings. It seeks to maintain that international political structures are used to enhance the dominance of what the author and critical geopolitics adherents regard as Western democratic and capitalist nations over the international political and security orders.

Ó Tuathail presents his theories by seeking to describe how traditional geopolitical theorists such as Halford Mackinder, Friedrich Ratzel (1849–1904), Nicholas Spykman (1893–1943), and others sought to impose systems of ideological geopolitical hegemony on other countries and on the international political system. He uses Bosnia, and to a lesser extent Ireland, as examples of how purportedly hegemonic Western powers have used geopolitics to impose their preferred policy and security arrangements on these countries.

Parker, W. H. *Mackinder: Geography as an Aid to Statecraft*. Oxford: Clarendon Press, 1982. ISBN: 0-19-823235-7.

This work describes how Halford Mackinder sought to incorporate geography into his international relations and geopolitical theories. Besides providing biographical information on this geopolitical luminary, Parker analyzes the importance of Mackinder's geopolitical thought, with particular emphasis on the Heartland theory and how this theory has been supported, criticized, and modified by various factions within the scholarly community. This support, criticism, and modification of Mackinder's writings have also been influenced by prevailing geopolitical issues present at the time of their writing such as the relationship between NATO and the Warsaw Pact prevalent at the time this work was published.

Rowe, Elana Wilson, ed. *Russia and the North*. Ottawa: University of Ottawa Press, 2009. ISBN: 978-0-7766-0700-9.

This compendium of essays, written primarily by Scandinavian scholars, seeks to examine and analyze the increasing importance of the north in Russian geopolitics. Chapter topics include policy aims and political realties in the Russian north, the increasing importance of the north in Russian military activities, cross-border cooperation in northwest Russia involving Norway, real and potential threats caused by climate change in the Russian north, recent developments in the Russian fisheries sector, the increasing importance of offshore oil and natural gas resources in Russian economic policy making, areas of population growth and decline in the Russian north, the rights of indigenous populations in the Russian north, how oil and gas development affects these indigenous populations, and intersections between Russian regional northern policies and overall Russian diplomatic, economic, natural resources, and natural security policy making.

Rumley, Dennis. *The Geopolitics of Australia's Regional Relations*. Boston: Kluwer, 1999. ISBN: 0-7923-5916-X.

Rumley seeks to examine the geopolitical factors influencing Australia's relationships with other Asia-Pacific countries. The two distinct parts of this work describe what the author sees as the international relations structure of the Asia-Pacific region and Australian regional linkages with these countries. Topics addressed within these parameters include geopolitical challenges in the Asia-Pacific, the role played by the Association of Southeast Asian Nations and human rights in Australian policy making, the importance of economic linkages in Australian trade policies with particular emphasis on access to mineral resources, the role of immigration in assessing Australian national interests, Australian security relationships with regional powers such as Indonesia and Singapore, and how Australia views its relationships with China and Japan and how they affect Australia's critical relationship with the United States.

Sajima, Naoko, and Kyoicki Tackikawa. *Japan's Sea Power: A Maritime Nation's Struggle for Identity*. Foundations of International Thinking on Seapower. Canberra: Sea Power Centre, Australia Department of Defense, 2009. ISBN: 978-0-642-29705-1. http://www.navy.gov.au/w/images/INTSP_2_JapaneseSP.pdf.

Although published by the Australian Navy, this historical review of Japanese geopolitics is written by two Japanese academics. It provides information on Japan's background and evolution as a maritime nation, with particular emphasis on its economic, political, and strategic relationships with adjacent geographic powers such as China, Korea, and Russia. One section of this work describes the origins and evolution of Japanese sea power, which is described as consisting of three distinct historical eras: the coastal navy era, covering until the 1853 arrival of the United States' Perry Squadron; the oceanic navy era, lasting to the end of World War II; and the contemporary era of Japanese sea power, which has occurred since 1945.

This contemporary era has seen the creation of a Maritime Self-Defense Force between approximately 1945 and 1976, a period emphasizing countering cold war threats from the Soviet Union between 1976 and 1989, the development of a post–cold war maritime force between 1989 and 2001, and the development of an early-21st-century maritime force whose operational emphases including countering nuclear proliferation as part of the Proliferation Security Initiative and assisting U.S. forces in counterterrorism operations.

Appendices feature descriptions of important historical battles throughout Japanese history, including confrontations with American, Chinese, Korean, and Russian naval forces.

Shephard, Allan. *Seeking Spratly Solutions: Maritime Tensions in the South China Sea*. Canberra: Department of the Parliamentary Library, 1993. ISSN: 1037-2938. http://www.aph.gov.au/library/pubs/bp/1993/93bp06.pdf.

This work examines how the Spratly Islands in the South China Sea may become a focus of international conflict due to their potential oil reserves and the competing claims of various regional powers. Countries with immediate claims on various portions of the Spratlys and their adjacent seabed resources include China, Vietnam, Taiwan, the Philippines, Malaysia, and Brunei. Additional powers with interests in the Spratlys, due to their proximity to key international shipping routes, include Australia, Japan, and the United States.

Seeking Spratly Solutions presents possible ways of resolving these issues involving bilateral consultation between interested countries, regional consultation, and United Nations participation. Appendices feature maps of these islands and chronological listings of which islands have been occupied by individual countries and their military personnel.

Singh, Bilveer. *Defense Relations between Australia and Indonesia in the Post–Cold War Era*. Contributions in Military Studies. Westport, CT: Greenwood Press, 2002. ISBN: 0-313-322260-0.

Singh provides an overview of Australian-Indonesian security relations from the end of World War II until the beginning of the 21st century. This relationship has evolved between confrontation and cooperation during this time period, with the late 1990s rebellion producing East Timor's independence being an instance of confrontation between these countries. Singh describes how Indonesia's proximity to international sea lanes has made Australia acutely sensitive to any political and military instability in Indonesia that might threaten the ability of international trade to reach Australian ports.

Additional sections of this work examine how Australian-Indonesian relations were conducted in the 1990s by prime ministers Paul Keating (1991–1996) and John Howard (1996–2007). Keating sought to pursue closer relations with Indonesia based on his belief that Australia should seek to integrate its national interests more closely with Asia, while Howard believed Australia's most important strategic relationship was with the United States and that Indonesia was less critical to Australia's long-term foreign policy and national security interests.

Stulberg, Adam N. *Well-Oiled Diplomacy: Strategic Manipulation and Russia's Energy Statecraft in East Asia*. SUNY Series in Global Politics. Albany: State University of New York Press, 2007. ISBN: 978-0-7914-7063-3.

This work examines how Russia has experienced mixed results using its energy resource advantages to influence its Eurasian policies between 1992 and 2002. Topics addressed in this appraisal examine the theoretical foundations of Russian energy policy and the federation's strategic energy predicament, which includes impressive energy resources but is hampered by complicated and opaque legal and regulatory structures and infrastructure deficiencies that keep it from reaching its optimum economic potential.

Additional chapters examine successful Russian natural gas diplomacy to coerce compliance from Turkmenistan and Kazakhstan, problems developing effective petroleum policies for the Caspian Sea region, and Moscow's efforts to restore and enhance its nuclear energy programs as part of its bilateral relationship with former Soviet republics such as Kazakhstan and Kyrgyzstan.

Thomas, Nicholas, ed. *Re-orienting Australia-China Relations: 1972 to the Present*. Burlington, VT: Ashgate, 2004. ISBN: 0-7546-3245-8.

This collection of essays analyzes the development and evolution of Australian-Chinese relations in the three decades since these two countries established formal diplomatic relations in 1972. The authors describe how bilateral relations between these countries have experienced various ups and downs since their initial establishment under Australian prime minister Gough Whitlam (1972–1975), their evolution under Malcolm Fraser's premiership (1975–1983), upheaval during Bob Hawke's premiership (1983–1991) as evidenced by Australia's hostile reaction to the 1989 Tianamien Square massacre, and more recent developments during the premierships of Paul Keating (1991–1996) and John Howard (1996–2007).

Essays address the critical importance played by economics and trade in fostering and sustaining this bilateral relationship, how Australia has sought to balance its relationships with China and the United States, Australian-Chinese interactions in the World Trade Organization, ways Australia has presented its viewpoints on human rights issues in its interactions with Chinese officials, the promotion of educational links between the two countries, and how Australia has been able to cultivate and maintain a mutually advantageous relationship with Taiwan without incurring much Chinese displeasure due to Australian affirmation of the "one China" policy and Taiwan being careful not to push Australia for a greater level of formal diplomatic recognition.

Thornton, Judith, and Charles E. Ziegler, eds. *Russia's Far East: A Region at Risk.* Seattle: National Bureau of Asian Research in Association with University of Washington Press, 2002. ISBN: 0-295-98210-1.

This work is a compilation of essays on political and economic developments in the Russian Far East since the fall of the Soviet Union and how developments in this large geographic area affect Russia, China, Japan, South Korea, and the United States.

Following introductory contextual overviews, thematic topics scrutinized in this work include the impact of Russian market–oriented economic reforms on this region, studies of this area's natural resource assets and development potential, the impact of the Russian military and its recent defense conversion activities on the region's economy, perspectives of adjacent countries with particular emphasis on Chinese migration into the Russian Far East and the multiple impacts of this migration, and how the East Asian balance of power is being altered by China's increasing prosperity and Russia's declining power in this region.

Todd, Emmanuel. *After the Empire: The Breakdown of the American Order.* European Perspectives. Trans. C. Jon Delogu. New York: Columbia University Press, 2003. ISBN: 9780231131025.

Written before the 2003 U.S. military action in Iraq, Todd argues that America does not have the military or economic power to be an empire and that structural weaknesses in the U.S. economy and societal demographics also signal declining U.S. influence on global political, economic, and military arenas. Todd argues that this declining American power will result in closer cooperation between France and Germany and Europe and Russia. He also believes increasing Japanese economic investment in Europe signifies that continent's increasing importance in international economic policy making at U.S. expense. He ultimately envisions the emergence of an Eurasian alliance consisting of Europe, Russia, Japan, and the Arab-Islamic world as a counterweight to U.S. economic and military power, which allegedly angers allies and enemies with its military power.

Trenin, Dimitrii. *The End of Eurasia: Russia on the Border between Geopolitics and Globalization*. Washington, DC: Carnegie Endowment for International Peace, 2002. ISBN: 0-8700-3190-2. http://www.carnegie.ru/en/pubs/books/2129dt0103all.pdf.

Trenin, representing a liberal or Western-oriented perspective in contemporary Russian geopolitical thinking, seeks to examine the meaning of Russia with emphasis on its borders. He believes the end of the Soviet/Russian empire stems from a long self-determining process instead of mistakes, crimes, or greed and that the Russian federation faces new and different challenges along its European, central Asian, and Far Eastern borders.[8]

He goes on to examine why Russia broke up and whether the Commonwealth of Independent States could have served as a mechanism for reasserting Russian national power; characteristics of the federation's relationship with western former Soviet republics such as Belarus, Ukraine, and Moldova; and Russian's southern tier relationships with countries such as Georgia and Azerbaijan in the South Caucuses, separatist Chechnya in the North Caucasus, and diverse central Asian countries. He also examines conditions in the Russian Far East, including the status of the Sino-Russian border, Russian relations with China, and Russo-Japanese relations concerning the Southern Kuril islands, and also examines the tension between Westernization and preserving traditional cultural identity in debates over Russian foreign policy.

Possible geopolitical options for Russia to follow include pursuing a revisionist policy in which Russia will have to restore its historic empire to survive; a multipolar policy reminiscent of 18th-century European balance of power politics in which Russia pursues ad hoc coalitions with the United States, Europe, and China as its interests dictate; national disintegration due to internal regional pressures and external threat from China; or enhancing national prosperity through economic development and information technology advances.[9]

Turk, Richard W. *The Ambiguous Relationship: Theodore Roosevelt and Alfred Thayer Mahan*. Contributions in Military Studies. New York: Greenwood Press, 1987. ISBN: 0-313-25644-6.

Study examining the relationship between Theodore Roosevelt (1858–1919) and naval strategist Alfred Thayer Mahan (1840–1914) while also seeking to determine the extent to which each of these individuals influenced the other's geopolitical thought. Topics examined by Turk include how each of these individuals viewed the emergence of the U.S. Navy at the beginning of the 20th century, how each felt the United States should exert its increasing military power, policies both men thought the United States should follow in global arenas as diverse as the Caribbean and the Asia-Pacific, their attitudes toward England, and how they viewed Germany and Japan's rising power in the early decades of the 20th century. Correspondence between Mahan and Roosevelt is also included to further illuminate their relationship and provide insights into their perspectives on current geopolitical and military issues.

Woolley, Peter J. *Geography and Japan's Strategic Choices: From Seclusion to Internationalization*. Washington, DC: Potomac Books, 2005. ISBN: 1-5748-8667-3.

This work emphasizes the critical importance of geography in determining any country's political and strategic behavior. Woolley stresses Japan's location and topography in comparison with other countries and examines how Japanese leaders throughout its history interpreted and acted on Japan's geographic strengths and weaknesses. His work chronologically several distinct historical eras, including the Tokugawa era (1603–1868), Japan's opening to the West, the Meiji Restoration, Japan's rise and decline through World War II, postwar occupation, the cold war, and the post cold war era, which is seeing Japan address international security issues as varied as international terrorism, a rising China, and the threat of a nuclear North Korea.

Notes

1. Jakub R. Grygiel, *Great Powers and Geopolitical Change* (Baltimore: Johns Hopkins University Press, 2006): 1–4.
2. Simon Dalby, "Critical Geopolitics," in *Dictionary of Geopolitics*, ed. John O'Loughlin (Westport, CT: Greenwood Press, 1994): 56–58.
3. Zbigniew Brzezinski, *The Grand Chessboard: American Primacy and Its Geostrategic Imperatives* (New York: Basic Books, 1997): xii–xiv.
4. Ibid., 31.
5. Jack Child, *Geopolitics and Conflict in South America: Quarrels among Neighbors* (New York: Praeger Press, 1985).
6. Philip Kelly, *Checkerboards and Shatterbelts: The Geopolitics of South America* (Austin: University of Texas Press, 1997): 1–2.
7. Bobo Lo, *Axis of Convenience: Moscow, Beijing, and the New Geopolitics* (Washington, DC: Brookings Institution Press, 2008).
8. Dmitrii Trenin, *The End of Eurasia: Russia on the Border between Geopolitics and Globalization* (Washington, DC: Carnegie Endowment for International Peace, 2002): 13.
9. Ibid., 313–18.

CHAPTER 6

Indexes and Scholarly Journals

Articles published in scholarly journals are an essential component for conducting research on geopolitics or any other topic. Performing effective scholarly research on any subject involves thoroughly searching for individual journal article citations on this subject, and this is best accomplished by searching print indexes or electronic databases rather than perusing bookshelves for articles. Some indexes are freely available on the Internet, and their URLs will be listed here. Other indexes are produced by commercial companies and may be available in selected academic and public libraries that pay to subscribe to these services. An example of a freely available periodical index is Air University Library Index to Military Periodicals, produced by Air University Library at Maxwell Air Force Base in Alabama. This long-standing international politics and military science literature index covers 1988 to the present and is freely accessible at http://purl.access.gpo.gov/GPO/LPS3260.

This index features detailed citations and links to subject headings for additional research. On retrieving citations from this and other databases, users will need to check their local libraries to see if they have paper or electronic copies of the articles cited in these resources. Some of the databases listed here may provide links to the Online Public Access Catalogs of host libraries to determine if these libraries provide their users with direct access to articles from these journals.

America: History and Life, produced by ABC-CLIO, indexes articles, book chapters, books, and dissertations on American and Canadian history from 1450 to the present. It will be available in many academic libraries, and general information on it is available at http://www.abc-clio.com/.

Columbia International Affairs Online (CIAO) is produced at Columbia University and provides access to international affairs research from 1991 to present. Its contents will include materials from university research institutes, nongovernment organizations, foundation-funded research projects, conference proceedings, course packs, books, journals, and policy briefings. Information on CIAO can be found at http://www.ciaonet.org/.

Ebsco's Military and Government Collections is another resource produced by a prominent libraries serial vendor. It provides full-text access to articles from nearly 300 journals and periodicals, along with numerous pamphlet resources with retrospective coverage dating back to the mid-1980s. General information on this is accessible at http://www.ebsco.com/.

Google Scholar is a freely available search engine for finding scholarly literature on many subjects including excerpts from books and journal articles. Access to the full text of some of these resources may be provided if you are a faculty, staff member, or student at a college or university whose library subscribes to that journal. Google Scholar also tracks how many times individual works have been cited and provides information on these citations and links to them in some cases. This resource has received varying assessments of its quality and desirability and impact on academic research.[1] It can be accessed at http://scholar.google.com/.

Historical Abstracts is another ABC-CLIO database indexing articles, book chapters, books, and dissertations on national and international history outside North America from 1450 to the present. It is available in many academic libraries, and general information on it is accessible at http://www.abc-clio.com/.

Public Affairs Information Service (PAIS) is produced by Cambridge Scientific Abstracts in Bethesda, Maryland. Its focus is providing access to scholarly public policy literature from journal articles, books, book chapters, and selected U.S. government documents from over 120 countries. Many academic libraries subscribe to its print or online services and, general information on it can be found at http://www.csa.com/factsheets/pais-set-c.php.

Staff College Automated Periodicals Index (SCAMPI) is produced collaboratively by the Joint Forces Staff College Library, National Defense University Library, and Defense Technical Information Center. It provides bibliographic access to popular and scholarly military publications from 1985 to the present. SCAMPI is freely accessible at http://www.dtic.mil/dtic/scampi/.

Worldwide Political Science Abstracts (WPSA) is published by Cambridge Scientific Abstracts. It indexes articles from approximately 1,700 political science journals from 1975 to the present, with 67 percent of these being published outside the United States, in addition to some retrospective coverage from 1960 to 1974. General information on this database is accessible at http://www.csa.com/factsheets/polsci-set-c.php.

Scholarly Journals

Articles on geopolitics, political geography, international relations, national and international security, political theory, and similar topics can be found in an interdisciplinary variety of scholarly journals from disciplines such as geography, history, military science, and political science. These journals publish articles that have gone through the peer review process in which the journal's editorial board, consisting of experts and scholars in the field, review the proposed articles to determine their suitability for publication. Scholarly journals are distributed in print and electronic formats and are available in varying degrees at U.S. and foreign academic libraries. Prevailing practices in academic libraries, however, are emphasizing electronic access and holdings as the preferred method for users to access these resources and for libraries to retain them.[2]

A small number of these journals published by government agencies and nonprofit organizations may be freely available on the Internet. Most of these journals, however, are published by commercial for-profit publishers and are not freely available in print or electronic format. College or university libraries that have print and electronic access to these journals have paid for this access by negotiating contractual agreements with these periodicals publishers. Such agreements may restrict electronic access to these journals to users who are part of a university community such as faculty and students with university identification numbers. These agreements may stipulate that only computers in the university library or university's IP range may be used to access electronic journal contents.

A helpful directory of scholarly periodicals is *Ulrich's Periodicals Directory*. This annual multivolume set, published by R.R. Bowker, is a key source in many academic libraries for locating periodical information, and online access to it may be provided in these libraries.

Two subscription-based projects that provide subscribing academic libraries with numerous electronic journals on various subjects are JSTOR and ExLibris MetaLib. JSTOR provides access to recent and historical issues of scholarly journals in several social science disciplines, and information on it is available at http://www.jstor.org/.[3] ExLibris MetaLib is an international information service provider delivering access to electronic journal articles in multiple subjects at many academic and research institutions. General information on this service is accessible at http://www.exlibrisgroup.com/catagory/MetaLibFAQ.

An increasingly important aspect of scholarly journal publishing is the growth of the open access movement. This initiative seeks to provide a counterpoint to the sometimes restrictive access policies commercial publishers place on their works. Open access movement proponents advocate that scholars publish their work in journals that do not have restrictive public access policies or do not charge high and continually rising international subscription prices for their journals, which have become increasingly burdensome for the academic library community.[4] Information on this increasingly important scholarly publishing movement can be found at http://www.publicknowledge.org/issues/openaccess/, and an international and multidisciplinary directory of open access journals is freely available at http://www.doaj.org/.

The following sections present a representative sampling of important scholarly journals that produce articles on geopolitics. The information provided includes the journal's name, publisher, paper and electronic International Standard Serial Numbers (ISSNs), publication frequency and history, and general information about accessibility, including a URL if it is freely available to the general public.

African Security Review

African Security Review is published by the Institute for Security Studies in Pretoria and Cape Town, South Africa, with additional facilities in Nairobi, Kenya, and Addis Ababa, Ethiopia. It is published quarterly, its ISSN is 1024-6029, and it has been published since 1992. General information about this journal and access to its contents are accessible through the ISS Web site (http://www.iss.co.za/). Sample geopolitical articles include "China's Ventures in Africa" (2008), "Climate Change: A New Threat to Stability in West Africa? Evidence from Ghana and Burkina Faso" (2008), "Sea Piracy and Maritime Security in the Horn of Africa: The Somali Coast and Gulf of Aden in Perspective" (2009), and "Bad Order at Sea: From the Gulf of Aden to the Gulf of Guinea" (2009).

Air and Space Power Journal

Air and Space Power Journal or *Aerospace Power Journal* is the U.S. Air Force's preeminent military journal, and it is produced quarterly by Air University at Maxwell Air Force Base, Alabama. Its ISSNs are 0897-0823 and 1555-385X, and it has been published since 1947. Current and many historical issues are accessible at http://purl.access.gpo.gov/GPO/LPS25494. Sample articles on geopolitics as applied to aerospace forces include "Back to the Future: Thoughts on a Bipolar World Redux" (2002), "Offensive Airpower with Chinese Characteristics" (2007), "Deterrence and Space-Based Missile Defense" (2009), and "Guarding the High Ocean: Towards a New National-Security Space Strategy through an Analysis of US Maritime Strategy" (2009).

Alternatives: Turkish Journal of International Relations

Alternatives: Turkish Journal of International Relations is published quarterly by Fatih University in Istanbul, Turkey. It has been published since 2002, its ISSN is 1303-5525, and its contents are freely available at http://www.alternativesjournal.net/.

Geopolitics-oriented articles include "The Russian, Caucasian, and Central Asian Aspects of Turkish Foreign Policy" (2003), "Competition over Caspian Oil Routes: Oilers and Gamers Perspective" (2006), "Transboundary Water Cooperation in Africa: The Case of the Nile Basin Initiative (NBI)" (2008), and "Tectonic Shifts and Systemic Faultlines: A Global Perspective to Understand the 2008–2009 World Economic Crisis" (2009).

AntePodium: Online Journal of World Affairs

AntePodium: Online Journal of World Affairs is an open access ejournal published at Victoria University of New Zealand. It has been published irregularly since 1995, its ISSN is 1173-5716, and it can be accessed at http://www.victoria.ac.nz/atp/. Relevant articles include "Nationality and Sovereignty in the New World Order" (1996), "The Republic of Lebanon after Taif: An Analysis of Four Scenarios on the Emergence of a New Lebanon" (2001), "The Enigmatic Figure of the Non-Western Thinker in International Relations" (2008), and "China's African Policy and Its Soft Power" (2009).

Annals of the Association of American Geographers

Annals of the Association of American Geographers is published five times a year by Routledge, has been published since 1911, and is one of the world's premier geographic journals. Its ISSNs are 0004-5608 and 1467-8306, and general information about it can be found at http://www.tandf.co.uk/journals/titles/00045608.asp. Examples of geopolitical articles in this journal include "Offshore Threats: Liquefied Natural Gas, Terrorism, and Environmental Debate in Connecticut" (2008), "Globalization and New Geographies of Conservation" (2008), "Spaces of Water Governance: The Case of Israel and Its Neighbors" (2009), and "Oil Prices, Scarcity, and Geographies of War" (2009).

Asian Affairs: An American Review

Asian Affairs: An American Review focuses on U.S. policies toward Asia and Asian countries, domestic politics, economics, and international relations. It has been published quarterly since 1973 by Heldref Publications, its ISSNs are 0092-7678 and 1940-1590, and general information about it can be found at http://www.heldref.org/pubs/aa/about.html. Examples of recent geopolitical articles in this journal include "Uyghur Ethnic Separatism in Xinjiang China" (2008), "How to Approach the Elephant: Chinese Perceptions of India in the Twenty-first Century" (2008), "Fueling Crisis or Cooperation? The Geopolitics of Energy Security in Northeast Asia" (2009), and "Beijing's New Approach and the Rapprochement in the Taiwan Strait" (2009).

Baltic Security and Defence Review

Baltic Security and Defence Review is published annually by the Baltic Defence College in Tartu, Estonia. It has been published since 1999, its print and electronic ISSNs are 1736-3772 and 1776-3780, and its contents are accessible at http://www.bdcol.ee/?id=63. Geopolitics-related articles it has published include "Russian Military Reform: An Overview" (2001), "NATO's Role in the Post-modern European Security Environment: Cooperative Security and the Experience of the Baltic Sea Region" (2006), "Energy Security: Applying a Portfolio Approach" (2008), and "Strategy and Geopolitics of Sea Power throughout History" (2009).

Cambridge Review of International Affairs

Cambridge Review of International Affairs is published quarterly by Routledge. It has been published since 1986, its ISSNs are 0955-7571 and 1474-449X, and general information about this publication can be found at http://www.tandf.co.uk/journals/titles/09557571.asp. Examples of recently published articles include "Disputing the Geopolitics of the States System and Global Capitalism" (2007), "Balancing against Threats or Bandwagoning with Power: Europe and the Transatlantic Relationship after the Cold War" (2008), "The Globalization of Intelligence since 9/11: Frameworks and Operational Parameters" (2008), and "The ASEAN Regional Forum: From Dialogue to Practical Security Cooperation" (2009).

Comparative Politics

Comparative Politics is published quarterly by the City University of New York's Political Science Program. It has been published since 1968, its ISSNs are 0010-4159 and 2151-6227, and general information on it can be found at http://web.gc.cuny.edu/jcp/. Examples of recent *Comparative Politics* articles include "Following the Money: Muslim versus Muslim in Bosnia's Civil War" (2008), "Politics, Poverty, and Policies in Latin America" (2009), "Community Policing and Latin America's Citizen Security Crisis" (2009), and "What Explains Corruption Perceptions: The Dark Side of Political Competition in Russia's Regions" (2010).

Comparative Strategy

Comparative Strategy is published five times annually by Taylor and Francis. It has been published since 1978, its ISSNs are 0149-5933 and 1521-0448, and general information on it can be found at http://www.tandf.co.uk/journals/titles/01495933.asp. Recently published articles on geopolitics appearing here include "Nuclear Weapons and Iranian Strategic Culture" (2008), "An End to U.S. Hegemony? The Strategic Implications of China's Growing Presence in Latin America" (2009), "Creating Instability in Dangerous Global Regions: North Korean Proliferation and Support to Terrorism in the Middle East and South Asia" (2009), and "Strongman, Constable, or Free-Rider? India's 'Monroe Doctrine' and Indian Naval Strategy" (2009).

Diplomacy and Statecraft

Diplomacy and Statecraft is published quarterly by Routledge. It has been published since 1990, its ISSNs are 0959-2296 and 1557-301X, and general information about its contents can be found at http://www.tandf.co.uk/journals/titles/09592296.asp. Relevant recent articles in this journal, which cover historical and international relations aspects of geopolitics, include "National Security and Imperial Defence: British Grand Strategy and Appeasement, 1930–1939" (2008), "Theodore Roosevelt: Imperialist or Global Strategist in the New Expansionist Age?" (2008), "The British Are 'Taking to the Boat': Australian Attempts to Forestall Britain's Military Disengagement from Southeast Asia, 1965–1966" (2009), and "Sharing Water, Preventing War—Hydrodiplomacy in South Asia" (2009).

Eurasian Geography and Economics

Eurasian Geography and Economics is published bimonthly by Bellwether Publishing, has been published since 1960, its ISSN is 1538-7216, and general information about it can be found at http://bellweather.metapress.com/content/120747/. The journal's focus is economic and geographic issues facing China and the former Soviet Union. Examples of recent articles include "The Influence of High Oil Prices on the Russian Economy: A Comparison with Saudi Arabia" (2009), "Eurasian Natural Gas Pipelines: The Political Economy of Network Interdependence" (2009), "Understanding Land Development Problems in Globalizing China" (2010), and "Placing Pandemics: Geographical Dimensions of Vulnerability and Spread" (2010).

Europe-Asia Studies

Europe-Asia Studies is published 10 times annually by Routledge, and it focuses on historical and current political, social, and economic affairs of former

Communist bloc countries in the Soviet Union, Eastern Europe, and Asia. It has been published since 1949, its ISSNs are 0966-8136 and 1465-3427, and general information about its contents can be found at http://www.tandf.co.uk/journals/titles/09668136.asp. Examples of recently published articles focusing on geopolitical aspects of these regions include "Illegal Economic and Transit Migration in the Czech Republic: A Study of Individual Migrants Behavior" (2009), "Oil and Gas: A Blessing for the Few: Hydrocarbons and Inequality within Regions in Russia" (2009), "The Thawing of a Frozen Conflict: The Internal Security Dilemma and the 2004 Prelude to the Russo-Georgian War" (2010), and " A Comparative Study of Resource Nationalism in Russia and Kazakhstan 2004–2008" (2010).

European Journal of International Relations

European Journal of International Relations is published quarterly by Sage Publications. It has been published since 1995, its ISSNs are 1354-0661 and 1460-3713, and general information on its contents can be found at http://ejt.sagepub.com/. Examples of recently published articles covering geopolitics include "Remapping the Boundaries of 'State' and 'National Identity': Incorporating Diasporas into IR Theorizing" (2007), "Institutional Balancing and International Relations Theory: Economic Interdependence and Balance of Power Strategies in Southeast Asia" (2008), "The Geography of Fear: Regional Ethnic Diversity, the Security Dilemma, and Ethnic War" (2009), and "Identity, Foreign Policy, and the 'Other': Japan's 'Russia'" (2009).

European Security

European Security is published quarterly by Taylor and Francis. It has been published since 1992, and its paper and electronic ISSNs are 0966-2839 and 1746-1545. General information is available at http://www.tandf.co.uk/journals/titles/09662839.asp. Recently published articles on geopolitics include "Constructing the Mediterranean in the Face of New Threats: Are the EU's Words Really New?" (2008), "A Drop in the Ocean: Bulgaria's NATO Membership and Black Sea Geopolitics" (2008), "Energy and Security in Long-Term Defence Planning: Scenario Analysis for the Swedish Armed Forces" (2009), and "The Russian Case for Military Intervention in Georgia: International Law, Norms and Political Calculation" (2009).

Foreign Affairs

Foreign Affairs is one of the United States' and world's preeminent foreign policy journals. It is published bimonthly by the Council on Foreign Relations and has been published under different names since 1910. Its ISSNs are 0015-7120 and 1665-1707, and general information and excerpts from some recent articles can be found at http://www.foreignaffairs.org/. Examples of recently published *Foreign Affairs* articles focusing on geopolitical aspects of international affairs include "America's Edge: Power in the Networked Century" (2008), "The Great Crash, 2008: A Geopolitical Setback for the West" (2009), "The Key to Kiev" (2009), and "In The Quicksands of Somalia" (2009).

Foreign Policy

Foreign Policy is published bimonthly by the Carnegie Endowment for International Peace. It has been published since 1971, its ISSNs are 0015-7228 and 1945-2276, and general information on it and some online content can be found at http://www.foreignpolicy.com/. Sample articles covering geopolitical aspects of international affairs include "Empires with Expiration Dates" (2006), "[Oil] It's Still the One" (2009), "The Revenge of Geography" (2009), and "The Most Dangerous Place in the World" (2009).

Futures: The Journal of Policy, Planning, and Futures Studies

Futures: The Journal of Policy, Planning, and Futures Studies is published by Pergamon Press. It has been published since 1968, its ISSNs are 0016-3287 and 1873-6378, and general information on this title can be found at http://www.elsevier.com/wps/find/journaldescription.cws_home/30422/description#. Articles in this journal cover future studies and projections emphasizing business, defense planning, and international relations. Representative articles include "Future of Turkey-EU Relations: A Civilisational Discourse" (2005), "Scenarios to Challenge Strategic Paradigms: Lessons from 2025" (2006), "Renewable Scenarios for Major Oil-Producing Nations: The Case of Saudi Arabia" (2009), and "The Emergence of a New International Competitor in the Commercial Aircraft Sector: The China Syndrome" (2009).

Geographical Journal

Geographical Journal is published quarterly by Wiley-Blackwell for the Royal Geographical Society. It has been published since 1857, its ISSNs are 0016-7398 and 1475-4959, and general information about it can be found at http://www.wiley.com/bw/journal.asp?ref=0016-7398. Considered one of the world's premier scholarly geographic journals, its articles cover a wide variety of geography-oriented topics, including political geography and geopolitics. Sample articles include "Halford Mackinder and the 'Geographical Pivot of History': A Centennial Retrospective" (2004), "Laos and the Making of a

'Relational' Resource Frontier" (2009), "Climate Change–Induced Migration in the Pacific Region: Sudden Crisis and Long-Term Developments" (2009), and "Natural and Human Dimensions of Environmental Change in the Proximal Reaches of Botswana's Okavango Delta" (2010).

Geopolitics

Geopolitics is the premier scholarly journal examining geopolitical aspects of international relations. It has been published quarterly by Routledge since 1996, its ISSNs are 1465-0045 and 1557-3028, and general information about this journal can be found at http://www.tandf.co.uk/journals/titles/14650045.asp. Recently published articles include "Space and the Atom: On the Popular Geopolitics of Cold War Rocketry" (2008), "The Struggle for the Heartland: Hybrid Geopolitics in the Transcaspian" (2009), "The Geopolitics of Energy Security and the Response to Its Challenges by India and Germany" (2009), and "Geopolitics, Eurasianism, and Russian Foreign Policy under Putin" (2009).

Geopolitics, History, and International Relations

Geopolitics, History, and International Relations is a new journal published by Addleton Academic Publishers that began in 2009. It is published annually, its ISSN is 1948-9145, and general information on it can be found at http://www.addletonacademicpublishers.com/journals/general/info/journals.html. Sample inaugural articles from this journal include "Geopolitics, Power, and Governmentality" (2009), "Globalization, Political Geography, and Deterritorialization" (2009), "The Geopolitics of Europe's Borders" (2009), and "The Geopolitics of Church" (2009).

Global Economic Review

Global Economic Review is published quarterly by Routledge, it has been published since 1973, and its articles emphasize global issues including economic and political developments impacting East Asia. Its ISSNs are 1226-508X and 1744-3873, and general information about it can be found at http://www.tandf.co.uk/journals/titles/1226508x.asp. Sample articles include "The Geopolitics of Caspian Oil: Rivalries of the United States, Russia, and Turkey in the South Caucasus" (2008), "China and India in World Trade: Are the Asia Giants a Threat to Malaysia" (2008), "Location Strategies of Foreign Investors in China: Evidence from Japanese Manufacturing Multinationals" (2009), and "Linkages among US Interest Rates and East Asian Purchases of US Treasury Securities" (2009).

International Affairs

International Affairs is published by Wiley for the Royal Institute of International Affairs in London. It has been published since 1922, is published bimonthly, and its ISSNs are 0020-5850 and 1468-2346. General information about this journal can be found at http://www.wiley.com/bw/journal.asp?ref=0020-5850. Sample articles include "AIDS and Global Security" (2004), "Japan's Response to China's Rise: Regional Engagement, Global Containment, Dangers of Collision" (2009), "The Geopolitics of the Arctic Melt" (2009), and "From Constants to Variables: How Environmental Change Alters the Geopolitical and Geo-Economic Equation" (2009).

International Affairs: A Russian Journal of World Politics, Diplomacy, and International Relations

International Affairs: A Russian Journal of World Politics, Diplomacy, and International Relations is produced by Russia's Foreign Ministry and published in North America by East View Information Services. It is published bimonthly, it has been published since 1955, its ISSNs are 0130-9641 and 0130-9625, and general information on it can be found at http://www.eastviewpress.com/Journals/InternationalAffairs.aspx. Recent articles dealing with geopolitics in this journal include "The Baltics and Geopolitics" (2007), "Russia's Geopolitical Horizons" (2007), "Competing for Africa's Natural Resources" (2009), and "CSTO Upgrades Its Collective Security System" (2009).

International Security

International Security is produced at the Belfer Center for Science and International Affairs at Harvard University's John F. Kennedy School of Government. It has been published quarterly by Massachusetts Institute of Technology Press since 1976, and its paper and electronic ISSNs are 0162-2889 and 1531-4804. General information on *International Security* can be found through the Belfer Center Web site (http://belfercenter.ksg.harvard.edu/) and the publisher's Web site (http://mitpressjournals.org/loi/isec). Pertinent *International Security* articles on geopolitics include "Ten Years of Instability in a Nuclear South Asia" (2008), "How Smart and Tough Are Democracies: Reassessing Theories of Democratic Victory in War" (2009), "Bad Debts: Assessing China's Influence in Great Power Politics" (2009), and "Understanding Support for Islamist Militancy in Pakistan" (2010).

Journal of Strategic Studies

Journal of Strategic Studies is published six times per year by Frank Cass. It has been published since 1988, and its ISSNs are 0140-2390 and 1743-937X.

General information about its contents is available at http://www.tandf.co.uk/journals/titles/01402390.asp. Examples of geopolitical articles in this journal include "'Calmly Critical': Evolving Russian Views of US Hegemony" (2006), "China's Naval Ambitions in the Indian Ocean" (2008), "China's Theater and Strategic Missile Force Modernization and Its Implications for the United States" (2009), and "Who Really Dictates What an Existential Threat Is? The Israeli Experience" (2009).

Mediterranean Quarterly: A Journal of Global Issues

Mediterranean Quarterly: A Journal of Global Issues is published quarterly by Duke University Press. It has been published since 1989, its ISSNs are 1047-4552 and 1527-1935, and general information on it can be found at http://mq.dukejournals.org/.

Examples of articles focusing on this region's geopolitical and strategic issues include "Pax Americana or Multilateralism? Reflecting on the United States' Grand Strategic Vision of Hegemony in the Wake of the 11 September Attacks" (2007), "Disarming Hezbollah" (2008), "Defining Strategic Priorities: Ballistic Missile Defense, Iran, and Relations with Major Powers" (2009), and "Life after Oil: Economic Alternatives for the Gulf Arab States" (2009).

Military Thought

Military Thought is a Russian military theory and strategy journal produced by the Russian Federation's Ministry of Defense. It is published quarterly by East View Information Services and has been published since 1918. Its ISSN is 0236-2058, and general information on it is accessible at http://www.eastview.com/evpj/evjournals_new.asp?editionid=555. Sample articles on geopolitical issues include "China's Military-Economics Strategy and Its Armed Forces Restructuring" (2007), "Central Asian Vector of the Russian Federation's Military Policy" (2009), "Conditions for Armed Conflicts Arising on RF Territory in the 21st Century and Their Likely Characteristics in a Deteriorating Military-Political Situation" (2009), and "International Military Cooperation of Central Asian States" (2009).

The National Interest

The National Interest is published by the Nixon Center, is published bimonthly, and has been published since 1985. Its ISSNs are 0884-9382 and 1938-1573, and general information and access to some content is available at http://www.nationalinterest.org/. An inventory of pertinent articles includes "Putin's Third Way" (2009), "Bridge on the Dnieper" (2009), "Death Cometh for the Greenback" (2009), and "Spoils of Babylon" (2010).

Naval War College Review

Naval War College Review is published quarterly by the U.S. Naval War College Press. It has been published since 1948, its ISSN is 0028-1484, and access to articles from 2001 to the present and an index of articles from 1948 to the present is accessible at http://www.usnwc.edu/Publications/Naval-War-College-Review.aspx. Examples of geopolitics-oriented articles from this key journal of navy strategic and operational thinking include "The New Security Drama in East Asia: The Responses of U.S. Allies and Security Partners to China's Rise" (2009), "Piracy and Armed Robbery in the Malacca Strait: A Problem Solved?" (2009), "Great Britain Gambles with the Royal Navy" (2010), and "Australia's 2009 Defense White Paper: A Maritime Focus for Uncertain Times" (2010).

Orbis: A Journal of World Affairs

Orbis: A Journal of World Affairs is produced by the Foreign Policy Research Institute and is published by Elsevier Science. It is published quarterly, it has been published since 1957, and its ISSNs are 0030-4387 and 1873-5282. General information about its contents can be found at http://www.elsevier.com/wps/find/journaldescription.cws_home/620205/description#description.

Recent *Orbis* articles on geopolitics include "China and Global Energy Markets" (2007), "The Bush Doctrine: The Foreign Policy of Republican Empire" (2009), "The 'Mega-Eights': Urban Leviathans and International Instability" (2009), and "History Rhymes: The German Precedent for Chinese Seapower" (2010).

Parameters: U.S. Army War College Quarterly

Parameters: U.S. Army War College Quarterly is published by the U.S. Army War College and serves as the key U.S. Army professional journal. It has been published since 1971, its ISSN is 0031-1723, and access to articles from 1971 to the present are available at http://www.carlisle.army.mil/usawc/parameters/. Examples of this journal's rich corpus of geopolitical analysis include "The Future of Canada's Role in Hemispheric Defense" (2006), "The Strategic Importance of Central Asia: An American View" (2008), "China's New Security Strategy for Africa" (2009), and "Unlocking Russian Interests on the Korean Peninsula" (2009).

Political Geography

Political Geography is published eight times a year by Pergamon Press and has been published since 1982. Its ISSNs are 0962-6298 and 1873-5096, and general information about it can be found at http://www.elsevier.com/wps/find/journaldescription.cws_home/30465/description#description. This journal is a major journal of political geography and research on spatial dimensions of politics. Recently published articles include "Geographies of State Failure and Sophistication in Maritime Piracy Hijackings" (2009), "Border Thinking: Rossport, Shell and the Political Geographies of a Gas Pipeline" (2009), "Of Plagues, Planes, and Politics: Controlling the Global Spread of Infectious Diseases by Air" (2009), and "The Making and Breaking of Dubai: The End of a City-State?" (2010).

The Professional Geographer

The Professional Geographer is published quarterly by Routledge and has been published since 1949. Its ISSNs are 0033-0124 and 1467-9272, and general information about it can be found at http://www.tandf.co.uk/journals/titles/00330124.asp. Pertinent geopolitics articles it has published, which often emphasize geographic aspects of domestic aspects in individual countries, include "An Analysis of the Relationship between Residents' Proximity to Water and Attitudes about Resource Protection" (2007), "Land, Labor, and Rural Development: Analyzing Participation in India's Village Dairy Cooperatives" (2008), "Rethinking Geographies of Assimilation" (2009), and "The Suburbanization of Water Scarcity in the Barcelona Metropolitan Region: Sociodemographic and Urban Changes Influencing Domestic Water Consumption" (2010).

Review of African Political Economy

Review of African Political Economy is published quarterly by Routledge and has been published since 1973. Its ISSNs are 0305-6244 and 1740-1720, and general information about it can be found at http://www.tandf.co.uk/journals/titles/03056244.asp. Sample articles include "Enter the Dragon: Chinese Oil Companies and Resistance in the Niger Delta" (2008), "The Role of Private Military Companies in US-Africa Policy" (2008), "The Ethiopia-Eritrea Conflict and the Search for Peace in the Horn of Africa" (2009), and "Violence and National Development in Nigeria: The Political Economy of Youth Restiveness in the Niger Delta" (2009).

Review of International Political Economy

Review of International Political Economy is published by five times per year by Routledge and has been published since 1994. Its ISSNs are 0969-2290 and 1466-4526, and general information on it can be found at http://www.

tandf.co.uk/journals/titles/09692290.asp. Examples of recently published articles covering geopolitics include "HIV/AIDS, Security and the Geopolitics of US-Nigerian Relations" (2007), "The Global Political Economy of Social Crisis: Towards a Critique of the 'Failed State' Ideology" (2008), "A Rivalry in the Making? The Euro and International Monetary Power" (2008), and "Contested Terrains: Politics of Scale, the National State and Struggles for the Control over Nature" (2009).

Security Dialogue

Security Dialogue is published bimonthly by Sage Publications. It has been published since 1970, its ISSNs are 0967-0106 and 1460-3640, and general information on it can be found at http://sdi.sagepub.com/. Recent articles in this journal examining geopolitical issues include "The Responsibility to Protect and the Conflict in Darfur: The Big Let-Down" (2009), "Consensus and Governance in Mercosur: The Evolution of the South American Security Agenda" (2009), "Gangs, Urban Violence, and Security Interventions in Central America" (2009), and "The Security and Development Nexus in Cape Town: War on Gangs, Counterinsurgency and Citizenship" (2010).

Studies in Conflict and Terrorism

Studies in Conflict and Terrorism is published 12 times per year by Routledge. It has been published since 1992, its ISSNs are 1057-610X and 1521-0731, and general information about it can be found at http://www.tandf.co.uk/journals/titles/1057610X.html. Relevant articles analyzing the linkages between geopolitics, conflicts, and terrorism include "Identifying Urban Flashpoints: A Delphi-Derived Model for Scoring Cities' Vulnerability to Large-Scale Unrest" (2008), "Making Money in the Mayhem: Funding Taliban Insurrection in the Tribal Areas of Pakistan" (2009), "The al-Houthi Insurgency in the North of Yemen: An Analysis of the Shabab al Moumineen" (2009), and "Afghanistan's Insurgency and the Viability of a Political Settlement" (2010).

Turkish Studies

Turkish Studies is published quarterly by Routledge. It has been published since 1999, its ISSNs are 1468-3849 and 1743-9663, and general information on this journal can be found at http://www.tandf.co.uk/journals/titles/14633849.asp. Its primary area of coverage is Turkey's international relations with surrounding countries, and pertinent geopolitics articles include "Middle Easternization of Turkey's Foreign Policy: Does Turkey Dissociate from the West" (2008), "Turkey's Role in the Alliance of Civilizations: A New Perspective in Turkish Foreign Policy" (2008), "Turkey as a Trans-Regional Actor" (2009), and "NATO and Turkey in Afghanistan and Central Asia: Possibilities and Blind Spots" (2009).

Notes

1. See Williams H. Walters, "*Google Scholar* Search Performance: Comparative Recall and Precision," *Portal: Libraries and the Academy*, 9 (1)(January 2009): 5–24; Jared L. Howland, Thomas C. Wright, Rebecca A. Boughan, and Brian C. Roberts, "How Scholarly Is Google Scholar: A Comparison to Library Databases," *College and Research Libraries*, 70 (3)(May 2009): 227–34; Charles Martell, "A Citation Analysis of College and Research Libraries Comparing Yahoo, Google, Google Scholar, and ISI Web of Knowledge with Implications for Promotion and Tenure," *College and Research Libraries*, 70 (5)(September 2009): 460–72, for examples of Google Scholar assessments.

2. See Stephen Prothers, Margaret Prabhu, and Shirley Sullivan, "Electronic Journal Delivery in Academic Libraries," *Acquisitions Librarian*, 19 (37/38)(2006): 15–45; Chandra Prabha, "Shifting from Print to Electronic Journals in ARL University Libraries," *Serials Review*, 33 (1)(2007): 4–13; Golnessa Galyani Moghddam, "Archiving Challenges of Scholarly Electronic Journals: How Do Publishers Manage Them?" *Serials Review*, 33 (2)(2007): 81–90; and Christina Torbert, "Purchasing of Electronic Backfiles: Results of a Survey," 57 (4)(2009): 410–22.

3. Roger C. Schonfeld, *JSTOR: A History* (Princeton, NJ: Princeton University Press, 2003).

4. See Charles A. Schwartz, "Reassessing Prospects for the Open Access Movement," *College and Research Libraries*, 66 (6)(2005); Emma McCulloch, "Taking Stock of Open Access: Progress and Issues," *Library Review*, 55 (6)(2006): 337–43; and Kristi L. Palmer, Emily Dill, and Charlene Christie, "When There's a Will There's A Way? Survey of Academic Librarian Attitudes about Open Access," *College and Research Libraries*, 70 (4)(2009): 315–35.

CHAPTER 7

Gray Literature: Dissertations, Theses, Technical Reports, Think Tank Publications, Conference Proceedings, and Blogs and Social Networking Utilities

Gray literature is a significant corpus for conducting scholarly geopolitical research. There are numerous ways of defining gray literature and the role it plays in scholarly literature and research libraries collection development policies.[1] Gray literature generally refers to literature not found in conventional formats, such as books, journal articles, or government or military documents, or through the print indexes or electronic databases normally used to find conventional scholarly research literature. This chapter examines literature on geopolitics as appearing in doctoral dissertations, master's theses, technical reports, think tank publications, conference proceedings, and blogs and other social networking utilities.

Most of this literature will not be freely available on the Internet, although this chapter will emphasize freely available think tank information resources and blogs. Effective access to these resources will best be provided in academic research libraries that have purchased often expensive commercial databases. Besides including overviews of these gray literature resource types, this chapter will also include bibliographic citations and annotations for representative samplings of gray literature in these particular genres.

Dissertations and Theses

Doctoral dissertations and master's theses represent written documentation of their authors' intellectual mastery of various subjects, as well as the successful defense of their findings in oral examinations conducted by their thesis and dissertation supervisors in the process of obtaining their degrees. Writing a thesis or dissertation is an intellectually and physically demanding process that helps enhance the knowledge of intellectual disciplines and branches within these disciplines. This process also requires the thesis or dissertation writer to examine and evaluate an interdisciplinary variety of resources in reaching their conclusions, and such interdisciplinarity is becoming an increasingly common component of academic research. A significant body of literature exists on the role of doctoral dissertations in the academic research process.[2]

Once dissertations have been successfully defended, they are eventually deposited in university libraries. In most cases, dissertations are only likely to be housed in libraries at the institutions where they were written. However, some academic research libraries will make efforts to purchase dissertations and theses to enhance the quality of their collections in selected areas. Providing efficient bibliographic access to dissertations and theses has been problematic for academic libraries, as various studies document. The Internet's growth has helped improve access to these resources as many libraries have developed digital institutional repositories to provide varying levels of access to theses and dissertations with some success.[3]

Scholars doing master's and doctoral work on geopolitics and related topics produce theses and dissertations as part of their degree requirements in disciplines such as geography, history, political science, and other fields. Sometimes theses dissertations may be revised and published as scholarly books. There are many ways to access these resources. University Microfilms International (UMI), located in Ann Arbor, Michigan, is a major repository for theses and dissertations. Most theses and dissertations are only available in nonelectronic formats, but many are available electronically through UMI's ProQuest Dissertations and Theses (PQDT) service. General information about this service is available online (http://www.proquest.com/en-US/catalogs/databases/detail/pqdt.shtml). This is a paid subscription service, and access to it will generally be restricted to academic library users.

There are some additional caveats to consider when trying to locate theses and dissertations. A limited number of universities participate in UMI's theses and dissertations programs, so you cannot be sure that your literature search will retrieve all relevant documents. Only dissertations produced within the last decade or so are likely to be available online through these services. Dissertation authors may choose not to make their dissertations electronically available to PQDT or to make them available for purchase or borrowing through interlibrary loan. It is difficult to obtain theses and dissertations from countries outside the United States, Canada, Australia, and the United Kingdom because documents from these countries are not readily available through international bibliographic service providers such as UMI or the Online Computer Library Consortium.

Useful online repositories to search for and in some cases to help find the full text of theses and dissertations include the Theses Canada Portal, produced and maintained by Library and Archives Canada (http://www.collectionscanada.gc.ca/thesescanada/index-e.html), which provides bibliographic citations for Canadian university theses and dissertations from 1965 to the present; the Australasian Digital Theses Program (http://adt.caul.edu.au/), which is a collaboration of Australian and New Zealand universities that originated in 1998–1999 and that is supported by the Council of Australian University Libraries; the Networked Digital Library of Theses and Dissertations (http://www.ndltd.org/), which consists of various U.S. and European universities whose origins date from 1987–1996 at Virginia Tech University; and Index to Theses (http://www.theses.com/), which indexes and provides limited abstracting and no full-text access to theses produced in Great Britain and Ireland since 1716.

The next section of this chapter covers a partial selection of theses and dissertations on various aspects of geopolitics from numerous universities in recent years. Entries will include requisite bibliographic citations and excerpts from the abstracts or summaries of these documents. Documents which are freely available will include URLs. Readers should check to see if these documents are available electronically through their libraries database subscriptions or interlibrary loan.

These documents were written for various degree programs; represent diverse theoretical, ideological, and methodological research perspectives; and use multifaceted research sources in their bibliographies; their authors may have gone on to careers in academe or the military. Selection of these resources does not mean the author endorses or opposes the conclusions reached in these documents. Their selection and inclusion illustrates the author's contention that theses and dissertations can be valuable sources for conducting substantive research on the geopolitics of the United States and other countries.

Ademola, Adeleke. *Ties without Strings? The Colombo Plan and the Geopolitics of International Aid, 1950–1980*. PhD diss., University of Toronto, 1996. http://www.nlc-bnc.ca/obj/s4/f2/dsk3/ftp04/NQ35427.pdf.

Ademola studies international aid politics with particular emphasis on the Colombo Plan initiated by British Commonwealth countries in 1950 and targeted toward non-Communist Asian countries. The author argues that the Colombo Plan was motivated by cold war geopolitics and was premised on the belief that poverty, underdevelopment, and large populations made these countries vulnerable to Communist subversion. This dissertation scrutinizes the politics and diplomacy of program membership expansion and the security, strategic, and economic motivations of participating countries.

Essig, Andrew M. *Managing Instability: America's Pursuit of an "Expansion" Policy in the Caspian Sea Region*. PhD diss., Pennsylvania State University, 2001.

Essig examines the importance of expanding democracy promotion and free-market economic systems in U.S. post–cold war foreign policy. He views NATO's expansion into Eastern Europe and the formation of Asia-Pacific Economic Co-operation as examples of enlargement in U.S. foreign policy, then uses these initiatives as applied to the Caspian Sea Region. Particular emphasis is placed on U.S. policies toward adjacent countries, including Armenia, Azerbaijan, Georgia, Kazakhstan, and Turkmenistan. The role of ethnic politics in this region is examined, as is regional development of oil and other natural resources, with the author seeing oil has being historically inimical to democracy and economic development in the early stages of national political development.

Gerhardt, Hannes. *The Geopolitics of Distant Suffering: United States Government and Faith-Based Responses to "Genocide" in Sudan*. PhD diss., University of Arizona, 2007.

Treatise examining the role of what the author regards as "bio-normative" responses to geopolitical developments such as the humanitarian crisis in Darfur, Sudan. Gerhardt is particularly interested in the roles played by the Christian Right and other faith-based movements in their efforts to promote the cause of the victims of Sudanese government policies.

Hughes, Rachel Bethany. *Fielding Genocide: Post-1979 Cambodia and the Geopolitics of Memory*. PhD diss., University of Melbourne, 2006. http://repository.unimelb.edu.au/10187/1605.

Thesis examining the relationship between place, memory, and geopolitics, with particular emphasis on Cambodian memorial sites dedicated to the victims of Khmer Rouge genocide in that country between 1975 and 1979. It goes on to examine various domestic political and cultural factors contributing to the development of these sites, the desire of the Cambodian government to promote the tourism value of these sites as a means of enhancing economic development, and that government's desire to use these commemorative practices as a means of being readmitted into the international political system.

Kathman, Jacob. *The Geopolitics of Civil War Intervention*. PhD diss., University of North Carolina at Chapel Hill, 2007.

This dissertation examines why the interests of third-party interveners are decisive determinants of external intervention in civil war. Kathman contends that third parties are more likely to intervene in conflicts that threaten their regional stability interests. Such interventions can increase the likelihood of short-term regional contagion while decreasing such contagion over the long term.

Koo, Min Gyo. *Scramble for the Rocks: The Disputes over the Dikdo/Takeshima, Senkaku/Diaoyu and Paracel and Spratly Islands*. PhD diss., University of California, Berkeley, 2005.

Examination of three prominent island territorial disputes in East Asia involving countries such as China, Japan, the Philippines, and Vietnam. Koo believes that a combination of resource competition, fluid geopolitics, and unstable domestic power dynamics produces the initiation and escalation of these three island disputes. Koo also asserts that the calming influence of economic interdependence continually keeps such sovereignty disputes from escalating into full-scale diplomatic or military crises. The author concludes by contending that the best way to hedge against potentially disruptive behaviors is for the concerned countries to engage more with each other and work to achieve greater economic interdependence.

Pietsch, Samuel. *Australia's Military Intervention in East Timor, 1999*. PhD diss., Australian National University, 2009. http://thesis.anu.edu/public/adt-ANU 20091214.122004/.

Presented from a Marxist perspective, this work argues that Australia's 1999 military intervention in East Timor was motivated by Australia's strategic interests to maintain stability in the Indonesian archipelago. The author maintains that this Australian intervention has helped facilitate public consensus in favor of subsequent Australian military interventions in Pacific Island nations that have enhanced Australian military influence in Southeast Asia and the southwest Pacific.

Powers, Shawn. *The Geopolitics of the News: The Case of the Al Jazeera Network*. PhD diss., University of Southern California, 1991.

Study examining how the Al Jazeera network has enabled the small Persian Gulf country of Qatar to become a regional geopolitical force by becoming a key player in ongoing regional political and religious conflicts. Based on interviews with Al Jazeera Arabic and English news broadcasters and other network officials, this work examines strategies behind the network's growing regional popularity within the context of the geopolitical aspirations of Qatar and surrounding countries.

Pritchard, Denise Diane. *Representing Jerusalem: A Critical Geopolitical Analysis of the Role of Orient House in the Constitution of Palestinean National Identity, 1993–1999*. MA thesis, University of Victoria, 2000. http://www.nlc-bnc.ca/obj/se/f2/dsk1/tape4/PQDD_0008/MQ52806.pdf.

This work presents a critical geopolitics methodological perspective on media portrayals of the Israeli-Palestinian political struggle at the Palestinian Orient House site in Jerusalem between 1993 and 1999. Pritchard examines the role played by Jerusalem in Palestinian nationalist political ideology and believes that boundaries play a particularly important role in determining specific national identities.

Rao, Gautham. *The Creation of the American State: Customhouses, Law, and Commerce in the Age of Revolution*. PhD diss., University of Chicago, 2008.

Rao describes the important geopolitical and economic roles played by customs officials and buildings in constructing the United States' national economic infrastructure during the country's initial decades. Topics examined include the interaction between customs officials and merchant capitalists and the development of revenue generation methods to enhance governmental treasury resources and fund early U.S. expansion activities.

Schulman, Zachary Nathan. *Cryopolitics: The New Geopolitics of the Northwest Passage and Implications for Canadian Sovereignty*. MA thesis, George Washington University, 2009.

Study examining the role of the Northwest Passage in Canadian government sovereignty ideology and how this region is becoming more important geopolitically due to the advent of ice-free summers. There is increasing transportation in that region and interest in the area's large volume of untapped natural resources, including oil and manganese, which is placing an increased burden on the Canadian government's and military's efforts to enforce national sovereignty.

Schulman also stresses the concept of cryopolitics, which is the competition between states to control emerging resources from territory created by melting ice. It emphasizes that the Canadian government has instituted a policy of coopting environmental concerns such as climate change for geopolitical gain and argues that the 1982 United Nations Convention on the Law of the Sea fails to meet the requirements of the Arctic's emerging international geopolitical and legal environment.

Shen, Yi. *The Rise of China and Its Impact on Australia's Relations with the United States*. MA thesis, University of New South Wales, 2009. http://handle.unsw.edu.au/1959.4/41553.

Shen examines Australia's ability to maintain strong long-term relationships with China and the United States. Thesis findings contend that Australia may be able to maintain good relations with both countries in the long term, despite Sino-U.S. strategic rivalry. While the author feels that this strategic competition increases the chance of conflict, it does not mean Sino-U.S. conflict is inevitable. Shen goes on to acknowledge the real risks of such a conflict over Taiwan, but he believes its likelihood of occurring is small due to the United States' continuing regional strategic presence and military superiority. In addition, Australia would probably side with the United States despite China's economic importance to Australia because of the United States' critical importance to Australian economic interests and national security.

Slaibi, Ahmad Ali. *Three Empirical Studies on the Geopolitics of Petroleum Pricing, Revenue Sharing, and Macroeconomic Implications of Petroleum Revenues on Developing Countries*. PhD diss., Cornell University, 2007.

Research analyzing oil price variability within an international geopolitical context and the potential impact of price windfalls on sub-Saharan economic development. Specific sections of this work examine how political and military factors interact with oil exporter and importer economic considerations to define a target price zone, how different sub-Saharan Africa oil production costs and revenue sharing agreements between oil companies and African governments impact oil production, and how government petroleum revenues have impacted economic development in these countries.

Smith, Sara Hollingsworth. *A Geopolitics of Intimacy and Anxiety: Religion, Territory, and Fertility in Jammu and Kashmir*. PhD diss., University of Arizona, 2009.

Feminist perspective on how geopolitical, religious, and territorial perspectives play out in the Leh district of India's disputed Jammu and Kashmir state. Smith examines political conflict between Buddhists and Muslims in this district, with activist Buddhists encouraging Buddhist women to maximize fertility and avoid marrying Muslim men in order to maintain their religion's electoral control in this area.

Wright, Laurie Jennifer. *Security Concerns and the Potential for Stability in the Black Sea Region: Relations among Russia, Ukraine and Turkey*. MA thesis, Royal Military College of Canada, 1997. http://www.nlc-bnc.ca/obj/s4/f2/dsk2/ftp04/mq22786.pdf.

Analysis of security concerns and the potential for regional stability in the Black Sea region, with particular emphasis on relations between the Russian Federation, Turkey, and Ukraine between 1991 and 1996. Military concerns are discussed, as are the Black Sea region's economic potential and the potential role of oil in broader regional economic development. Wright believes that existing concerns can be overcome in the long term and that the potential exists to achieve economic prosperity through regional cooperation.

Xiaodi, Wu. *Back to the Heartland? Transformation of Chinese Geopolitics and the "Renewed" Importance of Central Asia*. PhD diss., Syracuse University, 2005.

Analysis and interpretation of Chinese geopolitics from premodern times to the present, with emphasis on whether there is a Chinese threat to central Asia in the post–cold war era. The author concludes that Confucian geopolitical thinking and behavior, including a China-centric worldview and order, cannot be a basis for understanding and interpreting modern Chinese geopolitics. Instead, the author believes contemporary interactions and the capitalist world system are primarily responsible for determining the general trend and center of gravity for modern Chinese geopolitics and China's central Asian geopolitical objectives.

Technical Reports

Technical reports from government agencies such as the National Technical Information Service (NTIS) and the Defense Technical Information Center's (DTIC) Scientific and Technical Information Network (STINET) can also be useful resources for those conducting research on gray literature concerning geopolitics and other scientific and technological subjects. NTIS is a U.S. Commerce Department agency whose purpose is providing and simplifying access to the multitudinous data files and scientific and technical reports produced by federal agencies and their contractors. Initially established as the Publications Board in 1945 to manage the release of captured German documents and technical reports to U.S. industry, NTIS received its present name in 1970. Since NTIS receives no congressional appropriations, it charges for costs associated with collecting, abstracting, storing, reproducing, and selling its information resources through public sales.[4]

NTIS's Web site (http://www.ntis.gov/) provides information about its products and services and how to search for and locate these items. NTIS materials are useful if you desire to purchase copies of their publications. Many of these resources, however, are available freely elsewhere, with DTIC STINET being a prime example.

DTIC began after World War II due to the need to translate captured German and Japanese military, scientific, and technical information. The secretaries of the navy and air force established it as the Central Documents Office on October 13, 1948, and it became known as DTIC in October 1979. DTIC serves as a specialized provider of domestic and international scientific and technical reports, with particular emphasis on those having military applications for the Defense Department. General information about DTIC and its products and services is available at http://www.dtic.mil/.[5]

STINET (http://www.dtic.mil/dtic/search/tr/) provides the ability to search for and retrieve the abstracts and full text of many technical reports on geopolitics and related topics. Reports that are not available in full text may be ordered through NTIS. Examples of these reports, many produced by students at military war colleges or research institutes like the RAND Corporation or Institute for Defense Analyses, include the following citations with URLs:

Cheek, Paul. *ASEAN's Constructive Engagement Policy toward Myanmar (Burma)*, http://handle.dtic.mil/100.2/ADA483273 (2008).

Katzman, Kenneth. *Iran: U.S. Concerns and Policy Responses*, http://handle.dtic.mil/100.2/ADA472432 (2006).

Larson, Christopher. *China's Energy Security and Its Military Modernization Efforts: How China Plans to Dominate the World*, http://handle.dtic.mil/100.2/ADA468854 (2007).

Moon, Thomas D. *Rising Dragon: Infrastructure Development and Chinese Influence in Vietnam*, http://handle.dtic.mil/100.2/ADA501507 (2009).

Northern, Natalie D. *Energy Sustainability and the Army: The Current Transformation*, http://handle.dtic.mil/100.2/ADA511558 (2009).

Perez, Mario. *The Chavez Challenge: Venezuela, the United States and the Geopolitics of Post–Cold War Inter-American Relations*, http://handle.dtic.mil/100.2/ADA497231 (2009).

Schmaglowski, Dieter. *The Israeli-Palestinean Conflict: A Hopeless Case for U.S. Policy in the Middle East?*, http://handle.dtic.mil/100.2/ADA470891 (2007).

Swanson, Michael. *A New Great Game: A Phase Zero, Regional Engagement Strategy for Central Asia*, http://handle.dtic.mil/100.2/ADA479438 (2007).

Think Tank Publications

Research institutions or think tanks are prodigious producers of geopolitical research and analysis. Experts from these organizations may be hired by government departments or military services to conduct research or design projects, and many of them may be invited to testify before governmental forums in support of or in opposition to particular policy proposals. Funding for these institutions may come from individual, nonprofit, governmental, and commercial sources that represent a variety of ideological or philosophical perspectives.[6]

A wide variety of U.S. and international think tanks produce analyses of geopolitical literature that are freely available in English. The Foreign Policy Research Institute's Think Tank Directory (http://thinktank.fpri.org/) is a good place to start. This section provides brief descriptions of U.S. and international think tanks conducting geopolitical research and analysis that is freely available in English. Entries are arranged alphabetically by country and think tank name and will provide a variety of ideological and methodological approaches to their analyses. Many of these institutions will focus on international political and security trends and developments in their immediate geographic areas, while others will analyze these topics on a global scale.

Argentina

Argentine Council for International Relations

This Buenos Aires–based organization was founded in 1978 to examine various aspects of international relations. Its Web site, http://www.cari.org.ar/, provides links to various Spanish-language publications, including *Soberanía como Condición: los límites de la intervención humanitarian* (2010).

Australia

Australian Strategic Policy Institute

The Australian Strategic Policy Institute (ASPI) is located in Barton, Australian Capital Territory, and was founded in 2000. It is an independent nonpartisan policy institute established by the Australian government to inform and provide the public with fresh ideas on Australian defense and strategic policy matters. ASPI's Web site, http://www.aspi.org.au/, provides a rich variety of information resources and the opportunity to comment on specific publications. Examples of these publications include *Connecting the Dots: Towards an Integrated National Security Strategy* (2009), *A Delicate Issue: Asia's Nuclear Future* (2009), and *Time for a Fresh Approach: Australia and Fiji Relations Post-abrogation* (2010).

Lowy Institute for International Policy

Located in Sydney, the Lowy Institute for International Policy was founded in 2003 and is an independent international policy organization seeking to generate ideas and discussion about international developments and Australia's international role. Its Web site, http://www.lowyinstitute.org/, features a variety of information resources including geopolitically oriented research reports such as *Confronting the Hydra: Big Problems with Small Wars* (2009), *A Focused Force: Australia's Defence Priorities in the Asian Century* (2009), and *The Mekong: River under Threat* (2009).

Brazil

Centro Brasileiro De Relações Internacionais

The Brazilian Center for International Relations (CEBRI) was established in 1998 and is located in Rio de Janeiro. Its institutional purpose is studying and analyzing Brazilian foreign policy and international relations. Its Web site, http://www.cebri.com.br/, provides access to a variety of information resources (primarily in Portuguese), including *The Geopolitics of Energy: The View from Latin America* (2008) and *Brazil's International Agenda Revisited: Perceptions of the Brazilian Foreign Policy Community* (2008).

Canada

Centre for Security and Defence Studies (Carleton University)

This organization is located in Ottawa and is part of Carleton University's Norman Paterson School of International Affairs. Its missions include interdisciplinary graduate and undergraduate teaching on international affairs and defense and security studies and enhancing public discussion of these issues. Its Web site, http://www.carleton.ca/csds/, features publications such as *Maritime Security and the Culture of Prevention* (2004) and *After the Fall: Theory and Practice of Post-intervention Security Conference Report* (2006).

Centre for Military and Strategic Studies (University of Calgary)

The Centre for Military and Strategic Studies (CMSS) was established in 1981 and is committed to developing excellence in security and defense studies. Its Web site, http://cmss.ucalgary.ca/, provides access to publications such as the *Journal of Military and Strategic Studies* (1998 to present).

York Centre for International and Security Studies

Founded in 1967 at York University, YCISS conducts what it considers as critical and theoretically informed research on security within local, national, international, and global contexts and emphasizes the ethical and political dimensions of foreign, defense, and security policies. Its Web site, http://www.yorku.ca/yciss/, contains various publications on geopolitical aspects of international relations, including *Violent Interventions: Selected Proceedings of the Fifteenth Annual Conference of the York Centre for International and Security Studies* (2008) and *Geopolitics, the Revolution in Military Affairs, and the Bush Doctrine* (2008).

China

China Institute of Contemporary International Relations

This organization was founded in 1980 and is located in Beijing. It serves as a comprehensive international studies research institution founded by the Chinese government, and its research encompasses world economic, political, security, and strategic studies. Its Web site, http://www.cicir.ac.cn/, features the text of some English-language publications, including *The United States and the Islamic World* (2005), but most Web site content is in Chinese.

Shanghai Institute for International Studies

This organization was established in Shanghai in 1960. It is a comprehensive research organization whose areas of study include the United States, Japan, Europe, Russia, and the Asia-Pacific region, with additional emphasis on major power relations and the security environment of countries on China's periphery. The institute's Web site, http://www.siis.org.cn/, features English-language descriptions of reports and journals it produces.

Denmark

Danish Institute for International Studies

This organization was established in 2002 and is located in Copenhagen. It is an independent research institution studying international affairs and conducting research on topics affecting Danish foreign and security policy with particular emphasis on development policy. Its Web site, http://www.diis.dk/, provides a variety of English-language materials on geopolitical subjects, including *The Foreign Policy of Iran: Ideology and Pragmatism in the Islamic Republic* (2009) and *The Georgian-Russian Conflict: A Turning Point?* (2010).

Estonia

Estonia Foreign Policy Institute

The Estonia Foreign Policy Institute (EFPI) was established in 2000 and seeks to provide enhanced understanding of international affairs and Estonia's role in a changing world. It is located in Tallinn, and its key areas of research include European Union integration and enlargement, regional security, and Russian developments. Further information about EFPI activities can be found at http://www.evi.ee/, and examples of its publications include the annual *Estonian Foreign Policy Yearbook* (2003 to present), *The North and ESDP: The Baltic States, Denmark, Finland and Sweden* (2008), and *Molotov-Ribbentrop: Challenging Soviet History* (2009).

Finland

Finnish Institute of International Affairs

The Finnish Institute of International Affairs (FIIA) was established in 1961 and is located in Helsinki. Its institutional mission is producing high-quality and topical information on international relations and the European Union. General and specific information on FIIA can be found at http://www.upi-fiia.fi/. Examples of recent geopolitically oriented publications it has produced include *Controversies over Missile Defence in Europe* (2009), *Hitting a Moving Target: Implications of Japan's Missile Defence* (2010), and *The EU and the Global Climate Regime: Getting Back into the Game* (2010).

France

Institut de Relations Internationales et Strategiques

The Institute for International Relations and Strategic Relations (IRIS) was established in 1991, is located in Paris, and conducts research in a variety of international relations and security fields, including sport and geopolitics. Information about institute activity and some English-language resources can be found at http://www.iris-france.org/.

Descriptions are provided for French-language publications, including ordering information, with representative samples including *La Politique Américain au Moyen-Orient* (2006), *L'Eau, Source de Menaces?* (2008), and *Les Guerres Asymétriques* (2009).

Institute Français de Géopolitique

The French Geopolitics Institute was established in 1976 and is located at the University of Paris. It provides a multidisciplinary program for studying domestic and international examples of how geography affects national and international politics and policy making. Information about the institute can be found at http://www.geopolitique.net/. Examples of relevant French-language institute publications include abstracts of *Représentations anciennes et Situations Géopolitiques Contemporarines: Antioche Daris l'maginaire Collectif Syrien* (2008) and *Nouvelle Governance et Réalitiés Géopolitiques: Comment Réformer l'Organisation Territoriale de la République?* (2008).

Germany

German Institute for International Security Affairs
This organization was established in 1962 and is located in Berlin. It is an independent and governmentally funded organization advising the German government and parliament on foreign and national security policy issues. Its research divisions cover topics such as European Union integration and external relations, international security, the Russian Federation and Commonwealth of Independent States, Middle East and Africa, Asia, and global issues. Detailed information on the institute is available at http://www.swp-berlin.org/. Examples of English-language geopolitical information resources it has produced include *Russia-NATO Relations: Stagnation or Revitalization?* (2008), *Russia's Military Capabilities: "Great Power" Ambitions and Reality* (2009), and *Russian Gas, Ukrainian Pipelines, and European Supply Security: Lessons of the 2009 Controversies* (2009).

Institute for Strategic, Political, Security, and Economic Consultancy
This Berlin-based organization was founded in 2002 and conducts information on security-oriented research, with an emphasis on international relations. The institute's Web site is http://www.ispsw.de/, and examples of publications produced by organizational associates include *The Fight against Corruption, Industrial Espionage, and Economic Crime* (2010), *The Geopolitical Dimension of Resource Security: Germany and Europe Need a Resource Strategy* (2010), and *Hacktivism of Chinese Characteristics and the Google Inc. Cyber Attack Episode* (2010).

India

Institute for Defence Studies and Analysis
This organization was established in 1965, is located in New Delhi, and is an independent and nonpartisan organization seeking to conduct objective research and analysis on defense security topics. Its Web site, http://www.idsa.in/, provides access to information about institute activities, including publications such as *Trilateral Nuclear Proliferation: Pakistan's Euro-Chinese Bomb* (2006), *Journal of Defence Studies* (2007 to present), *Coastal Security Arrangement: A Case Study of Gujarat and Maharashtra Coasts* (2009), *A Study on Illegal Immigration into North-East India: The Case of Nagaland* (2009), and *The Dragon's Shield: Intricacies of China's BMD Capability* (2010).

Institute for Peace and Conflict Studies
This institute was founded in 1996, is located in New Delhi, and studies South Asian peace and security studies matters. Its Web site, http://www.

ipcs.org/, provides information about institute research areas and programs, and the text of its some of its information resources. Representative samples of these include *Af-Pak: A Strategic Opportunity for South Asia?* (2009), *The Dragon on Safari: China's Africa Policy* (2009), *Pakistan: Politics, Religion and Extremism* (2009), and *Meeting Maritime Challenges: Indian Navy Looks Skyward* (2010).

Indonesia

Center for Strategic and International Studies

Indonesia's Center for Strategic and International Studies was founded in 1971, is located in Jakarta, and conducts policy-oriented discussion and studies on domestic and international issues. Its Web site, http://www.csis.or.id/, provides access to various information resources, including working papers such as *Post Tsunami Reconstruction and Peace Building in Aceh: Political Impacts and Potential Risks* (2005) and *Economic Crisis, Institutional Changes and the Effectiveness of Government: The Case of Indonesia* (2007).

Iran

Institute for Political and International Studies

The Institute for Political and International Studies (IPIS) was founded in 1983, is located in Tehran, is part of the office of the Deputy Foreign Minister for Education and Research, and conducts research to benefit Iranian foreign policy. IPIS's English-language Web site, http://www.ipis.ir/english/, features information about institute programs and publications such as selected articles from the *Iranian Journal for International Affairs* (2007 to present), with representative samples including "The Israeli Impact on Standing Tensions between Iran and the United States" (Summer 2008) and "The Future of the Caspian Sea after Tehran Summit" (Winter–Spring 2008–2009).

Israel

Begin-Sadat Center for Strategic Studies

The Begin-Sadat Center for Strategic Studies (BESA) was established in 1993, is located at Bar-Ilan University in Ramat Gan, and strives to contribute to Middle Eastern peace and security by conducting pertinent policy research on strategic subjects affecting Israeli foreign policy and national security. BESA's Web site, http://www.besacenter.org/, presents a variety of free materials on these issues, including *From Omnipotence to Impotence: A Shift in the Iranian Portrayal of the "Zionist Regime"* (2008), *Is Gaza Occupied? Redefining the Legal Status of Gaza* (2009), *Despite Pundits, Netanyahu Wants Peace* (2010), and *Regional Alternatives to the Two-State Solution* (2010).

Institute for National Security Studies

The Institute for National Security Studies (INSS) was founded in 1977, is nonpartisan and independent, is located in Tel Aviv, and studies key issues concerning Israeli national security and broader Middle East affairs. INSS's Web site, http://www.inss.org.il/, provides information about institute activities and links to various information resources, including the periodical *Strategic Assessment* (1998 to present), *The US and Israel under Changing Political Circumstances: Security Challenges of the 21st Century Conference Proceedings* (2009), *Sino-Israeli Relations: Current Reality and Future Prospects* (2009), and *Withdrawal from the Golan Heights in Stages* (2010).

Italy

Institute of International Affairs

The Institute of International Affairs was founded in 1965, is located in Rome, and conducts research in various areas of international affairs, including Italian foreign policy and Mediterranean and Middle Eastern affairs. The institute's Web site, http://www.iai.it/, provides access to various English-language materials, including *Report of the Conference "Addressing the Resurgence of Sea Piracy: Legal, Political and Security Aspects"* (2009), *The Treaty on Friendship, Partnership and Cooperation between Italy and Libya: New Prospects for Cooperation in the Mediterranean* (2009), *European Neighborhood Policy and the Southern Mediterranean: Drawing from the Lessons of Enlargement* (2009), and *The New Turkish Foreign Policy and the Future of Turkey-EU Relations* (2010).

Japan

Japan Institute of International Affairs

The Japan Institute for International Affairs (JIIA) was established in 1959, is located in Tokyo, and is an academically independent institution affiliated with the Japanese Ministry of Foreign Affairs. Its institutional mission is conducting medium- to long-term research on international political and security affairs and promoting the exchange of relevant information in these areas. JIIA's Web site, http://www.jiia.or.jp/, provides further information about organizational activities and some English-language resources, including *Strategic Implications for Japan of the Relocation of US Marines from Okinawa to Guam* (2009), *Improving Cross-Strait Relations Confusing to the Japanese* (2009), *Japan's Peacebuilding Policy toward Afghanistan: The Need for a Civilian Surge to Improve Security* (2009), and *Japan's New Strategy toward the Mekong Region* (2010).

Jordan

Center for Strategic Studies

The Center for Strategic Studies (CSS) was established in 1984 and is located at Jordan University in Amman; its research foci are regional conflicts, international relations, and security. Its Web site, http://www.css-jordan.org/, provides information about center organizational components, including its Iranian and European-Mediterranean Studies units and programs encompassing domestic Jordanian economic and political developments. Examples of CSS publications addressing geopolitics include *The Dilemma of Politics in Arab-Iranian Relations: The Case of Jordan* (2007), *The Tehran-Washington Talks Dilemma and Possible Scenarios* (2009), and *Implementation of Jordan-EU Action Plan: A CSS Independent Evaluation* (2009).

Lithuania

Institute of International Relations and Political Science

The Institute of International Relations and Political Science (IIRPS) was founded in 1992, is located at Vilnius University, and conducts instructional and research programs dealing with domestic and international politics. Its Web site, http://www.tspmi.vu.lt/, includes publications such as the journal *Lithuanian Foreign Policy Review* (1998 to present) with representative articles, including *A Russian-Led 'OPEC for Gas'? Design, Implications, Countermeasures* (2008), *The Big, the Bad and the Beautiful: America, Russia and Europe's Mellow Power* (2008), and *Baltic Military Cooperation: Past, Present and the Future* (2009).

Malaysia

Council for Security Cooperation in the Asia-Pacific

CSCAP was founded in 1992 by representatives from two dozen strategic studies centers in the Asia-Pacific region based on their belief that there needed to be a nongovernmental structure for analyzing and discussing regional security issues. CSCAP is headquartered in Kuala Lumpur, and its Web site, http://www.cscap.org/, provides additional information about organizational activities and current research interests. Some of these research foci include Asia-Pacific naval enhancement, offshore gas and oil installation safety and security, establishing regional hubs for countering transnational organized crime, and climate change's security implications.

Examples of freely available full-text publications include the annually published CSCAP *Regional Security Outlook* (2007 to present), *Maritime Knowledge and Awareness: Basic Foundations of Maritime Security* (2007),

Regional Security Implications of the Global Financial Crisis (2009), and *Guidelines for Maritime Cooperation in Enclosed and Semi-enclosed Seas and Similar Sea Areas of the Asia-Pacific* (2009).

Institute of Strategic and International Studies

The Institute of Strategic and International Studies (ISIS) was founded in 1983, is located in Kuala Lumpur, and conducts research and disseminates research findings in defense, security, and foreign affairs, national and international economic affairs, nation building, science, technology, and natural resources, and international understanding and cooperation. ISIS's Web site, http://www.isis.org.my/, provides information about institute programs and access to multiple publications, including *Role of Non-state Actors in International Security and on Humanitarian Issues in Conflict Areas* (2008), *New Dimensions of Food Security: Implications on Self-Sufficiency and Other Concerns* (2009), and *Democracy, Free Markets and Ethnic Conflict in East Asia* (2009).

Mexico

Mexican Council on Foreign Relations

This organization was established in 2001, is located in Chapultepec, and is responsible for creating a framework so various sectors of Mexican society can become involved in analyzing and debating Mexico's role in international politics. Information about the council's activities can be found at http://www.consejomexicano.org/. Examples of accessible English-language publications include *The Cuba-Venezuela Challenge to Hemispheric Security: Implications for the United States* (2009), *The United States and Mexico: Towards a Strategic Partnership: A Report of Four Working Groups on U.S.-Mexico Relations* (2009), *The Outlook for Energy Reform in Latin America* (2009), and *Cuba: A New Policy of Critical and Constructive Engagement* (2009).

New Zealand

Centre for Strategic Studies (Victoria University)

The Centre for Strategic Studies (CSS) was founded in 1993, is located at Victoria University in Wellington, and is an independent organization with the mission of enhancing national understanding of the global environment New Zealand operates in. CSS's Web site, http://www.victoria.ac.nz/css/, provides information about center programs and the text of numerous publications, including *Pacific Island Security Management by New Zealand and Australia: Towards a New Paradigm* (2005), *Concepts of Maritime Security: A Strategic Perspective on Alternative Visions for Good Order and Security at Sea, with Policy Implications for New Zealand* (2009), and *What Journalists Need to Know about International Humanitarian Law* (2009).

Nigeria

Nigerian Institute of International Affairs

The Nigerian Institute of International Affairs (NIIA) was founded in 1961 and is located in Lagos; its missions include promoting international affairs research and study and training Nigerian diplomats and other nations in international affairs activities. NIIA's Web site, http://www.niianet.org/, provides further information about institute activities and descriptions of organizational publications, which are not provided in full text.

Pakistan

Islamabad Policy Research Institute

The Islamabad Policy Research Institute (IPRI) was founded in 1999 and is located in Islamabad; its institutional mission is analyzing and evaluating national and international political and strategic issues affecting Pakistan, south Asia, and international affairs. IPRI's Web site, http://ipripak.org/, provides access to a number of useful information resources, including articles from *IPRI Journal* (2001 to present), research papers such as *Federally Administered Tribal Areas of Pakistan* (2005) and *China's Peaceful Rise and South Asia* (2008), and the monthly news analyses *IPRI Factfile* (1999 to present).

Poland

Polish Institute of International Affairs

The Polish Institute of International Affairs (PIIA) was established in 1996 by parliamentary legislation and is responsible for conducting research on international affairs and providing expertise on this subject for the Polish government and public. PIIA's Web site, http://www.pism.pl/, provides access to various English-language information resources, including reports and analyses such as *Implications of the Russia-Ukraine Gas Dispute for the Construction of Nord Stream* (2009), *Missile Defense Program: Obama Administration's New Approach* (2009), *A New Strategy for Afghanistan: Political Reform First* (2009), and *NATO after the Georgian Conflict: A New Course or Business as Usual?* (2009).

Russia

Center for Analysis of Strategies and Technologies

The Center for Analysis of Strategies and Technologies (CAST) was established in 1997, is located in Moscow, and serves as an independent, noncommercial, and nongovernmental organization focused on conducting innovative research on the security challenges and implications of weapons and technology trade and defense restructuring. CAST's Web site, http://www.cast.ru/, provides the text of selected reports, including *The Chinese*

Syndrome in Russian Export (2004), and descriptions of articles from periodicals such as *Moscow Defense Brief* (2004–present).

There are several additional Russian think tanks whose work encompasses geopolitical issues, including the Russian Academy of Science's Institute of Far Eastern Studies (http://www.ifes-ras.ru/), this organization's Institute for the U.S. and Canada Studies (http://www.iskran.ru/), Russia's Institute for Strategic Studies (http://www.riss.ru/), and the Institute of World Economy and International Relations (http://www.imemo.ru/). Unfortunately, most of their resources are in Russian only and contain extremely limited free full-text materials, limiting global access to their geopolitical thinking and insights.

Singapore

Institute of Strategic Studies, S. Rajaratnam School of International Studies (Nanyang Technological University)

This institute, which is part of the Rajaratnam School of International Studies (RSIS), was established in 1996 and incorporated into its present organizational alignment in 2007. Institutional missions include providing rigorous graduate professional education in international affairs; conducting policy-relevant research in national security, defense and strategic studies, diplomacy, and international relations; and collaborating with comparable international relations schools to form global excellence networks.[7]

RSIS's Web site, http://www.rsis.edu.sg/, provides information about institute research emphases, including Asia-Pacific security, conflict and nontraditional security, international political economy, and country/area studies. Freely accessible institute research reports and conference proceedings include *Climate Insecurities, Human Security and Social Resilience* (2009), *Developing an Integrated Approach to Maritime Security through the Counter-terrorism Convention, Criminal and International Law: Legal Perspectives, Capacity Building* (2009), *How Geography Makes Democracy Work* (2009), *The Philippines as an Archipelagic and Maritime Nation: Interests, Challenges, and Perspectives* (2009), and *The Korean Peninsula in China's Grand Strategy: China's Role in Dealing with North Korea's Nuclear Quandry* (2010). This rich variety of reports makes RSIS materials essential reading for understanding Asia-Pacific geopolitical trends and developments.

South Africa

South African Institute for International Affairs

SAIIA was founded in 1934, is located in Braamfontein, a suburb of Johannesburg, and serves as a nongovernmental research institution analyzing

South African and African international relations. SAIIA's Web site, http://www.saiia.org.za/, provides access to information about institute research areas, including security and conflict resolution, and emerging powers and global challenges, with a section of this later area incorporating material on China in Africa. Examples of freely accessible publications include *China's Development Policy in Africa* (2007), *What's Urdu for Biltong: Can South Africa Help Pakistan* (2009), *Digging Deep for Profits and Development: Reflections on Enhancing the Governance of Africa's Mining Sector* (2009), and *The Oil Factor in Sino-Angolan Relations at the Start of the 21st Century* (2010).

South Korea

Institute for Far Eastern Studies

The Institute for Far Eastern Studies was established in 1972 and is located at Kyungnam University in Seoul. Its institutional mission is promoting peaceful Korean reunification by conducting research on North Korea, national reunification, and northeast Asia. Its English-language Web site, http://ifes.kyungnam.ac.kr/eng/default.asp, provides additional information about its activities and selected information resources, including the text of articles from its journal *Asian Perspectives* (2003 to present).

Taiwan

Taiwan Security Research

TSR was founded in 1997, is located in Taipei, and serves as an academic and nongovernmental resource for disseminating information on Taiwanese security and regional security issues. Its Web site, http://taiwansecurity.org/, features newspaper articles, academic papers, governmental policy statements, and reports from English-language sources. Examples of these resources include *China's Search for Military Power* (2008), *Cross-Strait Relations: First the Easy Steps, Then the Difficult Ones* (2008), and *China Tops List of Unfriendly Countries Despite Improved Relations: Survey* (2009).

Turkey

Foreign Policy Institute

The Foreign Policy Institute (FPI) was established in 1974, is located at Bilkent University in Ankara, and seeks to enhance foreign policy knowledge through research, meetings, and publications. Its Web site, http://www.foreignpolicy.org.tr/, provides additional information about FPI activities and lists of publications it has produced, including tables of contents. Examples of these books include *The Armenian Issues in Nine Questions and Answers* (1992),

Caspian Energy Diplomacy since the Fall of the Cold War (2006), and *Turkey's Neighborhood* (n.d.).

United Arab Emirates

Gulf Research Council

The Gulf Research Council was founded in 2000, is located in Dubai, and is an independent research organization conducting objective and scholarly research on political, economic, social, and security issues facing countries in the Persian Gulf region, including Gulf Cooperation Council (GCC) countries. Its Web site, http://www.grc.ae/, provides descriptions and abstracts, but not the full text of many English-language reports, with representative samples including *Water Scarcity in the GCC Countries: Challenges and Opportunities* (2007) and *Piracy: Motivation and Tactics: The Case of Somali Piracy* (2009).

United Kingdom

Chatham House

Chatham House, originally established in 1920 as the Royal Institute of International Affairs, is located in London and conducts independent and rigorous research and analysis of international affairs. Key areas of current emphasis include energy, environment, and resource governance, international economics, and regional and security studies on a global scale. The Chatham House Web site, http://www.chathamhouse.org.uk/, provides information on its multiple information resources, including *Thirst for African Oil: Asian National Oil Companies in Nigeria and Angola* (2009), *Transit Troubles: Pipelines as a Source of Conflict* (2009), *The Feeding of the Nine Billion: Global Food Security for the 21st Century* (2009), and *Beyond the Dollar: Rethinking the International Monetary System* (2010).

Crisis States Research Centre

CSRC was established in 2001 and is located in London. It serves as an interdisciplinary research center for examining war, state collapse, and reconstruction in fragile states and by identifying how conflict and war affect future state building policies while also analyzing the historical impact of state reconstruction and international intervention in failed states.

CSRC's Web site, http://www.crisisstates.com/, provides information about center research emphasis areas, including development as state making, cities and fragile states, and regional and global conflict axes. Numerous geopolitically relevant analyses are available here, including *The African Union as a Security Actor: African Solutions to African Problems?* (2009), *The Tormented Triangle: Regionalisation of Conflict in Sudan, Chad and the Central African Republic* (2009), *Buffer Zone, Colonial Enclave or Urban Hub? Quetta: Between*

Four Regions and Two Wars (2010), and *Negotiating with the Taliban: Toward a Solution for the Afghan Conflict* (2010).

Royal United Services Institute

This institute was established in 1831, is located in London, and serves as an independent think tank specializing in cutting-edge defense and security research. Its Web site, http://www.rusi.org/, provides information about institute programs and research activities. Examples of its accessible full-text resources include *Unmanned Combat Air Vehicles: Opportunities for the Guided Weapons Industry?* (2008), *Combating International Terrorism: Turkey's Added Value* (2009), *Towards Cross-Border Security* (2010), and *NATO's Tactical Nuclear Dilemma* (2010).

United States

Carnegie Endowment for International Peace

CEIP was founded in 1910, is located in Washington, D.C., and various international locations, and seeks to advance international cooperation and promote active U.S. international engagement. Its Web site, http://www.ceip.org/, provides access to a number of information resources on international relations and geopolitics. Recent examples of these include *Engaging Pakistan: Getting the Balance Right* (2008), *Fixing a Failed Strategy in Afghanistan* (2009), *The Arctic Climate Change and Security Policy Conference: Final Report and Findings* (2009), and *What Comes Next in Yemen? Al-Qaeda, the Tribes, and State-Building* (2010).

Center for a New American Security

CNAS was founded in 2007; is located in Washington, D.C.; and is an independent and nonpartisan research institute seeking to develop what it considers to be strong, pragmatic, and principled national security and defense policies to promote and protect American interest and values. Its Web site, http://www.cnas.org/, provides information about CNAS programs and access to numerous reports on geopolitical subjects, including *On the Knife's Edge: Yemen's Instability and the Threat to American Interests* (2009), *Promoting the Dialogue: Climate Change and the Maritime Services* (2010), *Arsenal's End? American Power the Global Defense Industry* (2010), and *Contested Commons: The Future of American Military Power in a Multipolar World* (2010).

Center for International Security and Cooperation (Stanford University)

CISAC was founded in 1970 and is part of Stanford University's Freeman Spogli Institute for International Studies. It serves as an interdisciplinary research and training center focusing on difficult international security–related problems by providing what it regards as policy-oriented solutions. Information on CISAC is accessible at http://cisac.stanford.edu/, with sample full-text resources, including *Fueling the Future: Mongolian Uranium and Nuclear Power Plant Growth in China and India* (2009), *Iran's Nuclear and Missile Potential: A Joint Threat Assessment by U.S. and Russian Technical Experts* (2009), and *Lessons Learned from the North Korean Nuclear Crises* (2010).

Center for Strategic and International Studies

This center was founded in 1962; is located in Washington, D.C.; and is one of the premier U.S. international security research institutes. It is bipartisan and nonprofit and conducts research and analysis and develops policy initiatives that seek to look into the future and anticipate change. Its Web site, http://www.csis.org/, provides access to a number of prescient geopolitical analyses, including *Declaration on U.S. Policy and the Global Challenges of Water* (2009), *A Healthier, Safer, and More Prosperous World: Report of the CSIS Commission on Smart Global Health Policy* (2010), *Russia-Europe Energy Relations: Implications for U.S. Policy* (2010), and *Geopolitics of the Iranian Nuclear Energy Program: But Oil and Gas Still Matter* (2010).

Council on Foreign Relations

The Council on Foreign Relations was founded in 1921, is located in New York City, and serves as one of the world's premier nonpartisan international relations advocacy and public information organizations. Its Web site, http://www.cfr.org/, provides information about council programs, experts, and numerous reports. Examples of these resources include *Independent Task Force Report No. 62: U.S. Nuclear Weapons Policy* (2009), *Alternative Views on Climate Change* (2010), *Al-Qaeda's Financial Pressures* (2010), and *Obama's Missed Opportunity in Indonesia* (2010).

Foreign Policy Research Institute

FPRI was founded in 1955 and is located in Philadelphia. It is a nonprofit organization seeking to use scholarship to develop policies advancing U.S. national interests. FPRI research areas include the war on terrorism; Middle East developments; nuclear proliferation; relations with China, Japan, and Russia; long-term issues such as the role of religion and ethnicity in Western politics; and the nature of Western identity and its implications for the United States and the Atlantic Alliance. FPRI's Web site, http://www.fpri.org/, provides further information about institute programs and the text of many publications, including *Counterterrorism and the Integration of Islam in Europe* (2006), *Teaching the Long War and Jihadism* (2009), *Civil-Military*

Relations and the U.S. Strategy Deficit (2010), and *The "Mega-Eights": Urban Leviathans and International Instability* (2010).

International Crisis Group

Founded in 1995 and located in Washington, D.C., and other international offices, this organization's creation grew from concern over the international community's failure to anticipate and respond to early 1990s humanitarian tragedies in Bosnia, Rwanda, and Somalia. ICG seeks to conduct research, policy analysis, and engage in political advocacy on behalf of potential and existing international crisis regions. Its Web site, http://www.crisisgroup.org/, provides information on its multifaceted activities, including the text of many of its research reports. Examples of these reports, which can be obtained after free registration for them, include *China's Thirst for Oil* (2008), *Jonglei's Tribal Conflicts: Countering Insecurity in South Sudan* (2009), *Nigeria: Seizing the Moment in the Niger Delta* (2009), *Venezuela: Accelerating the Bolivarian Revolution* (2009), *The Iran Nuclear Issue: The View from Beijing* (2010), and *Iraq's Uncertain Future: Elections and Beyond* (2010).

National Institute for Public Policy

Founded in 1982 and located in Fairfax, Virginia, the National Institute for Public Policy seeks to examine U.S. foreign and defense policies in view of continually changing global security environments. Its Web site, http://www.nipp.org/, provides information about institute analysts and the text of some of their research, including *A More Dangerous World: Nuclear Zero Goal Is Not Practicable* (2008) and *The START Treaty* (2010).

RAND Corporation

The RAND Corporation was founded in 1946 and is located in Santa Monica, California; it has various other offices in the United States, Europe, and the Middle East. Long considered one of the world's preeminent public policy research institutions, it conducts research in a variety of national and international security issues and international relations topics. Its Web site, http://www.rand.org/, is a treasure trove of information resources of interest to those studying geopolitics, with representative samples including *Greece's New Geopolitics* (2001), *Russian Foreign Policy: Sources and Implications* (2009), *The Geopolitical Consequences of World Economic Recession: A Caution* (2009), *Dangerous but Not Omnipotent: Exploring the Reach and Limitations of Iranian Power in the Middle East* (2009), *Security in Iraq: A Framework for Analyzing Emerging Threats as U.S. Forces Leave* (2010), and *Troubled Partnership: U.S.-Turkish Relations in an Era of Global Geopolitical Change* (2010).

Conference Proceedings

Conference proceedings can also be useful sources for finding information on geopolitics. Professional associations representing a variety of disciplines hold conferences on a regular basis, where members discuss and debate trends and developments in their fields and present their findings and data in speeches, presentations, and in some cases, through published papers. Some conference proceeding documents may eventually be published as scholarly journal articles or chapters in books. There are numerous assessments in library and information science literature on the role of conference proceedings in scholarly research and communication and on the challenges in accessing these materials.[8]

Most conference proceedings are not freely available to users who are not part of the professional associations in question or affiliated with a university with a major academic library. These resources tend to be selectively or sporadically cataloged in academic library online public access catalogs and often are not cataloged with as high a level of bibliographic access as books and journals.[9]

Two major databases for accessing conference proceedings that are available in some academic libraries include the Institute for Scientific Information's ISI Web of Science: Proceedings and Cambridge Scientific Abstracts's Conference Papers Index. General information about these resources may be found at http://pcs.isiknowledge.com/ and http://www.csa.com/, respectively.

Conference proceedings represent an interdisciplinary variety of subjects. Those covering geopolitics and political geography may be produced as part of the scholarly research process in disciplines such as environmental science, geography, history, military science, political science, and various scientific and technology fields. The following is a selective annotation of relatively recently published conference proceedings on geopolitics topics. Bibliographic citations are provided, including information on the organization at which the paper was initially presented and book International Standard Bibliographic Number (ISBN) or serial International Standard Serial Number (ISSN). A representative sampling of these papers arranged in chronological order by conference date includes the following:

Arsenault, Daniel, and Jamie Green. "Effects of the Separation Barrier on the Viability of a Future Palestinean State." In *2nd Israeli-Palestinean Conference on Water for Life in the Middle East*. Antalya, Turkey, October 2004. ISBN: 978-3-540-69508-0.

Baldwin, Andrew. "Carbon Nullius and Racial Rule: Race, Nature and the Cultural Politics of Forest Carbon in Canada." In AAG *Conference on Critical Explorations in Nationalism and the Environment*. Bali, Indonesia, December 2007.

de Fraiture, Charlotte, Mark Giordano, and Yongsong Liao. "Biofuels and Implications for Agricultural Water Use: Blue Impacts of Green Energy." In *International Conference on Linkages between Energy and Water Management for Agriculture*. Hyderabad, India, January 29–30, 2007. ISSN: 1366-7017.

Ingram, Alan. "HIV/AIDS, Security and the Geopolitics of US-Nigerian Relations." In *Annual Conference of the Royal Geographical Society/Institute of British Geographers Conference*. London, August 31–September 2, 2005. ISSN: 0969-2290.

Iqbal, Zaryab, and Harvey Starr. "Bad Neighbors: Failed States and Their Consequences." In *40th Annual Meeting of the Peace Science Society*. Columbus, OH, November 10–12, 2006. ISSN: 0738-8942.

Kriviliev, Vladimir A. "Geopolitics and Environmental Security." In *NATO Advanced Research Workshop on Geographical Information Processing and Visual Analytics for Environmental Security*. October 13–17, 2008, Trento, Italy. ISBN: 978-90-481-2897-6.

Liu, Liwei, Peng Wang, and Zhao Erdong. "Research of Chinese Oil Companies' Investment in Eurasia Region." In *2007 International Conference on Wireless Communications, Networking and Mobile Computing*. Shanghai, September 21–25, 2007. ISBN: 978-1-4244-1311-9.

Scott, James Wesley. "Bordering and Ordering the European Neighbourhood: A Critical Perspective on EU Territoriality and Geopolitics." In *Conference on Regional Development Challenges of EU Border Regions in the Context of the Interaction between the EU and Countries of Its Immediate Neighbourhood*. Tartu, Estonia, June 16–17, 2008. ISSN: 1406-0922.

Suen, Xiaoli, Jianping Li, and Chen Wang. "The Energy-Triangle Region around China: Regional Co-operation of Energy Security." In *Proceedings of the 2008 International Conference on E-Risk Management*. Nanjing, China, June 27–30, 2008. ISBN: 978-0-78677-08-6.

Tagaranski, Mario, and Andrius Aviziust. "Energy Security for the Euro-Atlantic Region." In *NATO Advanced Research Workshop on Energy and Environmental Challenges to Security*. Budapest, November 21–23, 2007. ISBN: 978-1-4020-9451-4.

Wu, Gang, Yi-Ming Wei, and Ying Fan. "An Empirical Risk for the Import Risk of China's Petroleum Products Based on the Improved Portfolio Approach." In *2008 IEEE Conference on Sustainable Energy Technologies (ICSET)*. Singapore, November 24–27, 2008. ISBN: 978-1-4244-1887-9.

Blogs and Social Networking Utilities

Blogs and social networking utilities such as Facebook and Twitter are increasing their influence in disseminating scholarly information and political advocacy. Any assessment of geopolitical gray literature must include these emerging information dissemination venues.[10] This subsequent section will present a representative sampling of how geopolitics is being analyzed in these emerging Internet venues.

Energy and Geopolitics

This Facebook group is run from Belgium's University of Antwerp and the Flemish Centre for International Policy by David Criekemans, a professor in foreign policy at these institutions. It seeks to stimulate debate about energy questions and their relationship to global and regional geopolitics. The group had 313 members as of March 2010, and discussion topics included geopolitical consequences of the 2008 Caucasus War and whether Brazilian petroleum reserves could make it a new Saudi Arabia. This resource can be accessed at http://www.facebook.com/group.php?gid=13326203842.

Exploring Geopolitics

This English-language academic site provides access to geopolitical insights provided by a global array of approximately 50 scholars. It seeks to increase awareness of geopolitics and relevant information sources; provide information about geopolitical schools of thought; and narrow the information gap between the academic world, policy makers, the business community, and journalists. This Web site is arranged into five categories: education, geopolitical traditions, world politics, international security, and resource scarcity, featuring various writings, interviews, and op-eds. It can be accessed at http://www.exploringgeopolitics.org/ and features the AllGeopolitics Twitter service (http://twitter.com/AllGeopolitics), which had 18 followers as of March 2010.

Geo-Graphics

This is an international economics–oriented blog hosted by the Council on Foreign Relations and its Center for Geo-Economic Studies. It features postings and statistics from August 2008 to the present on a variety of international economic issues and their relationship to geopolitics. Examples of posting topics include China's international economics role, how central banks influence international economic and political policies, the international impact of the global economic downturn, and how international trade affects national and international economic and political development. This resource can be accessed at http://blogs.cfr.org/geographics/.

Global Geopolitics Net

This is a noncommercial education project of the Eurasia Research Center that seeks to study political developments in countries part of the former

Soviet Union, the Middle East, and south Asia. As an information resource and blog network, Global Geopolitics Net seeks to present information analysis and opinion on global politics, intelligence gathering and analysis, counterterrorism, human rights, globalization, and other international issues, along with the domestic politics of numerous countries.

Mackinder Forum

Inspired by the life and work of noted geopolitical writer Halford Mackinder, this international organization seeks to promote geopolitical study and increase its academic standing; bring together military officers, diplomats, policy makers, academics, and business personnel to debate contemporary geopolitical issues; exchange and disseminate new geopolitical ideas and concepts; and investigate the geopolitical foundations of democratic institutions and ideals. The forum's Web site, http://www.mackinderforum.org/, features information about leading members, the text of recent documents and reports on geopolitics from government agencies, information about a forthcoming online open access journal *Projections*, written analyses such as *The Afghanistan Reassessment: Geopolitical Dilemmas, Tactical Curiosities, and Strategic Consequences* (2009) and *The Geopolitical Containment of China* (2009), and recent newspaper articles on geopolitics.

Politicalgeog

This is a Twitter feed run by Professor Klaus Dodds at the Royal Holloway University of London's Department of Geography. It contains links to geopolitics news stories from a global variety of sources and has 32 followers as of March 2010. Tweet topics include the controversy over whether to call the Persian Gulf the Arabian Gulf, Argentina trying to gain broader support for its claim to the Falkland Islands, and Secretary of State Hillary Clinton taking a "tough line" on Iranian nuclear aspirations. This service can be accessed at http://twitter.com/politicalgeog.

Thomas P.M. Barnett Blog

Barnett is a consultant on international security issues who has served as a U.S. Naval War College Professor, worked in think tanks such as the Center for Naval Analysis, and authored international and political strategic analysis works such as *The Pentagon's News Map: War and Peace in the 21st Century* (2004), *The Pentagon's New Map: Blueprint for Action: A Future Worth Creating* (2005), and *Great Power: America and the World after Bush* (2009). He currently serves as the senior management director for Enterra Solutions, an international management and technology consultant firm. His blog, http://thomaspmbarnett.com/weblog/, features his observations on geopolitical and related topics from May 2004 to the present, which may also have been published in *Esquire* magazine and various other venues, including video webcasts.

Notes

1. Works describing gray literature and its role in library collections include Paolo de Castro and Sandra Salinetti, "Quality of Grey Literature in the Open Access Era: Privilege and Responsibility," *Publishing Research Quarterly*, 20 (1)(2004): 4–12; Heather Lehman and Janet Webster, "Describing Grey Literature Again: A Survey of Collection Policies," *Publishing Research Quarterly*, 21 (1)(Spring 2005): 64–72; and Bertrum H. McDonald, Ruth E. Cordes, and Peter G. Wells, "Assessing the Diffusion and Impact of Grey Literature Published by International Intergovernmental Scientific Groups: The Case of the Gulf of Maine Council on the Marine Environment," *Publishing Research Quarterly*, 23 (1)(Spring 2007): 30–46.

2. For representative samples, see Calvin James Boyer, *The Doctoral Dissertation as an Information Source* (Metuchen, NJ: Scarecrow Press, 1973); Edward S. Balian, *How to Design, Analyze, and Write Doctoral Research: The Practical Guidebook* (Lanham, MD: University Press of America, 1982); and Peggy L. Maki and Nancy A. Borkowski, eds., *The Assessment of Doctoral Education: Emerging Criteria and New Models for Improving Outcomes* (Sterling, VA: Stylus, 2006). See the following for the increasing interdisciplinarity of academic research and writing: Molly Molloy, "The Internet in Latin America," *Journal of Library Administration*, 43 (3/4)(2005): 129–47; and Bradley Brazzeal and Robert Fowler, "Patterns of Information Use in Graduate Research in Forestry: A Citation Analysis of Masters Theses at Mississippi State University," *Science and Technology Libraries*, 26 (2)(2005): 91–106.

3. A partial sampling of these works includes Jean-Pierre Herubel and Ann Buchanan, "Comparing Materials Used in Philosophy and Political Science Dissertations: A Technical Note," *Behavioral and Social Sciences Librarian*, 12 (2)(1993): 63–70; L. Hoover, "Cataloging Theses and Dissertations: An Annotated Bibliography," *Technical Services Quarterly*, 19 (3)(2001): 21–39; Newkirk Barnes, "The Use of U.S. Government Publications as Bibliographic References in Doctoral References," *Journal of Academic Librarianship*, 32 (5)(2006): 503–11; and C. Rockelle Strader, "Author Assigned Keywords versus Library of Congress Subject Headings: Implications for the Cataloging of Electronic Theses and Dissertations," *Library Resources and Technical Services*, 53 (4)(2009): 243–50.

4. Bert Chapman, *Researching National Security and Intelligence Policy* (Washington, DC: CQ Press, 2004): 75.

5. S. Rajatnam School of International Studies, "Mission of the RSIS," http://www.rsis.edu.sg/about_rsis/rsis_objective.html.

6. Lane Wallace, *The Story of the Defense Technical Information Center: 1945–1995* (Fort Belvoir, VA: Defense Technical Information Center, 1995): 10–15, 46.

7. See Barbara L. Berman, "Coping with Conference Proceedings," *Cataloging and Classification Quarterly* 10 (3)(1990): 19–34; S. M. DeSilva and A. N. Zainab, "An Advisor for Cataloguing Conference Proceedings: Design and Development

of CoPAS," *Cataloging and Classification Quarterly* 29 (3)(2000): 63–80; B.M. Russell and R.L.B. Hutchison, "Official Publications at Texas A&M University: A Case Study in Cataloging Archival Material," *American Archivist*, 63 (1)(2000): 175–84; and Suhyeon Yoo, Kijeong Shin, and Heeyoon Choi, "Collecting Foreign Digital Grey Literature through a Consortium in Korea: An Example of Conference Proceedings," *The Grey Journal*, 5 (3)(2009): 142–46.

8. See Chapman, *Researching National Security*, 296–326, for a listing of prominent U.S. national security oriented think tanks. There are many Web-based links to international geopolitically oriented think tanks, including http://thinktanks.frpi.org/, produced by the Foreign Policy Research Institute.

9. See Kimberly Douglas, "Conference Proceedings at Publishing Crossroads," *Science and Technology Libraries*, 22 (3/4)(2002): 39–50; James Hartley, "On Requesting Conference Papers Electronically," *Journal of Information Science*, 30 (5)(2004): 475–79; Yannis Manolopoulos and Antonis Siridiropoulos, "A New Perspective to Automatically Rank Scientific Conferences Using Digital Libraries," *Information Processing and Management*, 41 (2)(2005): 289–312; and Wolfgang Glanzel, Balazs Schlemmer, Andreas Schubert, and Bart Thus, "Proceedings Literature as Additional Data Source for Bibliometric Analysis," *Scientometrics*, 68 (3)(2006): 457–73.

10. Examples discussing the potential impact of social networking utilities on political research in U.S. politics and comparative international politics include Maurice Vergeer and Liesbeth Hermans, "Analysing Online Political Discussions: Methodological Considerations," *Javnost/The Public*, 15 (2)(2008): 37–56; Ashley Esarey and Xiao Qing, "Political Expression in the Chinese Blogosphere: Below the Radar," *Asian Survey*, 48 (5)(2008): 752–72; Nigel Jackson, "Representation in the Blogosphere: MPs and Their New Constituents," *Parliamentary Affairs*, 61 (4)(2008): 642–60; and Amanda Lenhart and Susannah Fox, *Twitter and Status Updating* (Washington, DC: Pew Internet and American Life Project, 2009), http://www.pewinternet.org/~/media//Files/Reports/2009/PIP Twitter MemoFinal.pdf.

CHAPTER 8

Current Geopolitical Scholars

A number of scholars representing classical and critical geopolitical perspectives are influencing this discipline's research and analysis while representing disciplinary fields such as geography, history, international economics, military science, and political science. This chapter will present a representative sampling and description of their works without evaluating the quality or significance of their writings. These entries will include brief biographical descriptions, including their employment information, and selected listings of their works.

Thomas P.M. Barnett

Thomas P.M. Barnett has developed a prominent career analyzing geopolitical trends and strategies in academe and in corporate consulting. He received his BA in international relations and Russian literature from the University of Wisconsin, a master's degree in Harvard University's Soviet Union Program, and a PhD in political science from Harvard University. His career has consisted of being the project director for the CAN Center for Naval Analysis, a professor and senior strategic researcher at the Naval War College, and a consultant in the U.S. Department of Defense (DOD), including service as an assistant for strategic futures in the DOD's Office of Force Transformation from 2001 to 2003. He currently runs his own consultancy firms Barnett Consulting and Enterra Solutions, which provide independent policy and management consultations and briefing presentations to private corporations and research organizations.[1]

Barnett has written for popular, business, and scholarly audiences. His first prominent book, *The Pentagon's New Map: War and Peace in the 21st Century*, contended that the United States and other developed areas he calls the core needed to reduce threats to their security by connecting with areas such as Africa, Asia, and South America, which he calls the gap that has not been reached by global economic development. He goes on to maintain that the U.S. military needs to be restructured to enhance its suitability for peace-keeping and nation-building operations.

His second book, *The Pentagon's New Map: Blueprint for Action—A Future Worth Creating*, argues that the United States equates its national security with globalization's continued survival and success. His third and most recent book, *Great Powers: America and the World after Bush*, states his belief that the United States still has the power and ability to shape its global destiny and that globalization will face crucial tests in the next few years.

Samples of Barnett's writings include the following:

Great Powers: *America and the World after Bush*. New York: Putnam, 2009.

The Pentagon's New Map: Blueprint for Action—A Future Worth Creating. New York: Berkeley Trade, 2006.

The Pentagon's New Map: War and Peace in the 21st Century. New York: Putnam, 2004.

He also writes on international affairs issues for popular magazines like *Esquire* and op-eds for a numerous newspapers as well as maintaining a regularly updated blog at http://www.thomaspmbarnett.com/weblog/ covering from March 2004 to the present and a Twitter feed at http://twitter.com/thomaspmbarnett.

Simon Dalby

Simon Dalby is a professor in the Department of Geography and Environmental Studies at Carleton University in Ottawa, Canada. He is one of the leading figures in critical geopolitics studies, which seeks to look beyond factors in classical geopolitics to include ethnic politics and what its proponents regard as racism and environmental and economic exploitation and "hidden messages" in political rhetoric to explain how geography can influence domestic and international policy making.

Dalby received his undergraduate degree in geography at Trinity College in Dublin, and his activism saw him become involved in a campaign to prevent construction of a nuclear reactor in southeast Ireland. He received his master's degree at British Columbia's University of Victoria; his thesis was a historical and sociological analysis of the protest movement against nuclear power plant construction in Ireland. He received his PhD at Simon Fraser University in 1983 and wrote his dissertation on how Washington intellectuals reconstructed the Soviet threat to Western security interests. This dissertation influenced his interest in critical geopolitics and geopolitical discourse and would ultimately be revised and published in 1990 as *Creating the Second Cold War*.

He has been at Carleton since 1993 and has edited the journal *Geopolitics* since 2009. His research into critical geopolitics has covered topics as identity politics in the Australian–New Zealander–U.S. alliance, environmental security, the impact of American foreign policy in areas such as geopolitics, globalization, and empire, and allegedly American imperial themes in debates concerning the war on terror, national missile defense, and global consumption patterns as they relate to military strategies.[2]

Samples of Dalby's writings include the following:

"Environmental Security and Climate Change." In *International Studies Online/ International Studies Encyclopedia*, 12 vols., ed. Robert A. Denemark. Oxford: Blackwell, 2010.: 1580–97

"The Pentagon's New Imperial Cartography: Tabloid Realism and the War on Terror." In *Violent Geographies: Fear, Terror, and Political Violence*, ed. Derek Gregory and Allen Pred. New York: Routledge, 2007: 295–308.

"Geopolitics, the Bush Doctrine, and the War on Iraq." *Arab World Geographer*, 6 (1)(2003): 7–18.

Environmental Security. Minneapolis: University of Minnesota Press, 2002.

"Jousting with Malthus' Ghost: Environment and Conflict after the Cold War." *Geopolitics*, 5 (1)(2000): 165–75.

"Ecological Metaphors of Security: World Politics in the Biosphere." *Alternatives: Social Transformation and Humane Governance*, 23 (3)(1998): 291–319.

Continent Adrift: The Changing Strategic Geoparameters of Australian Security Discourse. Working Paper 35. Canberra: Australian Defence Studies, 1995.

"Critical Geopolitics: Discourse, Difference, and Dissent." *Environment and Planning D: Society and Space*, 9 (3)(1991): 261–83.

Creating the Second Cold War: The Discourse of Politics. London: Pinter and Guilford, 1990.

Further information about Dalby and his work can be found at http://httpserver.carleton.ca/~sdalby/.

Andrew S. Erickson

Andrew Erickson is an associate professor in the U.S. Naval War College's Strategic Research Department and one of the founders of that department's China Maritime Studies Institute. He has also worked as a Chinese translator and technical analyst for Science Applications International Corporation and has been employed with the U.S. Embassy in Beijing, U.S. Consulate in Hong Kong, U.S. Senate, and White House. He received his BA in history and political science from Amherst College and an MA and PhD in international relations and comparative politics from Princeton University. His research specialties include Chinese military and foreign policy, Japan/East Asia security and international relations, maritime and aerospace technology development, energy resources and geostrategy, military basing, and power projection.[3]

Erickson has published books, articles, and reports in a variety of venues, including journals such as *Joint Force Quarterly*, *Journal of Strategic Studies*, *Naval War College Review*, and *Orbis*. Examples of his multifaceted writings on Chinese and East Asian geopolitical issues, with particular emphasis on maritime matters, include the following:

"China's Oil Security Pipe Dream: The Reality and Strategic Consequences of Seaborne Imports." *Naval War College Review*, 62 (2)(Spring 2010): 88–111.

Andrew S. Erickson, Lyle J. Goldstein, and William S. Murray. *Chinese Mine Warfare: A PLA Navy "Assassins Mace" Capability*. Newport, RI: Naval War College Press, 2009.

"Using the Land to Control the Sea? Chinese Analysts Consider the Anti-ship Ballistic Missile." *Naval War College Review*, 62 (4)(Autumn 2009): 53–86.

"Gunboats for China's New 'Grand Canals'? Probing the Intersection of Beijing's Naval and Energy Security Policies." *Naval War College Review*, 62 (2)(Spring 2009): 43–76.

"Chinese Theater and Strategic Missile Force Modernization and Its Implications for the United States." *Journal of Strategic Studies*, 32 (1)(February 2009): 67–114.

"Can China Become a Maritime Power?" In *Asia Looks Seaward: Power and Maritime Strategy*, ed. Toshi Yashihara and James R. Holmes. Westport, CT: Praeger Security International, 2008: 70–110.

Andrew S. Erickson, Gabriel B. Collins, Lyle J. Goldstein, and William S. Murray, eds. *China's Energy Strategy: The Impact of Beijing's Maritime Policies*. Annapolis, MD: Naval Institute Press, 2008.

Additional information on Erickson can be found at http://www.andrewerickson.com/ and http://twitter.com/andrewerickson.

Colin Gray

Colin Gray is one of the scholarly community's premier and prolific military strategists and geopolitical writers. He received his BA in economics from Manchester University and a DPhil from Oxford University's Lincoln

College. He has advised the British and American governments and NATO on military and strategic matters and has held academic appointments at the University of Reading, where he directs the Centre for Strategic Studies within the Department of Politics and International Relations, the U.S. Army War College, and the National Institute for Public Policy in Fairfax, Virginia.

His research interests, falling firmly into the classical geopolitics tradition, include strategic theory and strategic history, strategy for contemporary geographic environments, nuclear proliferation, counterinsurgency, and technological innovation. Gray seeks to incorporate historical lessons in advocating contemporary military strategy and believes political and military leaders need to understand the advantages and disadvantages of their military power, not be overly impressed with technological advances, and not place excessive reliance on any military branch to achieve national security objectives.[4]

Examples of Gray's multifaceted journal and monographic writings include the following:

After Iraq: The Search for a Sustainable National Security Strategy. Carlisle, PA: Strategic Studies Institute, U.S. Army War College, 2009. http://purl.access.gpo.gov/GPO/LPS107731.

Recognizing and Understanding Revolutionary Change in Warfare: The Sovereignty of Context. Carlisle, PA: Strategic Studies Institute, U.S. Army War College, 2006. www.strategicstudiesinstitute.army.mil/pdffiles/PUB640.pdf.

The Sheriff: America's Defense of the New World Order. Lexington: University Press of Kentucky, 2004.

Strategy for Chaos: Revolutions in Military Affairs and the Evidence of History. London: Frank Cass, 2002.

"Thinking Asymetrically in Times of Terror." *Parameters*, 32 (1)(Spring 2002): 5–14.

"Strategic Culture as Context: The First Generation of Theory Strikes Back." *Review of International Studies*, 25 (1)(January 1999): 49–69.

The Geopolitics of the Nuclear Era: Heartland, Rimlands, and the Technological Revolution. New York: Crane, Russak, 1977.

Additional information on Gray can be found at http://www.reading.ac.uk/spirs/about/staff-c-s-gray.aspx.

Jakub Grygiel

Jakub Grygiel is the George H.W. Bush Associate Professor of International Relations at Johns Hopkins University's School of Advanced International Studies. He received his PhD in politics at Princeton University, and his research interests include Eastern Europe, Russia and the former Soviet Union, U.S. foreign policy, and strategic and security issues. He is particularly interested in the revival of Russian nationalism and other topics on central and Eastern Europe economics, history, and politics.[5]

Examples of Grygiel's writings include the following:

"The Costs of Respecting Sovereignty." *Orbis*, 54 (2)(March 2010): 268–83.

Great Powers and Geopolitical Change. Baltimore: Johns Hopkins University Press, 2006.

"Empires and the Powers of Barbarians." Conference Papers-American Political Science Association Annual Meeting, 2006: 1–20.

"Imperial Allies." *Orbis*, 50 (2)(Spring 2006): 209–21.

"The Dilemmas of U.S. Maritime Security in the Early Cold War." *Journal of Strategic Studies*, 28 (2)(April 2005): 187–216.

Additional information on Grygiel can be found at http://www.sais-jhu.edu/faculty/directory/bios/g/grygiel.htm.

Peter Hugill

Peter Hugill is professor of geography at Texas A&M University and also holds an appointment in that institution's George Bush School of Public Service. He received his BS at the University of Leeds, his MS at Simon Fraser University, and his PhD at Syracuse University. His research interests focus on the historical relationship between people and their environment as technology mediates. His writings have focused on telecommunication and transportation systems in the world system, the role played by agricultural commodities in sculpting world trade flows, industrial development, and consumer markets, with particular geographic interests in the relationships these issues play involving Anglo-America and Europe.[6]

Examples of Hugill's prolific array of geopolitical publications include the following:

"Historical Geographies of Trade, Transport and Communications." In *The International Encyclopedia of Human Geography*, ed. Rob Kitchen and Nigel Thrift. Amsterdam: Elsevier, 2010: 338–44.

"The Geopolitical Implications of Communication under the Sea." In *Communications under the Sea: The Evolving Cable Network and Its Implications*, ed. Bernard Finn and Daqing Yang. Cambridge, MA: MIT Press, 2009: 257–77.

"The American Challenge to British Hegemony, 1861–1946." *Geographical Review*, 99 (3)(July 2009): 403–25.

"German Great Power Relations in the Age of Simplicissimus, 1896–1914." *Geographical Review*, 98 (1)(January 2008): 1–23.

"Trading States, Territorial States, and Technology: Mackinder's Unexplored Contribution to the Discourse on State Types." In *Global Geostrategy: Mackinder and the Defence of the West*, ed. Brian W. Blouet. London: Frank Cass, 2005: 107–24.

Global Communications since 1844: Geopolitics and Technology. Baltimore: Johns Hopkins University Press, 2004.

Additional information on Hugill can be found at http://geography.tamu.edu/profile/PHugill.

J. Mohan Malik

J. Mohan Malik is a professor at the U.S. military's Asia-Pacific Center for Security Studies (APCSS) in Honolulu. His education includes a MPhil in Chinese from Delhi University and a PhD in international relations from Australian National University. Malik has been a faculty member or lecturer at institutions such as the Australian Defence College and directed the postgraduate Defense Studies Program at Australia's Deakin University before coming to APCSS in 2001. His research interests include Asian geopolitics, China's Asian strategy, and Asia-Pacific nuclear proliferation. He has also testified before U.S. and Australian government agencies and performed consultancies for the Australian Army, Jane's Information Group, and Science Applications International Corporation.[7]

Malik has produced a political corpus of geopolitical writings, with many of them accessible through his Web site (http://www.apcss.org/core/BIOS/malik/malik.htm). Examples of these multifaceted works include the following:

"India-China Relations." In *Berkshire Encyclopedia of China: Modern and Historic Views of the World's Newest and Oldest Global Power*, 5 vols., ed. Linsun Cheng and Mary Bragg. Great Barrington, MA: Berkshire, 2009: 3:1143–50.

"India's Response to China's Rise." In *The Rise of China and International Security: America and Asia Respond*, ed. Kevin J. Cooney and Yoichiro Sato. London: Routledge/Taylor and Francis, 2009: 177–212.

"The East Asia Community and the Role of External Powers: Ensuring Asian Multilateralism Is Not Shanghaied." *Korean Journal of Defense Analysis*, 19 (4) (Winter 2007): 29–50.

"Security Council Reform: China Signals Its Veto." *World Policy Journal*, 22 (1) (Spring 2005): 19–29.

The China Factor in the India-Pakistan Conflict. Honolulu, Hawaii: Asia-Pacific Center for Security Studies, 2002.

"Dragon on Terrorism: Assessing China's Tactical Gains and Strategic Losses after 11 September." *Contemporary Southeast Asia*, 24 (2) (2002): 252–93.

Mackubin Thomas Owens

Mackubin Thomas Owens is associate dean of academics for electives and directed research and a professor of strategy and force planning at the U.S. Naval War College. He received his BA from the University of California, Santa Barbara, an MA in economics from the University of Oklahoma, and a PhD in politics from the University of Dallas. He has served in the Marine Corps, and his academic career includes service at the University of Rhode Island, University of Dallas, Catholic University, and Marine Corps School of Advanced Warfighting. He has also served as a consultant to Los Alamos National Laboratory, Marine Corps Headquarters, Joint Chiefs of Staff, Claremont Institute, Ashbrook Center, and Foreign Policy Research Institute.

His research specialties include U.S. strategy and force planning, with particular emphasis on naval and power projection forces, the political economy of national security, national security organization, and American civil-military relations. He served as editor in chief of the journal *Strategic Review* from 1990 to 1997 and currently serves as editor of *Orbis*; he also writes regularly for *National Review Online*.[8]

Examples of Owens's writings include the following:

"The Bush Doctrine: The Foreign Policy of Republican Empire." *Orbis*, 53 (1) (January 2009): 23–40.

"Reflections on Future War." *Naval War College Review*, 61 (3)(Summer 2008): 61–76.

"Strategy and the Strategic Way of Thinking." *Naval War College Review*, 60 (4) (Autumn 2007): 111–24.

"Rumsfeld, the Generals, and the State of U.S. Civil-Military Relations." *Naval War College Review*, 59 (4)(Autumn 2006): 68–80.

"In Defense of Classical Geopolitics." *Naval War College Review*, 52 (4)(Autumn 1999): 59–76.

"Technology, the RMA (Revolution in Military Affairs), and Future War." *Strategic Review*, 26 (2)(Spring 1998): 63–70.

Fundamentals and Force Planning. Newport, RI: Naval War College Press, 1992.

Additional information on Owens can be accessed at http://www.claremont.org/scholars/id.21/scholar.asp or www.fpri.org/about/people/owens.html.

Chris Seiple

Chris Seiple is the president of the Institute for Global Engagement, which is a research, education, and diplomatic institution seeking to build sustainable global religious freedom with local partners. He is a graduate of Stanford University, the Naval Postgraduate School, and the Fletcher School for Law and

Diplomacy at Tufts University. He also is a senior fellow at the Foreign Policy Research Institute, Council on Foreign Relations, and International Institute for Strategic Studies. His areas of expertise include national and homeland security, U.S. foreign policy, central and East Asia, humanitarian intervention, religion and international affairs, Christian-Muslim relations, and religious freedom. He speaks at U.S. military schools and within the intelligence community on national security and religious and cultural engagement.[9]

Seiple presents his geopolitical views through a variety of writings, including being a regular contributor to the *National Journal*'s National Security Blog (http://security.nationaljournal.com/), and he is the founder of the journal *The Review of Faith and International Affairs*-(http://rfiaonline.org/). Examples of his writings include the following:

"Ready . . . or Not? Equipping the U.S. Military Chaplain for Inter-religious Liaison." *Review of Faith and International Affairs*, 7 (4)(Winter 2009): 43–49.

Chris Seiple, Knox Thames, and Amy Rowe. *International Religious Freedom Advocacy*. Waco, TX: Baylor University Press, 2009.

Revisiting the Geo-political Thinking of Sir Halford John Mackinder: United States–Uzbekistan Relations 1991–2005. PhD diss., Fletcher School of Law and Diplomacy, 2006.

"Uzbekistan: Civil Society in the Heartland." *Orbis* 49 (2)(Spring 2005): 245–59.

Heartland Geopolitics and the Case of Uzbekistan. Philadelphia: Foreign Policy Research Institute, 2004.

The U.S. Military/NGO Relationship in Humanitarian Interventions. Carlisle, PA: U.S. Army War College, Peacekeeping Institute, 1996.

Additional information on Seiple can be found at http://www.globalengage.org/about/staff/771-dr-chris-seiple.html.

Francis P. Sempa

Francis P. Sempa is the assistant U.S. attorney for the Middle District of Pennsylvania and an adjunct professor of political science at Wilkes University and is also a prominent writer on geopolitical issues. He received his BS in political science from the University of Scranton and his JD from Pennsylvania State University. His writings focus on prominent geopolitical thinkers such as James Burnham, Halford Mackinder, and Alfred Thayer Mahan and on various historical and foreign policy topics, including the history of international relations.[10]

Examples of Sempa's writings include the following:

America's Global Role: Essays and Reviews on National Security, Geopolitics, and War. Lanham, MD: University Press of America, 2009.

"Presidential War Powers in Historical-Legal Context." *American Diplomacy*, 10 (2008). http://www.unc.edu/depts/diplomat/item/2008/1012/comm/sempa_war powers.html.

Geopolitics: From the Cold War to the Twenty-first Century. New Brunswick, NJ: Transaction, 2007.

"Spykman's World." *American Diplomacy*, 4 (2006). http://www.unc.edu/depts/diplomat/item/2006/0406/semp/sempa_spykman.html.

"The Geopolitics of the Post–Cold War World." *Strategic Review*, 20 (Winter 1992): 9–17.

"Why Teach Geopolitics?" *International Social Science Review*, 65 (1)(Winter 1990): 16–20.

"Geopolitics and American Strategy: A Reassessment." *Strategic Review*, 15 (Spring 1987): 27–38.

Geróid Ó Tuathail (Gerard Toal)

Gerard Toal is professor of government and international affairs and director of the masters of public and international affairs program at Virginia Tech University's Alexandria campus. A native of Ireland, Toal received a BA in history and geography from National University of Ireland, Maynooth, an MA in geography from the University of Illinois Urbana-Champaign, and a PhD in political geography from Syracuse University. He is one of the key scholars in the critical geopolitics movement in political geography and international relations, and his research interests include critical geopolitics, nationalism, political geography, post-Communism, and globalization.[11]

Toal currently serves as associate editor of the journal *Geopolitics* and has produced an extensive corpus of work reflecting his ideological perspectives, with representative samples including the following:

"Accounting for Separatist Sentiment in Bosnia-Herzegovina and the North Caucasus of Russia: A Comparative Analysis of Survey Responses." *Ethnic and Racial Studies*, 32 (4)(May 2009): 591–615.

A *Geopolitics Reader*. 2nd ed. London: Routledge, 2006.

"The 'West Bank of the Drina': Land Allocation and Ethnic Engineering in Republika Srpska." *Transactions of the Institute of British Geographers*, 31 (3)(September 2006): 304–22.

"The Frustration of Geopolitics and the Pleasures of War: Behind Enemy Lines and American Geopolitical Culture." *Geopolitics*, 10 (2)(Summer 2005): 356–77.

Gerard Toal, John O'Laughlin, and Vladimir Kolossov. "Russian Geopolitical Storylines and Public Opinion in the Wake of 9/11: A Critical Geopolitical Analysis and National Survey." *Communist and Post-Communist Studies*, 37 (3)(September 2004): 281–318.

Gerard Toal, John Agnew, and Katharyn Mitchell, eds. *A Companion to Political Geography*. Malden, MA: Blackwell, 2003.

"'Just Out Looking for a Fight': American Affect and the Invasion of Iraq."

Antipode: A Radical Journal of Geography, 35 (5)(November 2003): 856–70.

"Reasserting the Regional: Political Geography and Geopolitics in World Thinly Known." *Political Geography*, 22 (6)(August 2003): 653–55.

Critical Geopolitics. Minneapolis: University of Minnesota Press, 1996.

Further information about Toal and the text of some of his writings can be found at http://www.toal.net/ and www.psci.vt.edu/main/faculty/toal.html.

Notes

1. See Thomas P. M. Barnett, Biography Resource Center, http://galenet.group.com/servlet/BioRc?/; and http://www.thomaspmbarnett.com/biography.htm.
2. "Simon Dalby: Biography," http://http-server.carleton.ca/~sdalby/biography/biography.htm.
3. "Andrew S. Erickson: China Analysis from Original Sources," http://www.andrewerickson.com/.
4. See "Colin S. Gray," http://galenetgroup.com/servlet/BioRc?/; and University of Reading, "Staff Profile: Colin S. Gray," http://www.reading.ac.uk/spirs/about/staff/c-s-gray.aspx.
5. "Jakub Grygiel," http://www.sais-jhu.edu/faculty/directory/bios/g.grygiel.htm.
6. Texas A&M University, Department of Geography, "Profile: Peter Hugill," http://geography.tamu.edu/profile/PHugill/.
7. Asia-Pacific Center for Security Studies, "J. Mohan Malik, Ph.D. Professor," http://www.apcss.org/core/BIOS/malik/malik.htm.
8. Claremont Institute, "Mackubin Thomas Owens," http://www.claremont.org/scholars/id.21/scholar.asp.
9. Institute for Global Engagement, "Dr. Chris Seiple," http://www.globalengage.org/about/staf/771-dr-chris-seiple.html.
10. See Francis P. Sempa, *America's Global Role: Essays and Review on National Security, Geopolitics, and War* (Lanham, MD: University Press of America, 2009): 121; and Biography Resource Center, http://galenet.group.com/servlet/BioRc.
11. Virginia Tech University, Department of Political Science, "Gerard Toal (Gearóid Ó Tuathail)," http://www.psci.vt.edu/main/faculty/toal.html.

APPENDIX

Maps

Source: UN Cartographic Section.

Iran
Source: CIA World Fact Book.

Iraq
Source: CIA World Fact Book.

Strait of Hormuz
Source: CIA World Fact Book.

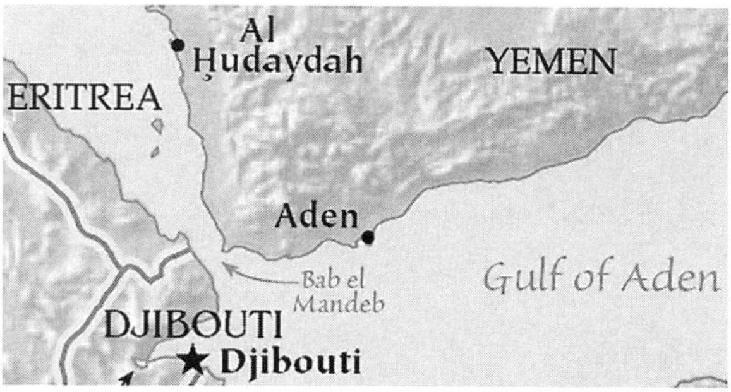

Strait of Bab el Mandeb
Source: CIA World Fact Book.

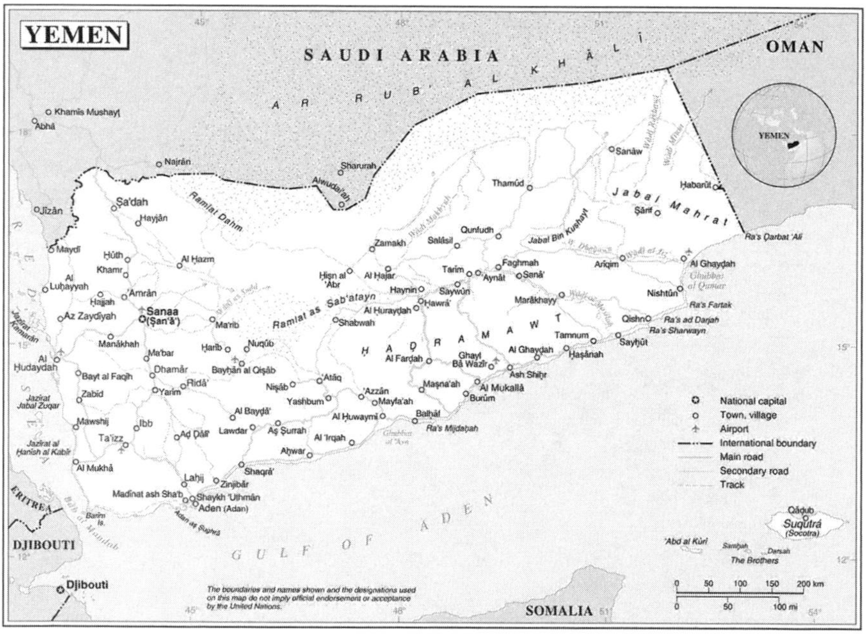

Source: United Nations Cartographic Department.

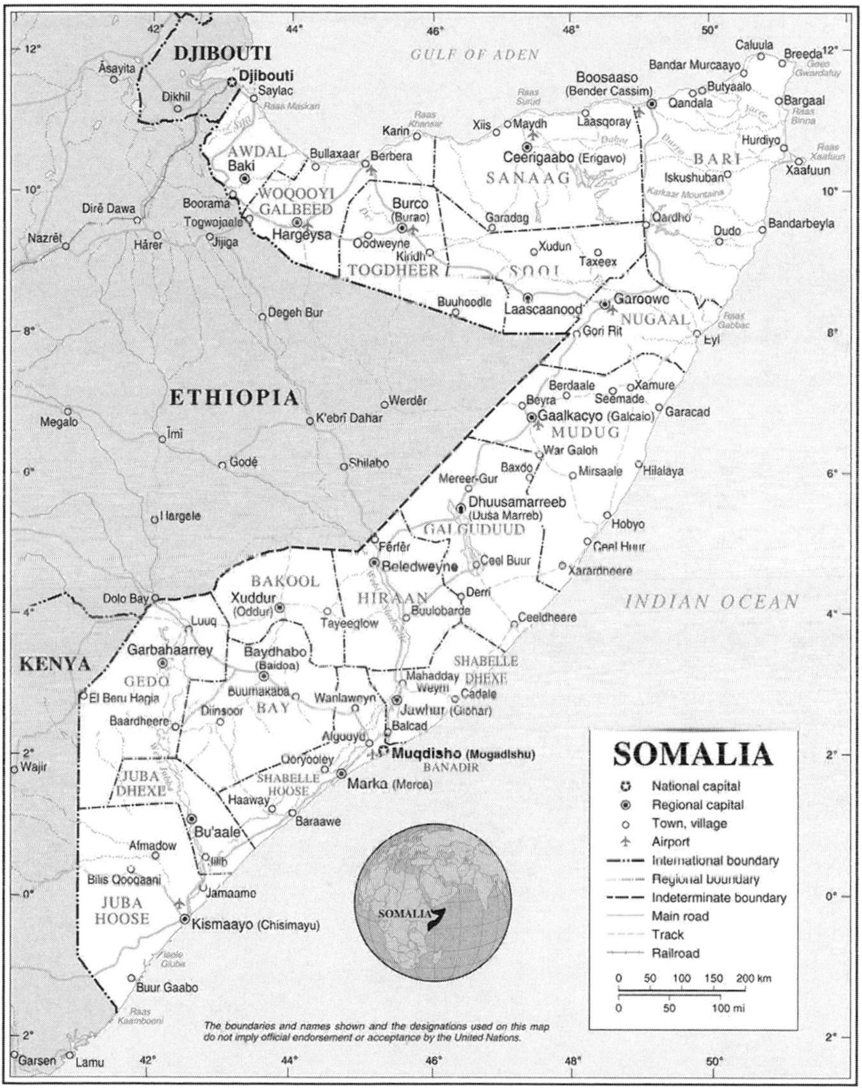

Source: United Nations Cartographic Department.

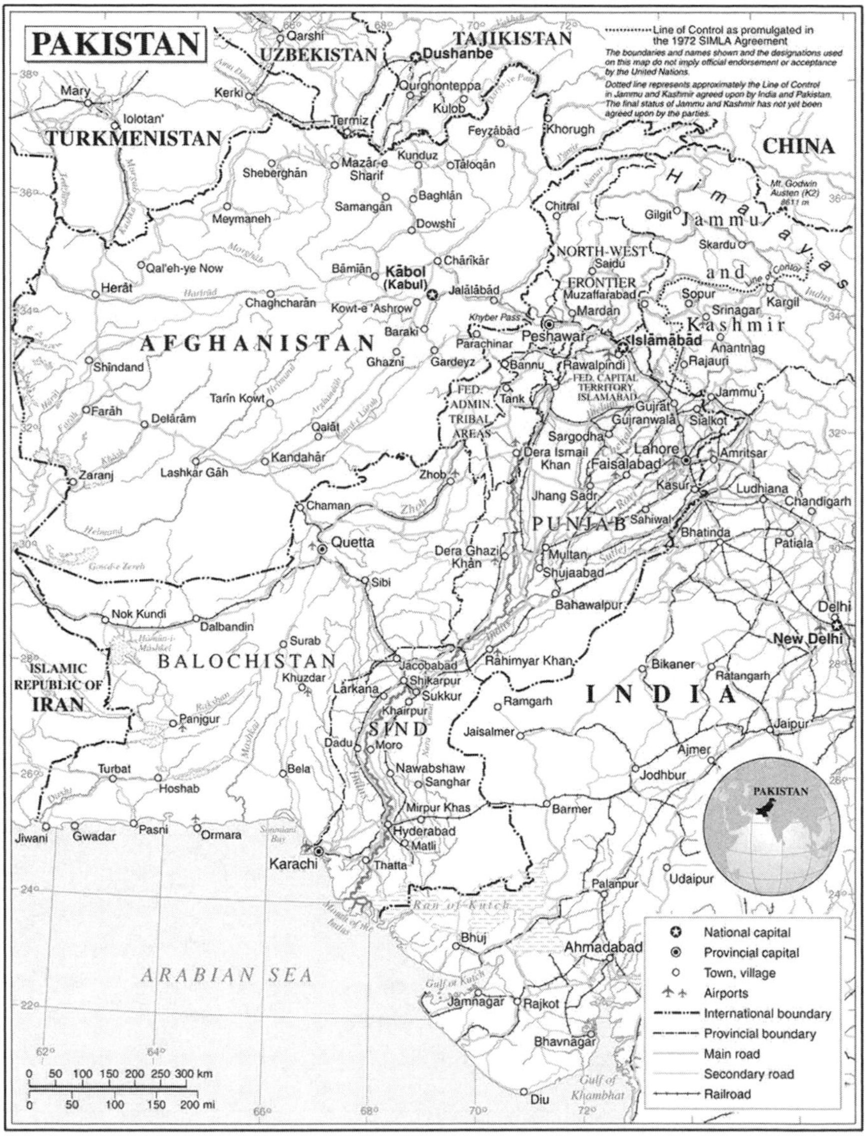

Source: United Nations Cartographic Department.

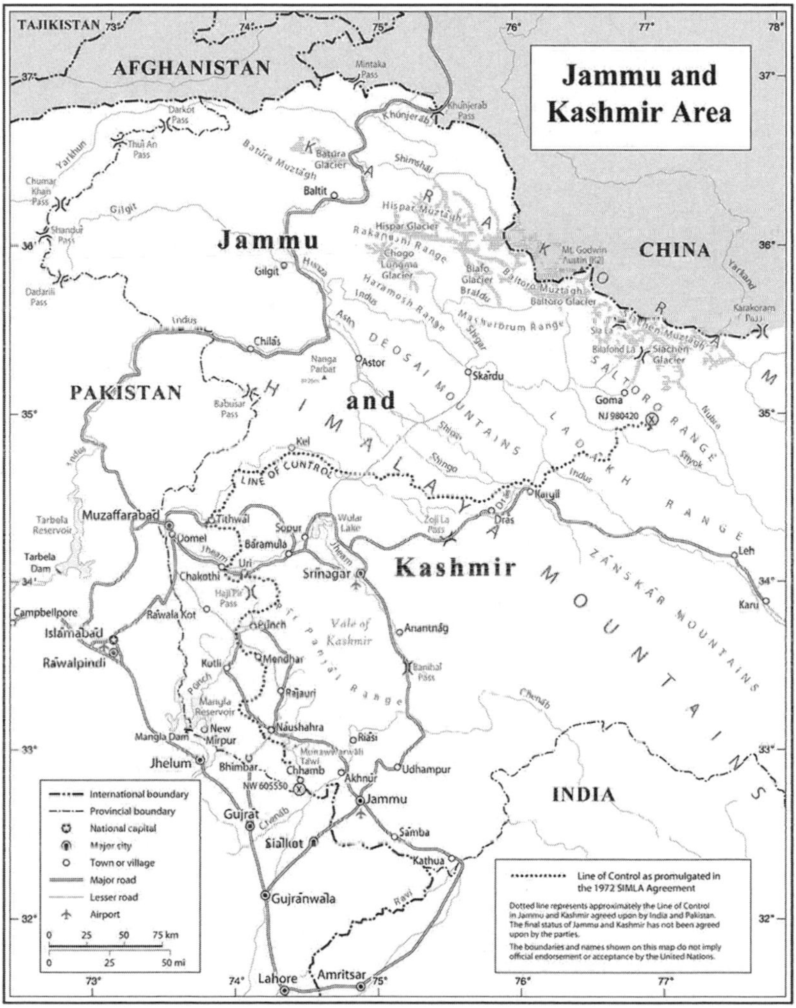

Source: United Nations Cartographic Department.

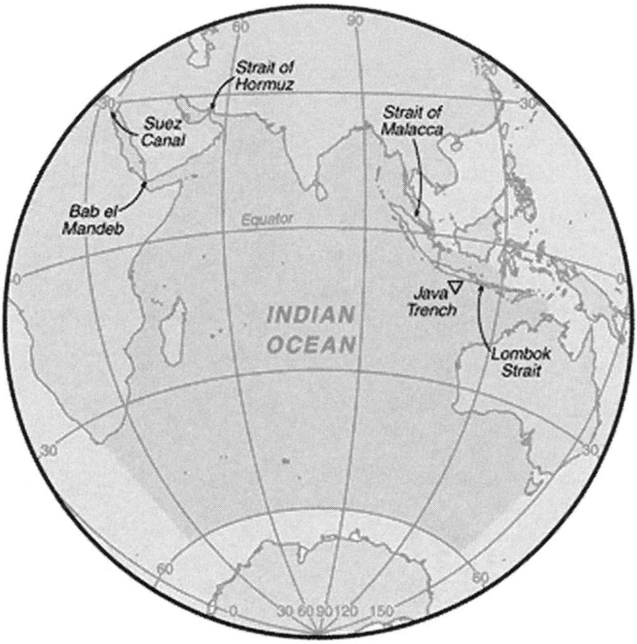

Source: CIA World Fact Book.

Source: CIA World Fact Book.

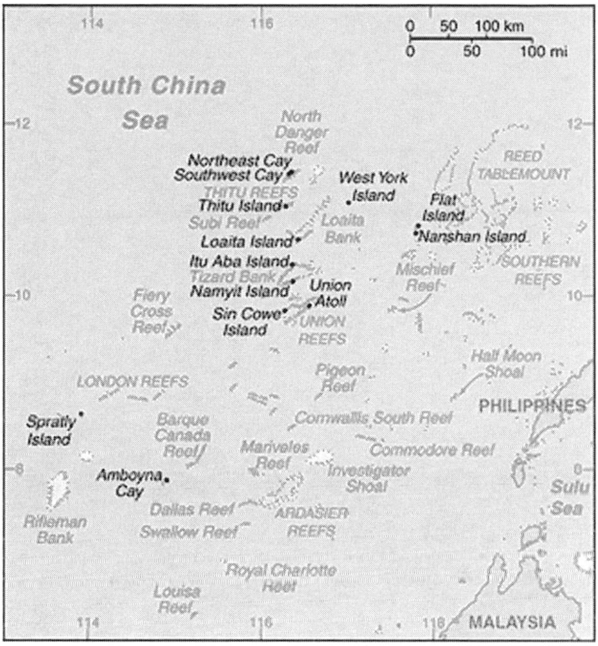

Spratly Islands
Source: CIA World Fact Book.

Taiwan
Source: CIA World Fact Book.

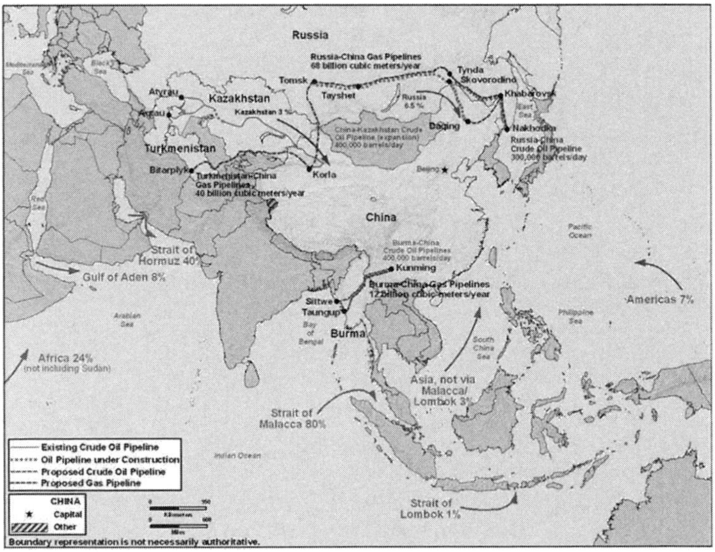

China's import transit routes/critical choke points and proposed/under construction SLOC bypass routes
Source: 2010 DOD China Military Report.

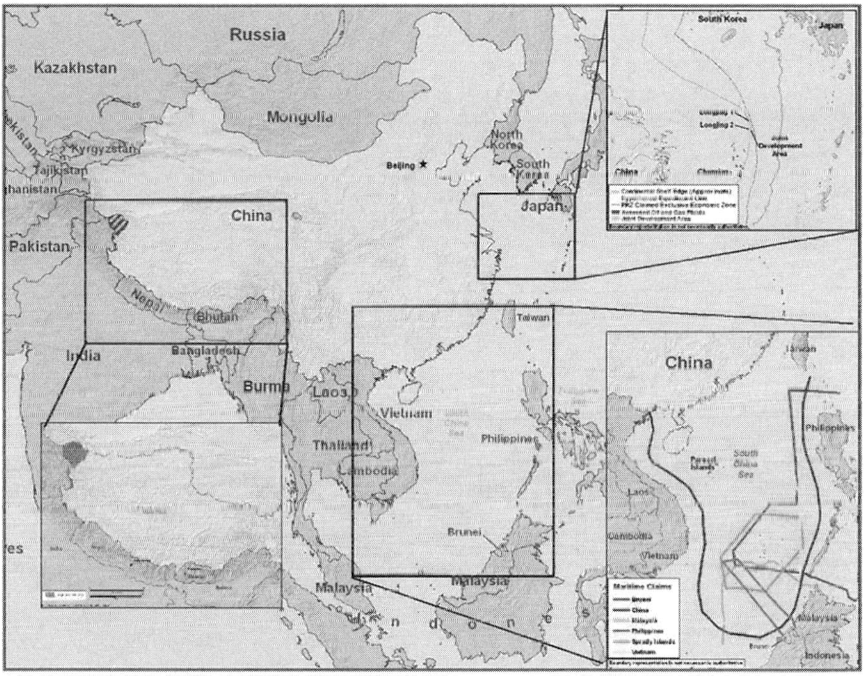

***China's Disputed Territories**. Although not exhaustive, three of China's major ongoing territorial disputes are based on claims along its shared border with India and Bhutan, the South China Sea, and with Japan in the East China Sea.*

Source: 2010 DOD China Military Report.

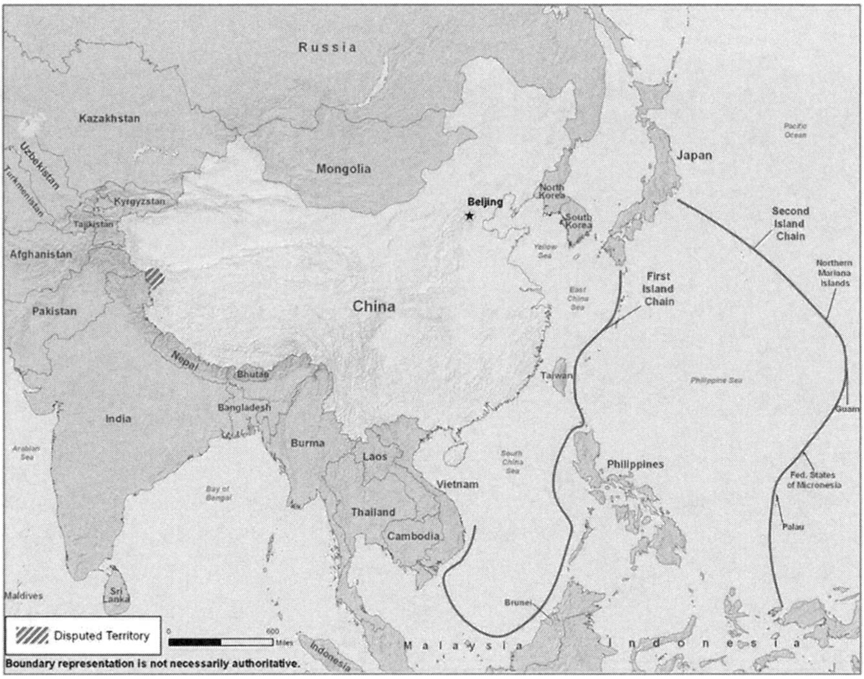

The First and Second Island Chains. *PRC military theorists conceive of two island "chains" as forming a geographic basis for China's maritime defensive perimeter.*

Source: 2010 DOD China Military Report.

North Korea
Source: CIA World Fact Book.

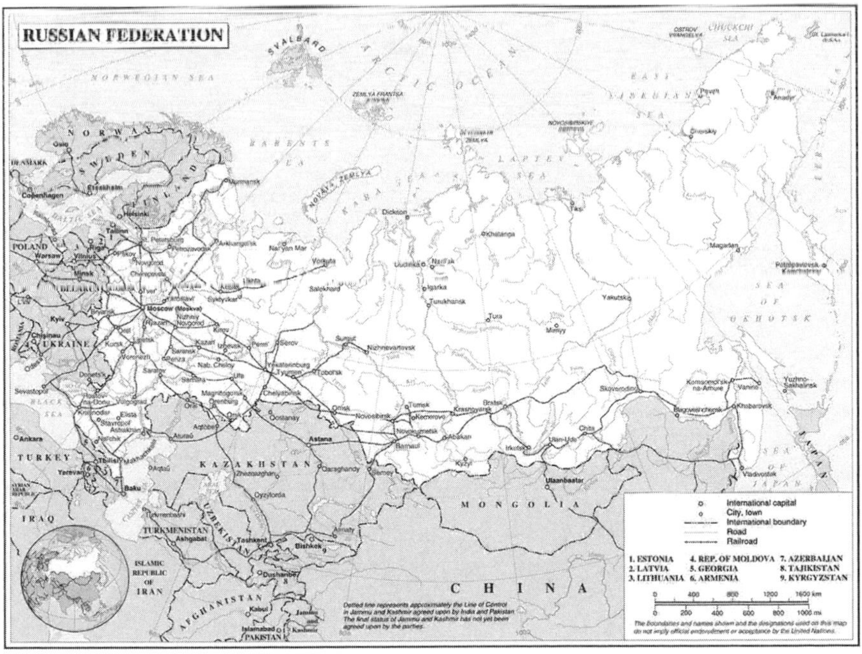

Source: United Nations Department.

ARCTIC REGION

Source: Central Intelligence Agency.

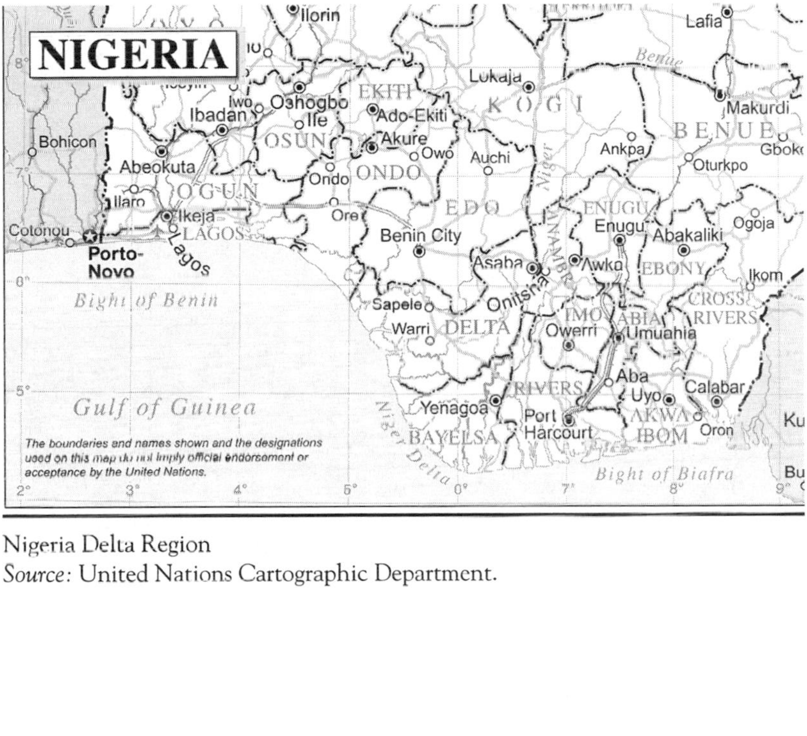

Nigeria Delta Region
Source: United Nations Cartographic Department.

Source: Central Intelligence Agency.

Glossary

This is a compilation of historical and current acronyms and terms often used in discussions and analysis of geopolitics and political geography.

Afghanistan/Pakistan	South Asian countries that are centers of major internecine and international military conflicts involving the United States and other members of NATO's International Security Assistance Force, Pakistani and Afghan branches of the Taliban, al-Qaeda, and Pakistani military and intelligence forces.
African Union	Founded in 1999, this is an organization of African countries seeking to promote greater economic and political cooperation among member countries.
Amazônia	Constituting approximately 40 percent of northwestern Brazil within the Amazon watershed, this region has been an area of intense and controversial economic development by the Brazilian government, which has produced concern by neighboring countries and the international environmental community.
Andean Community	Initially established in 1969, this is a South American international government organization whose members include Bolivia, Colombia, Ecuador, and Peru and that seeks to promote regional economic and social development.
Antarctica	Southern island continent used for scientific research by several countries, including the

United States, Norway, Argentina, and Australia. The continent is demilitarized and governed by the 1959 Antarctic Treaty. Antarctica possesses significant natural resources that may entice individual countries to exploit those resources and potentially produce international conflicts.

Archipelago — Group of many islands in a large body of water.

Arctic Council — Established by the 1996 Ottawa Declaration, this international governmental organization's membership consists of Arctic countries such as the United States, Canada, and Russia and indigenous residents of these countries. The council seeks to promote cooperation, cooperation, and consultation among member states, with particular emphasis on environmental protection and sustainable development issues.

Arctic Ocean — Ocean at the northern tip of the globe that surrounds Arctic countries and has extensive natural and wildlife resources. Although primarily covered in ice, it has experienced some climate change that has made more of it accessible to year-round shipping. The ocean's potential natural resources, including petroleum, may make it a source of international tension as powers such as Canada, Russia, and the United States may seek to claim the Arctic Ocean seabed as national territory.

Arms Trade — The manufacture, production, and selling of military equipment, which involves a variety of countries, including the United States, China, Russia, Brazil, France, and many others. This trade generates significant revenue and political influence for these countries and their commercial manufacturers.

Asia-Pacific Economic Cooperation (APEC) — International governmental organization of 21 Pacific Rim countries established in 1989, seeking to facilitate economic cooperation, growth, investment, and trade in the Asia-Pacific region.

Atlantic Narrows Region	Approximately 1,500-mile-wide section of the Atlantic Ocean and Brazil that Brazil seeks to keep free from domination by hostile powers.
Atlantic Ocean	One of the world's premier oceans, it geographically separates continents such as North and South America from Europe and Africa.
Australia	English-speaking island continent and democracy that is a major U.S. ally but also has and seeks to maintain close economic relationships with Asia. Its geopolitical interests encompass the Indian Ocean, stability in the Indonesian archipelago, and security and stability in the Pacific Rim region.
Baltic Sea	Northern European ocean that serves as a major trading route for Scandinavian, Central European, and some Eastern European countries.
Barents Euro-Arctic Council (BEAC)	International Governmental Organization established in 1993 to promote cooperation in this region adjacent to northern Scandinavia and northwest Russia. The region possesses significant fish, forest, gas, minerals, and oil resources.
Beagle Channel	Strait separating the southern end of continental South America from the island Tierra del Fuego and other smaller islands. Boundary disputes made the area a source of tension between Argentina and Chile, which nearly produced war in 1978. Papal mediation and a 1984 treaty between these countries resolved this conflict.
Black Sea	Historically and contemporarily significant ocean bounded by several southeastern European and Asian nations, including Azerbaijan, Bulgaria, Russia, and Turkey. Traffic exiting this body of water and heading southwest will eventually enter the Aegean and Mediterranean seas.
Boundaries or Borders	Determining the political boundaries between countries has been and remains a historical and contemporary source of geopolitical disputes.

	In some cases, boundaries are demarcated by natural barriers such as rivers, lakes, or mountains. In other cases, boundaries are imposed by outside powers or are determined and measured with inexact precision, which can cause later bilateral or multilateral disputes between countries.
Bush Doctrine	Various foreign and national security policy principles enunciated by President George W. Bush (2001–2009) in the aftermath of the 9/11 terrorist attacks. These included the United States' right to secure itself from countries harboring or aiding terrorist groups, the United States' right to attack and overthrow foreign governments it sees as being potential or real threats to U.S. security, spreading democracy around the world as an antiterrorism policy, and a willingness to pursue U.S. interests unilaterally even in the face of international opposition.
Cape of Good Hope	Point at the southwestern end of South Africa where Atlantic Ocean and Indian Ocean waters meet.
Caribbean Basin	The area encompassed by the Caribbean Sea, including countries within this body of water.
Caribbean Community (CARICOM)	Established in 1972, this organization of 15 Caribbean countries seeks to enhance economic development, improve living standards, and promote increased trade among member countries.
Caribbean Sea	Body of water extending from Florida's west coast to the east coast of Mexico and other Central American nations and continuing across South America's northern coast. Includes a large variety of countries in the West Indian archipelago.
Caspian Environment Programme	Established in 1991, this organization of Caspian Sea nations seeks to protect this area's marine and coastal environments.

Caspian Sea — The largest enclosed body of water on earth whose bordering countries include Azerbaijan, Iran, Kazakhstan, Russia, and Turkmenistan. Its enormous natural gas and oil resources, which are just beginning to be developed, make it an area of acute international geopolitical interest.

Charcas Triangle — Resource-rich and strategically located region of central South America that has sometimes been the source of tension involving surrounding countries such as Argentina, Bolivia, Brazil, Paraguay, and Uruguay.

Chechnya — A predominately Islamic region of Russia, this republic has sought to separate from Russia and has been the site of two wars between the Russian military and Chechen separatists since 1991.

Checkerboards — The process by which neighboring powers seek to enhance their security interests by allying with other powers which they believe will check the aspirations of neighboring countries which are hostile to them.

China in Africa — As part of its String of Pearls Strategy, this involves China's efforts to increase its economic assistance to and influence in African countries in order to secure access to natural resources such as oil and natural gas. Chinese assistance to these countries does not contain human rights or other accountability provisions characteristic of U.S. and other Western economic assistance programs. This assistance may eventually result in Chinese military and intelligence presence in these countries.

China in Latin America — China's efforts to increase its economic assistance to and influence in Latin American countries in order to secure access to natural resources such as oil and natural gas. Chinese assistance to these countries does not contain human rights or other accountability provisions characteristic of U.S. and other Western economic assistance programs. This assistance may eventually result in Chinese military and intelligence presence in these countries.

China	World's most populous nation, and its increasing economic wealth is increasing its political and military power throughout the world. Areas of Chinese geopolitical interests include Central Asia, northeast Asia, the Strait of Taiwan, the Korean Peninsula, the South China Sea, the Indian Ocean, Africa, Latin America, Tibet, and the Uighur Region, within its borders and where it faces a Muslim separatist movement.
Choke Points	Land or water geographic features such as bridges, peninsulas, or straits that commercial trade or military forces must pass through on a narrow front to reach their objectives.
Classical Geopolitics	A methodologically traditionalist interpretation of the role played by geography, natural resources, and transportation in formulating and implementing national and international political, economic, diplomatic, and military strategies.
Climate Change	Controversial belief that human-caused pollution may cause global warming, cause abnormal global temperature changes, alter existing environmental conditions and living standards, and produce sources of international conflict. In geopolitics, this has seen political and military planners address the possibility of year-round shipping access to previously inaccessible waterways such as the Northwest Passage and the emergence of national and international conflict over access to depleted natural resources such as water.
Colombia	Northwestern South American country located near on the Pacific Ocean and Caribbean Sea and near the Panama Canal. Geopolitical interests include territorial disputes with Venezuela and combating drug traffickers and paramilitary groups within national borders.

Common Foreign and Security Policy (CFSP) (European Union)	Mechanism used by European Union member countries to attempt to cooperate in the development and implementation of foreign and national security policies.
Conference on Security and Cooperation in Europe (CSCE)	This organization was established in 1973 and consists of the United States, Canada, and most European countries. It seeks to promote European cooperation on security issues affecting European countries.
Containment	Theory that a single nation or group of nations can use their combined political, diplomatic, economic, and military power to thwart the ambitions of a hostile power or group of hostile powers without actually using military force against those powers. The cold war policies of the United States and its allies toward the Soviet Union are often cited as an example. Containment has also been advocated by some as the best means of keeping Iran from acquiring and using nuclear weapons.
Correlation of Forces	A phrase used by the geopolitical strategists in the former Soviet Union to define and quantitatively measure all elements of national power, including economic and military forces and national will in relationship to other international powers.
Counterinsurgency Warfare	Armed conflict against an insurgency by forces opposed to recognized national governments in the territory where the conflict occurs. Insurgent forces seek to weaken or destroy the political authority of the defending authorities over the populations they seek to control, while counterinsurgent forces seek to protect and expand governmental authority by reducing or eliminating insurgent power.
Critical Geopolitics	A politically leftist approach to this subject that is heavily influenced by deconstructionist

	and postmodernist philosophical theories. It seeks to expose what it regards as deterministic, ethnocentric, exceptionalist, geographic, ideological, racist, and other flaws it claims exist in traditional or classical geopolitics.
Cryopolitics	Competition between states to control emerging resources and territory created by melting ice in areas such as the Arctic Ocean and Antarctica.
Dardanelles/Bosporus Straits	Narrow and strategically significant waterway in Turkey connecting the Black Sea with the Aegean and Mediterranean seas.
Delta Region (Nigeria)	An unstable and oil-rich area of Nigeria's Niger River delta which has been the scene of conflicts involving the Nigerian government, international oil companies, and disaffected residents who believe that they have not received oil royalty revenues to improve their personal living standards and achieve regional economic development. This conflict has also increased competition for public office in Nigeria and produced often ethnically derived violence in domestic Nigerian political campaigns and considerable public cynicism by region residents toward the Nigerian government.
Drang Nach Osten	Translated as "drive" or "push to the east," this was a 1920s-era German geopolitical term used to promote lebensraum or German expansion and settlement into Eastern Europe and Russia, which was believed to be the original homeland of Germans.
East African Community (EAC)	Established in 1999, this international governmental organization's members include Burundi, Kenya, Rwanda, Tanzania, and Uganda, and it seeks to expand economic, political, and social cooperation among member states.
Energy Information Administration (EIA)	Established in 1977, this organization serves as the U.S. Department of Energy's statistical and analytical arm preparing numerous reports on

	domestic U.S. and international energy market trends and developments.
Environmental Security	Developing policies intended to protect environmental integrity from human threats and preventing political conflict and war due to environmental change and degradation.
Eurasia	The landmass formed by the European and Asian continents and a term often used in geopolitics, international relations, and international security literature to describe the diplomatic, economic, environmental, political, and security relationships between and among countries in this large region.
Eurozone Countries	Economic and monetary union of 16 European countries that have adopted the euro as their currency.
Falkland Islands	British owned and settled islands which have been sought after by Argentina (which calls them the Malvinas Islands) and were the scene of a 1982 war won by the United Kingdom. British petroleum exploration and drilling in offshore waters in 2010 has increased Anglo-Argentine tensions.
Fjord	A long, narrow sea inlet between steep cliffs as occurs in countries like Norway.
Geopolitics	The study of the relationships between demography, economics, environment, geography, and politics and how they influence countries foreign and national security policies.
Georgia	Eastern European country that was formerly part of the Soviet Union. Lost the separatist territories of Abkhazia and South Ossetia to Russia in a 2008 war.
Golan Heights	Elevated and strategic mountainous region in the region adjoining Israel, Lebanon, and Syria. Israel acquired control of this region during the 1967 Arab-Israeli War. Syria seeks to reclaim this region, and Lebanon claims the Shebaa Farms section of this area.
Great Powers	Nations possessing the political, economic, and military resources, giving them enhanced

influence over international political and security affairs. Potential examples of early-21st-century great powers include the United States, China, India, Brazil, and Russia.

Heartland — Seminal political theory promoted by British geopolitical theorist Halford Mackinder that the central Eurasian region was the key to international political-military dominance and that the nation dominating this region would dominate the world. The theory has been criticized for excluding external powers such as Japan and the United States and for not adhering to current geopolitical realities. However, it was a major factor in launching geopolitics as an academic discipline, and its tenets can still be selectively applied to current and emerging geopolitical trends and developments.

Hegemony — The ability of one nation or a group of nations to dominate another nation or group of nations. Can be used synonymously with imperialism.

Homeland Security — A term used to describe efforts by the United States and other countries to protect themselves against internal and external threats.

Horn of Africa — Region where northeastern Africa intersects with the Arabian Peninsula and includes waters such as the Arabian Sea, Gulf of Aden, and Indian Ocean. Adjacent countries include Djibouti, Ethiopia, Eritrea, Somalia, and Yemen. Somalia-based maritime piracy attacks have made this an increasingly treacherous area for international shipping.

India — World's second most populous country and a rising international economic and military power. May become a rival to China and seek to deter Chinese expansion into the Indian Ocean.

Indian Ocean — The world's third largest ocean encompassing the five countries of the Indian subcontinent on the north, Africa on the west, the Southern Ocean or Antarctica on the south, and Indochina and Australia on the east.

Indonesia	Southeast Asian country which is the world's fourth most populous nation and consists of a large number of islands. Located in a strategically significant region adjacent to the Indian Ocean, South China Sea, and Pacific Ocean, Indonesia faces separatist movements in the provinces of Aceh and Papua.
International Energy Agency (IEA)	Established in 1974 as part of the Organization for Economic Cooperation and Development, this organization seeks to improve the world's energy supply and demand structure, promote globally rational energy policies, maintain and improve systems for coping with oil supply disruptions, and operate a permanent information system on the international oil market.
International Hydrographic Organization (IHO)	Initially established in 1921, this international governmental organization has 80 members. Its activities include coordinating national hydrographic office activities, achieving maximum uniformity in nautical charts and documents, adopting reliable and efficient methods for carrying out and using hydrographic surveys, and developing hydrographic and descriptive oceanographic sciences.
International Maritime Organization (IMO)	This United Nations–affiliated organization is responsible for developing and maintaining rules and regulations for international maritime shipping and maritime security.
International Seabed Authority (ISA)	Established in 1982 as part of the United Nations Convention on the Law of the Sea, this is the organization convention signatories use to adjudicate seabed and ocean floor disputes.
International Security Assistance Force (ISAF)	Afghanistan–NATO member led force of countries seeking to enhance the stability and viability of Afghanistan's government against Taliban insurrectionists through military and nonmilitary means.

Iran	Oil-rich and strategically important Middle Eastern country whose dictatorial Islamist regime, controversial aspirations to acquire nuclear weapons, and support for international terrorism pose acute security problems for regional and global countries, including the United States.
Iraq	Oil-rich and strategically important Middle Eastern country striving to rebuild its economic infrastructure, domestic stability, and political viability following U.S. military intervention and overthrow of Saddam Hussein's regime. Continues trying to address acute sectarian strife and Iranian interference in its internal affairs.
Isolationism	Nationalist ideology advocating noninvolvement in foreign alliances and nonintervention in other countries' external military affairs. Can be applied to U.S. relations with other countries or to other countries' bilateral or multilateral relationships.
Israel	Democratic ally of the United States that faces continuing security threats from surrounding countries such as Syria and Iran and domestic turmoil from Palestinian unrest in Gaza and the West Bank.
Japan	Major economic and political power in East Asia. Geopolitical interests include developments in the Korean Peninsula, China, and northeast Asia, ensuring free flow of oil and other international trade assets, and its territorial dispute with Russia over the Kuril and Sakhalin Islands.
Kashmir	Disputed region of the northwestern Indian subcontinent. Pakistan controls the northwest portion, India the central and southern portion, and China the northeastern portion of this area, which the United Nations calls Jammu and Kashmir. The most contentious disputes have been between India and Pakistan, and the Line of Control, dating from 1972, is a de facto military boundary between these two countries that is not recognized in international law.

Kurdistan — Large geographic region covering parts of eastern Turkey, northwestern Iran, northern Iraq, and a part of northern Syria. Various Kurdish political and military movements have sought to gain increased autonomy or outright independence from the countries they are currently part of. Kurds in northern Iraq have gained increased political influence in Iraq since the ouster of Saddam Hussein but still have contentious relationships with many Iraqi Arabs and the Iraqi government in Baghdad.

Latin America — Region of the Americas originally colonized by France, Portugal, and Spain. Encompasses most of Central and South America.

League of Arab States (Arab League) — Established in 1945, this is an organization of Arab states in southwest Asia and north and northeast Africa. It seeks to facilitate cultural, economic, political, scientific, and social programs to enhance collaborative relations between these countries.

Lebensraum — Translated as "space of life" or "living space," this German term sought to promote German expansion into Eastern Europe in the decades after World War I and during the Nazi era. It advocated cancellation of the Treaty of Versailles, which took away Germany's lost territories and colonies, and rationalized that Germany's surplus of births required it to acquire additional territory in Eastern Europe.

Littoral — Coastal regions or shores or the region or zone between the limits of high and low tides.

Maritime — Nautical term referring to seaborne ships, shipping, navigation, and law or to any activities conducted near the sea.

Mediterranean Sea — Large sea connected to the Atlantic Ocean and surrounded on the north by Anatolia and Europe, the south by Africa, and the east by countries such as Israel, Lebanon, and Syria.

Mekong River Commission — International governmental organization formed in 1995 by Cambodia, Laos, Thailand,

and Vietnam to jointly manage the Mekong River's shared water resources and economic potential. Burma and China became dialogue partners in 1996.

Neutrality and Neutralism: When a nation-state decides not to become involved or take sides in a political, diplomatic, or military dispute between other nation-states. Neutrality does not mean that the nation-state deciding to be neutral may not be drawn into the conflict against its will.

Nordic Council: Established in 1952, this organization promotes parliamentary and governmental cooperation between Denmark, Finland, Iceland, Norway, and Sweden in order to promote expanded economic and political cooperation between these countries.

North Atlantic Treaty Organization (NATO): Established in 1949, this collective military alliance of Western democracies sought to deter military attacks by the Soviet Union and its allies. Since the collapse of the Soviet Union, NATO has expanded its membership to include former Soviet bloc countries in Eastern Europe and has taken on new military missions in the Balkans and in Afghanistan with mixed results.

North Sea: Oceanic region ranging from the English Channel and Dover Strait on the south to the Norwegian Sea on the north with access to the Atlantic Ocean and Baltic Sea. Contains some oil and natural gas resources and is also being used to develop wave and wind energy.

Northwest Passage: Sea route connecting the Atlantic and Pacific Oceans through the Arctic Ocean along North America's northern coast using various waterways in the Canadian Arctic Archipelago. Canada's government considers the Northwest Passage to be Canadian territorial waters, but many countries consider it an international strait allowing free and unrestricted passage. Recent climatic warming is causing increased international shipping in the passage whose environmental impact is uncertain. Canada,

	Denmark, Norway, Russia, and the United States have territorial claims on various areas adjacent to the passage, which may contain significant natural resources.
Nuclear Nonproliferation	Seeking to stop the spreading of destructive nuclear weapons technology in the international political, diplomatic, and security arena. The same principle may also apply to nonnuclear weapons of mass destruction, including biological, chemical, and radiological weapons.
Nuclear Weapons	Explosive devices powered by nuclear fission and capable of causing considerable destruction and loss of life. Although there are numerous efforts to reduce nuclear weapons use in military environments and international forums, they are still necessary as deterrents in some geopolitical situations, and any attempt to eliminate them is likely to fail and have undesirable political and military-strategic consequences.
Organization for Economic Cooperation and Development (OECD)	Established in 1961, this organization of 30 of the world's most highly developed economies seeks to help governments foster prosperity and fight poverty through economic growth and financial stability, while also examining economic development's environmental and social implications.
Organization for Security and Cooperation in Europe (OSCE)	Established in 1975, this organization of 56 countries from central Asia, Europe, and North America has grown to become the world's largest regional security organization. It seeks to provide early warning, conflict prevention, crisis management, and postconflict rehabilitation through its 18 missions or field operations in eastern and southeastern Europe, the Caucasus, and central Asia.
Organization of American States (OAS)	Originally established in 1889, this organization's modern charter was established in 1948.

	It has 35 member states from North and South America and the Caribbean and seeks to support democracy, development, human rights, and security among member states.
Organization of the Black Sea Economic Cooperation (BSEC)	Established in 1992, this international government organization of 11 countries surrounding the Black Sea seeks to promote interaction and cooperation among member states.
Organization of Petroleum Exporting Countries (OPEC)	Established in 1960, this organization with 12 member countries seeks to coordinate oil production policies, help oil producers receive reasonable investment returns, and ensure oil consumers receive stable oil supplies.
Pacific Ocean	The world's largest ocean extending from the Arctic in the north to Antarctica in the south, bound on the east by North and South America, and on the west by Asia and Australia. Many islands of varying sizes are located here.
Pakistan's Tribal Areas	This region, consisting of tribal lands such as North and South Waziristan, is a semiautonomous area in northwestern Pakistan adjacent to Afghanistan that historically resisted British efforts to control it and currently resists similar Pakistani control efforts. Pashtun tribal identity is a key factor in this resistance to outside control, and the area is a sanctuary and training ground for al-Qaeda, Taliban, and other Islamist terrorist organizations.
Panama Canal	This 48-mile-long ship canal joins the Atlantic and Pacific Oceans and is a critical conduit for international maritime trade.
Peninsula	A large mass of land projecting into a body of water, for example, Mexico's Yucatan Peninsula.
Persian Gulf	An extension of the Indian Ocean located between Iran and the Arabian Peninsula. Generally called the Arabian Gulf by Arab states. A critical international economic and strategic waterway due to the enormous oil resources of

	surrounding countries and the large volume of shipping traffic required to transport this oil to global customers. Gulf waters are very shallow, and the Strait of Hormuz is the Gulf's narrowest point, with a width of 29 nautical miles.
Piracy	Warlike act committed on the high seas or skies by armed groups seizing control of ships or airplanes for criminal political and economic purposes. Particularly common off the coast of Somalia and in the Strait of Malacca.
Political Geography	Incorporates geographic analysis into political studies and emphasizes how geography can influence political and economic factors and perceptions, including unemployment rates and voter perceptions of local conditions. It examines political power's territorial constitution, including power sources, power shifts, and how political power is used in relation to territorial location and characteristics.
Rimland	Term coined by American geopolitical theoretician Nicholas Spykman. It refers to the Eurasian littoral from northwestern Europe to the Middle East and Southeast Asia. Spykman argued that the rimland was the world's most critical geopolitical region because it was involved in all major land and sea power conflicts and that the United States should maintain a global power balance by projecting its power into this area to prevent it from being dominated by other powers such as the Soviet Union.
Riparian	Located on the banks of a river or stream and the interface between land and a stream.
Russia	World's largest country with significant natural resources, military power, and geopolitical interests. These geopolitical interests encompass Europe, the Balkans, the Middle East, central Asia, China, northeast Asia, and developments within national borders.
Sea Lines of Communication (SLOC)	Primary maritime trade routes between ports. Also used to refer to naval operations to ensure

	that SLOCs are open in peacetime and closed in wartime.
Shanghai Cooperation Organization (SCO)	Founded in 2001, this Chinese-dominated intergovernmental security organization seeks to promote antiterrorism collaboration and mutual security cooperation among its member states, which include China, Kazakhstan, Kyrgyzstan, Russia, Tajikistan, and Uzbekistan.
Shatterbelts	Regions where military rivalries between outside powers tie into local disputes and produce the possibility of conflict escalation.
Somalia	A country located in the Horn of Africa that has become associated with the concept of failed state due to the absence of an effective government in recent decades. This lack of legal and governmental authority has made this area a base for maritime pirates and Islamist terrorist organizations that may be affiliated with al-Qaeda.
South Asian Association for Regional Cooperation (SAARC)	Established in 1985, this organization seeks to promote economic and social development in member countries including Bangladesh, Bhutan, India, Maldives, Nepal, Pakistan, and Sri Lanka.
South China Sea	A part of the Pacific Ocean encompassing an area from Singapore to the Strait of Taiwan and including an archipelago of several hundred islands and surrounding waters claimed by many surrounding countries. The area has significant oil and natural gas reserves and is a major international maritime shipping route for many countries.
Southern African Development Community (SADC)	Established in 1980, this organization of 15 countries seeks to enhance regional economic and human capital development. Its members include Angola, Botswana, Namibia, and South Africa.

Southern Common Market (Mercosur) — Established in 1991 by the Treaty of Asunscion, this organization of most South American countries seeks to promote free trade and the unimpeded movement of goods, people, and currency among its members.

Sovereign Debt — Government debt owned by countries to various creditors. Its repayment cannot be forced under the doctrine of sovereign immunity, but this repayment can be rescheduled, achieved through interest rate reductions, or forgiven by creditors. Failure to repay sovereign debt can result in the country losing its international credit rating and finding it more difficult to borrow in the future.

Sovereign Wealth Funds — State-owned investment fund consisting of financial assets such as stocks, bonds, real estate, or other foreign exchange financial asset funded instruments. Its purposes include budget and economic protection and stability from excessive revenue/export volatility, diversifying from nonrenewable commodity exports, enhancing returns on foreign exchange rate reserves, increasing future savings reserves, and funding economic and social development.

Spratly Islands — Series of islands in the South China Sea whose possession is contested by countries such as China, Indonesia, the Philippines, Taiwan, and Vietnam due to the belief that they and adjoining offshore waters contain significant natural gas and oil resources.

Strait of Malacca — A narrow 500-mile stretch of water between the Malaysian Peninsula and the Indonesian island of Sumatra. Serves as the major shipping channel between the Indian and Pacific oceans and is a critical economic artery for China, India, Japan, and South Korea. Several piracy attacks have occurred in this strait.

Strait of Taiwan — This 112-mile-wide section of the South China Sea has been the scene of numerous military confrontations between Taiwan and China since 1949. It remains a geopolitically

	contentious region due to the presence of Chinese ballistic missiles targeted at Taiwan as part of Beijing's desires to incorporate that country into China.
String of Pearls Strategy (China)	China's strategy to secure dependable access to natural resources by increasing commercial ties and developing civilian and military support infrastructures in areas along the Indian Ocean and extending to Africa.
Suez Canal	This 119-mile-long man-made sea-level waterway in Egypt connecting the Mediterranean Sea and Red Sea was opened in 1869. It allows water transportation between Europe and Asia without navigating around Africa. An international waterway, it can be used in war or peace by any ship without regard for its country of origin.
38th Parallel (Korean Peninsula)	Border dividing North and South Korea established after the 1953 ceasefire ending the Korean War. A heavily armed region featuring nearly two million North and South Korean and American soldiers, this is one of the world's politically and militarily tense regions.
Triple Border Points	Areas of potential security tension when three or more national frontiers intersect. Often used in South American geopolitical discussions.
U.S. Geological Survey Mineral Resources Program	The U.S. Geological Survey (USGS) was established in 1879 to conduct geological research. USGS's Minerals Resources Program does annual reports on domestic U.S. and foreign mineral industry trends and developments and relevant government mineral resources policies and programs.
United Kingdom	Once the world's largest empire, the United Kingdom remains an important regional global power with significant geopolitical interests in Europe, the Middle East, and South Atlantic. Generally cooperates closely with the United States.

United States — World's preeminent political, economic, and military power with significant geopolitical interests and presence in most global areas. Its increasing economic debt and strain on military forces due to operations in Afghanistan and Iraq may cause it to increase its collaboration with allied countries to achieve desired national strategic objectives.

Venezuela — Northern South American country with extensive petroleum resources. Its leader, Hugo Chavez, has become an adversary of the United States by seeking to develop close relations with countries as varied as China and Iran and by seeking to promote his anti-American views to other South American countries.

Wassenaar Arrangement on Export Controls for Conventional Arms and Dual-Use Goods and Technologies — Established in 1993, this organization of 40 countries, including the United States, Argentina, and the United Kingdom, seeks to enhance regional and international stability by promoting greater transparency and responsibility in international transfers of conventional arms and dual-use technologies.

World Island — Term coined by Mackinder to describe the combined Eurasian and African land masses. Mackinder contended that sea powers, especially Great Britain, should prevent any other power from controlling the World Island.

World Trade Organization — Established in 1995 from the General Agreement on Tariffs and Trade established in 1948, this organization of 153 member countries seeks to develop an international system of trade rules allowing governments to negotiate trade agreements and settle trade disputes.

Yellow Sea — Northern part of the East China Sea located between mainland China and the Korean Peninsula. Could play a critical role in any military confrontation or security crisis involving countries in this region including Japan.

Yemen — Southwestern Arabian Peninsula country. Has become of increased interest to U.S. antiterrorism policy makers as a result of al-Qaeda activities, including training Nigerian Umar Farouk Abdulmutallab, who attempted to explode a bomb on Northwest Flight 253 near Detroit on Christmas Day 2009.

Index

About the Author

BERT CHAPMAN is government information, political science, and economics librarian and professor of library science at Purdue University, West Lafayette, Indiana. He received his BA in history/political science at Taylor University, an MA in history at the University of Toledo, and an MSLS in library science at the University of Kentucky. Prior to his service at Purdue, he was reference/documents librarian at Lamar University. His research interests include using government documents to conduct military policy research and other forms of historical research. He is the author of *Military Doctrine: A Reference Handbook*, *Space Warfare and Defense: A Historical Encyclopedia and Research Guide*, and *Researching National Security and Intelligence Policy*.